Proverbs 16:9

OVERWHELMED
A Civilian Casualty of Cold War Poison

MITCHELL'S MEMOIR
As told by his Dad, Mom, Sister, and Brother

C. Mixon

Carrie Mixon

Shepherds
Publishing

OVERWHELMED

ISBN: 978-1-79298-256-9

Shepherds Publishing
515 6th St.
P.O. Box 267
Covington, IN 47932
765-793-2177

Book layout/design by:
    Word Services Unlimited
    loralee@wordservicesunlimited.com
    wordservicesunlimited.com

Cover layout/design by:
    Katie Klimek Neff – themeadowmarket.com
    Amanda Lawler Design – amlawler.com

Printed in the United States of America.

Table of Contents

Dedication

Mitchell Minor dedicates this book to all the future generations of his siblings and their spouses until the close of this age. May God's Word and this book inspire each of you "so that not one may be lost!" Amen!

Acknowledgments

Relationships are more important to our family than any worldly possession or accomplishment, and we consider our family and friends a blessing from God. On behalf of Mitchell, our family thanks everyone who has poured their love into our lives. This book is a testimony to this tangible love, and we look forward to adding new friends and family to Mitchell's eternal story.

At the center of our lives is Jesus, and it is our relationship with God's son that defines who we are today and where we will be at the close of this age. For this reason, we personally acknowledge our creator and thank him for giving us life and choosing us to serve his purposes through Mitchell. As we prepared *Mitchell's Memoir*, God sent us help along the way.

Pastor David Harkleroad of Faith Community Church in New Albany, Indiana prepared a heartfelt foreword to this book. His unique relationship growing up next door to our family gave him a front row seat to God's work in our lives. David and his wife, Christal, are dear friends, and the word's 'thank you' falls short of describing the gratitude that is in our hearts.

We would like to thank Sandra (Sandi) Harner for months of copy editing to prepare this book for every reader. Sandi is a retired senior professor of technical and professional communication from Cedarville University in Cedarville, Ohio. Sandi is an author and speaker in her own right and graciously gave her time to copy edit *Mitchell's Memoir*. Sandi also prepared the back cover narrative to invite others to discover for themselves Mitchell's Ministry between these pages. We have known and have been blessed by Sandi and her husband, Don, for twenty-five years.

Partway through writing *Mitchell's Memoir*, we realized that we may be misapplying some medical terms. Over the years, accurately describing and labeling Mitchell's lifetime diagnoses and numerous medical procedures was a challenge. We knew right away that JoAnn Davis, a pediatric nurse practitioner at Nationwide Children's Hospital in Columbus, Ohio, was the right person to consult. Many times as we agonized over Mitchell's health at Nationwide Children's Hospital, JoAnn would show up at just the right moment to encourage our family. We have known JoAnn and her husband, Brent, for nearly twenty years. The Davis' are a special family.

My friend, Jacob Estes, also stepped in the gap to help us with this book by screening its content for potential legal implications. I met Jacob six years ago on the first day of law school. We quickly became close friends as we studied and encouraged each other during our grueling night school experience while working full time during the day. Jacob is an attorney and partner at MacGillivray & Estes, LLP in Bellefontaine, Ohio. Since graduating from Capital University Law School, Jacob and I have phoned each other every Friday morning to encourage each other, pray, and study God's word. Many of our early morning discussions helped me solidify my own thoughts as I wrote my portion of *Mitchell's Memoir*. Jacob and his wife, Jennifer, are an amazing couple raising an amazing family. I consider Jacob closer than a brother, and I know God put this friendship together long before we were both born.

In the three short months we wrote *Mitchell's Memoir*, Sarah Dean Litten and Abigail (Abbey) Pyles Goins gave us real-time feedback as each chapter rolled off our minds and onto the screen. Sarah Litten is Carrie's cousin living in Nashville, Tennessee. Because Carrie and Sarah are both 'only children', they claim each other as a sister. We would both agree Abbey is like a daughter. Abbey is special because she lived with our family for many years and was one of Mitchell's caregivers. Abbey's story emerged to become its own chapter. Her unique perspective is a wonderful testimony to Mitchell's Ministry. Abbey is an amazing gift from God to our family, and we can never thank her enough for coming into our home to share the load of caring for Mitchell.

A special thanks is due to Katie Klimek Neff (themeadowmarket.com) along with Amanda Lawler Design (amlawler.com) for preparing the cover artwork. Katie, like her parents, is a close friend of the family and has known Mitchell his entire life. Katie is a talented artist and worked closely with Mitchell's sister, Grace Minor Becknell, to create a cover to reflect the controversy surrounding Mitchell's handicaps.

Finally, our family thanks the men and women of the armed forces and their families for their service to our country and we send our love and prayers to all those impacted by groundwater chemical contamination from US Department of Defense installations. We hope that Mitchell's story, in some small way, will increase public awareness of this silent battle still waging on the frontline of the Cold War. We also hope, that as you live our lives through these pages, you will see how God's love can be yours as you navigate your own circumstances that leave you, *Overwhelmed!*

Foreword

To say that I know the Minor family is an understatement. I grew up a short, ninety, barefoot-summer-steps from their front door. I have known the Minors since I was nine years old, and many of my oldest and dearest memories were made with them. Their oldest son, Taylor, was my best childhood friend and probably still holds that title to this day. I recall countless sunburnt, mosquito-bitten, joy-filled days of our childhood fun together. Our homes had revolving doors. Later, I lived with the Minors for a season in college. I have laughed and cried with this dear family. I remember when Levi (youngest son) was born, and I officiated his wedding. Yes, I know the Minor family well, and this resilient and wonderful family shaped my bedrock years deeply. We were neighbors.

It is an honor to introduce to you the Minor family and their story – a story you desperately need to know. Theirs is a visceral story that awakens the humanity in each of us. It sheds light on the chaos of the moment, and it will inform any dark days that may be ahead of you, like a lantern from the future to light your path. Although books rarely capture my attention, I can say with integrity that this book has captured my heart and attention. I read this manuscript in two sittings. (It would have been one had responsibilities not beckoned.) *Overwhelmed* has stirred dormant emotions that needed stirring in my soul. It has tilled hardened soil and planted seeds that will flourish. Somehow, in a way that only God can use something, this book has genuinely spoken to my moment. *Overwhelmed* has been a timely balm for me, and I believe that it will expose and heal you as well. I pray that this book will call out, "Come, let us return to the Lord. He has torn us to pieces but he will heal us; he has injured us but he will bind up our wounds" (Hosea 6:1).

Overwhelmed is a captivating story of the human condition. It has layers of value from a fascinating life story to deeper answers about providence, purpose, and love of neighbor. This is a book for the jaded, for those shell-shocked by life, and those who desire truly to love their neighbor. Overwhelmed challenged many of my latent biases and assumptions about people and life. This is an emotionally captivating read with life-altering truths and perspectives. This book is for you.

The Minors recently invited our family to a cookout. The calendar on their wall caught my eye. It said, "A smooth sea never made a skillful sailor." The Minors are truly skillful sailors, forged in the deepest and roughest seas, with a perspective and insight that is invaluable for anyone still in the storm. God has uniquely equipped and qualified the Minor family to tell the story of his grace and guidance. Solomon once said, "In their hearts humans plan their course, but the Lord establishes their steps" (Proverbs 16:9). The Minor's skillfully expose what this looks like over the course of a lifetime. May this book gently guide you from your plans to his path.

Mitchell, I have always envied your thick, black hair, knowing eyes, and your infectious laugh. You have a unique magnetism. You have such a special ministry. Thank you for the many lessons that you have taught me over the years. Thank you for teaching me, since we were children, what it means to love my neighbor. I love you, buddy!

David Harkleroad
_____

Pastor of Faith Community Church
New Albany, IN

Introduction

Mitchell Lee Minor was born October 6, 1989, at Wurtsmith Air Force Base (AFB), Michigan. The minute Mitchell was born, the doctor noticed he had a slightly smaller head than normal. It was another six months before doctors knew for sure something was wrong. One week later, Mitchell's initial diagnosis became microcephaly (small head) because his head and brain were growing slower than his body, causing his now obvious developmental delays. Mitchell's diagnosis was only the beginning of the Minor family's journey that would span nearly three decades.

Mitchell's dad was a Captain in the United States Air Force and B-52G Aircraft Commander, and Mitchell's mom was the anchor at home, already raising their two children. Since that life-altering day, Mitchell's full list of complications slowly emerged to reshape Craig and Carrie's family with each punctuated event. Over the years, Mitchell had five major surgeries to prolong his life, ease his discomfort, and improve his care. Mitchell's stature and head grew some, but his mental capacity never progressed past that of a baby.

When the dust settled, roughly twenty years later, Mitchell's complete diagnosis was microcephaly, infantile cerebral palsy, spastic quadriplegic cerebral palsy, scoliosis associated with his condition, generalized convulsive epilepsy with intractable epilepsy (Lennox-Gastaut syndrome), and respiratory insufficiency. Mitchell required around-the-clock care.

At the beginning, a doctor said Mitchell would not live past five. When Mitchell was six years old, doctors suggested Mitchell would not live to be a teenager. After Mitchell's thirteenth birthday, the doctors stopped guessing. Mitchell is fast approaching thirty and lives at home. Words like palliative care and Allow Natural Death (AND) orders are new terms in a long list of medical vernaculars that are now common in our household. Family and friends know that Mitchell has less time in front of him than behind, and today's goals for Mitchell are less about medical and more about his comfort in love.

The exact cause of Mitchell's condition will never be completely certain. When he was two years old, doctors speculated the culprit was a virus. Recent revelations strongly suggest another cause. At Wurtsmith AFB, the drinking water contained various amounts of fire-fighter foams, engine degreaser, jet fuel, and gasoline. Past health assessments suggest the amount of contamination present was not large enough to affect children and adults. Children in the womb were not part of these assessments. This assertion is far from being settled. Today, studies and reports are beginning to connect birth defects with drinking even small amounts of the types of chemicals found in the well water at Wurtsmith AFB. Craig, Carrie, and their two children moved into base housing during the first trimester of Mitchell's development and were not aware of the groundwater contaminations until part way through writing this book. The final chapter recalls the story of the Wurtsmith AFB groundwater contaminations, which led to that critical moment in the womb forever altering Mitchell's life and the life of his family. Although knowing exactly what caused Mitchell's condition may give us some closure value, we know that we serve a sovereign God who always has bigger plans.

From our vantage point today, high above the hills of adversity while looking back across the rough landscape of our lifetime, the question of why has come into focus. We understand now that our family was prepared in advance to serve Mitchell's ministry in order to display the heart of God through his people. Our God wants to teach his people how to value service to others over self-interest. The Mitchells of this world give us the choice to practice and learn this core character trait of God.

This book is our journey from our individual points of view shaped by our own biases and choices while serving Mitchell, each other, and our friends. Somewhere between all our stories is Mitchell's story, his memoir, his ministry, and God's challenge to us all. We leave it to you, the reader, to connect our stories and to God to speak to his people's hearts.

Mitchell's story is for every family that is overwhelmed no matter where you are in your journey. Also, we are confident Mitchell's life will help those whose lives intersect with the overwhelmed to discern when their service is helpful, harmful, or missing. It is important to understand that you do not need a special needs child to be overwhelmed. We have a saying in our family that "every family has a Mitchell". For this reason, we know that we all have some level of adversity in our lives and that we must be about the business of serving each other. Our stories are raw, reliving the emotions on paper for all to feel. If we did not do this, little of what we experienced could instruct others as they walk a similar path or instruct those whose lives may cross their paths. We edify and build up, by name, many who positively contributed to Mitchell's life. However, like real life, negative things have their place, and we relive them between these pages with equal clarity. In these instances, we do not name the individual or organization. No doubt, someone reading this book may figure out he or she is the person behind a less than positive experience. Our message to you is clear: We harbor no lingering bad thoughts, and from every fiber of our being we love you. The crazy thing about life is that our individual imperfections are constantly bumping into each other. Our family needed the good things and the bad things to make us who we are today, and we are abundantly thankful for both. One might state the purpose of our journey together this way: a profoundly handicapped child forced on a family and forced on a community to make us better people.

A MINISTRY IS BORN

(January 1989 – June 1990)

Chapter 1
Our Dreams Were Erased! – Dad

When Mitchell was born, I had no idea just how much our life was about to change. I was completely clueless as to the sacrifices we were about to make to accommodate that change. Carrie and I were not unlike any young couple; we had the standard hopes and dreams of working hard to build our nest and grow our family. You know what I mean, that white picket fence image with birds tweeting overhead. Sure, Carrie and I had different versions of that dream, but after seven years of marriage and two children, our dreams were beginning to merge. Looking back, building our dreams together was easy because we had plenty of examples to choose from in our church family. We carefully watched other families who were on the same path ahead of us. We were right behind them or so we thought. When we discovered Mitchell was profoundly handicapped, our plans were completely erased! Worse, we had no role models from which to make new plans! We had no idea what came next let-alone twenty years from now. From this moment on, our future lost all certainty, and we were overwhelmed.

When I began to write *Mitchell's Memoir*, I knew the idea was to put on paper my journey with Mitchell so that in some small way I could help other dads answer that first, second, third, ongoing question: "What do I do next?" However, as I began to unpack each memory, I was unprepared for the rush of emotions that seized (more like crushed) my heart. Quite simply, I cried. I felt fear, loneliness, anger, sadness, happiness, joy, and love, as disparate memories seemed to fight for control. I quickly realized that I was not as stable emotionally as I had supposed.

In general, I am very stoic, like Spock, as my sisters and brothers used to call me. In my early years, it was hard for family and friends to determine my mood. My family might have said it was downright impossible. Even today, I do not stray very far, left or right, from emotional center. I would also have said, fifty-eight years later, that I had kept a short account of unresolved emotional issues. Wow, was I ever mistaken! I realized that all those raw emotions were still there packed neatly away in the locked closet of my heart, mind, and soul. Some I hid in my heart because they were so painful it would harm those around me. Some emotions my mind simply rationalized away. Then there were the soul-wrenching memories that everyone knew, but I never let God help me resolve. What I am about to share with you is raw, and what began as a quest to help others has become a part of my healing.

My story serving Mitchell is incomplete without Carrie. Together, we were at the core of trying to hold it all together. We never talked about it, but we knew we had no choice. The alternative seemed even more uncertain. From the beginning, our other children shared in serving Mitchell. Early on, our daughter, Grace, led the charge with her selfless love toward Mitchell, standing with her parents to help the family make it through the next moment and the next crisis. Grace continues her service with her husband, Scott, and their three children. Levi, our youngest son, was born three years after Mitchell. Mitchell would later become one of Levi's closest friends and his best man in his wedding to Sarah. Today, Sarah selflessly attends to Mitchell, Carrie, and me while raising her young son. Finally, special family and friends have formed around us to complete the Mitchell story. At the center of his story is love. Without this love, our story is not compelling.

Mitchell's birth is burned into my memory. As I watched the birth of our third child, my heart swelled as tears predictably filled my eyes. The miracle of birth is simply overwhelming. I cannot help but praise God for letting Carrie and me share in creating a soul. Of course, Carrie did all the real work. However, in that moment, when all our children took their first breath, an unidentifiable new love filled my heart. I guess that started earlier for Carrie as she felt our children kicking and moving before they were born. For me, that moment came in an instant.

When the doctor and the nurse began to score Mitchell's first moments, all seemed well. The doctor looked up at me and said that his head was a little undersized, but I remember saying that my dad's head was small, and we all thought nothing more of it. By the way, my dad's head is not small. Growing up my dad was a large frontline football-sized man, and my perspective was all wrong. I laugh about it now. As the next six months progressed, we noticed small things. Mitchell did not push up with his arms or move his head as he should. Looking back, I think Carrie was in denial and missing all the clues. I kept saying, "Something is just not right." One Sunday evening while at a church potluck, Mitchell's birth doctor was in the food line with his baby son. His son was born roughly a week before Mitchell. I walked up to him, with Mitchell in my arms, and said "Doc, look at your son and now look at mine; tell me that something isn't wrong with Mitchell." His face and eyes exposed his concern instantly, and he said to make an appointment this week.

Steve and Sharon Baum were with us at the church potluck. By this time both Steve and Sharon shared a major part of our lives, and they already were our best friends. Our friendship is an eternal friendship, and Steve and Sharon providentially came alongside Carrie and me to share the journey. When the potluck was over, Carrie and I walked away with a cloud over our heads pretending like nothing was wrong.

Over the course of the next week, Carrie took Mitchell to the fateful doctor appointment while I was sitting on alert at Wurtsmith AFB. It was part of my job every three weeks to work and sleep in a building near our assigned B-52G loaded with nuclear bombs. Every 524th Bombardment Squadron (379th Bomb Wing) flight crewmember on alert was trained and ready to launch their B-52 if the President of the United States gave the order. I had a crew of five, including a co-pilot, navigator, radar navigator, electronic warfare officer, and gunner. Our alert tours lasted a week. When my daughter, Grace, only two years old at the time, passed the alert building, she would say, "That is where my daddy lives."

I knew Carrie was taking Mitchell to the doctor that morning, and with slight anxiousness, I was waiting for the call. The call finally came, and Carrie said that she, Sharon, and Steve wanted to meet me in the alert parking lot just outside the wire fence of the highly secure alert facility. Carrie offered nothing more; that they would be there in fifteen minutes. Of course, I knew it was about Mitchell, and from the sound of her voice, I was bracing myself for something bad. Getting in and out of the alert facility was not a fast process. The only entry and exit were through the layered security of a small guard shack forming a break in the tall chain link fence, complete with razor sharp wire that circled our bombers and half-underground lodging. The guards finally allowed me to pass, and I could see Steve and Sharon's van pulling into the parking lot. As I approached, a pit grew in my stomach with each step. It was a chilly day in May, and I could see my breath when I spotted Carrie first, then Steve, Sharon, and Mitchell.

I got in the van, and Carrie started to tell me about Mitchell. She choked out two unintelligible words before she began to sob. Her eyes were already red and swollen. Immediately Steve took charge and told me what was wrong. Everything Steve said after that moment is all a blur. My mind was all over the map as I comforted Carrie. I knew in that instant we would be leaving Wurtsmith AFB and that our lives were about to change in a way I could not predict. Stunned, I think my mind ran down every possible scenario in mere seconds. I do not remember crying at first as I sat there emotionless, stuck somewhere between all those emotions. It is like those nightmares where something is chasing you and you are running in ultra-slow motion unable to scream.

After Steve and Sharon comforted us some more, I told them that I needed to make a call to get off alert. I went back into the alert facility and called the Command Post. Within an hour, a replacement met me at the alert pad entrance. I left alert and never flew a B-52 again. In a few short weeks, I had military orders to relocate my family near a major medical facility at Wright Patterson AFB in Dayton, Ohio. My next job was to fly NT-39As with the 4953rd Test Squadron (4950th Test Wing).

In the span of seven weeks, I learned our son was severely handicapped, left our church family, left our best friends, began living in a new state, and started a new job. The dominant emotion at that moment was loneliness, followed closely by fear. I couldn't even imagine what Carrie was feeling, and I didn't have the bandwidth to do so. It was then, without saying a word to each other, Carrie and I adopted our two separate coping mechanisms. We did try to share our pain with each other, but as Carrie put it, "it was like two drowning people trying to save each other". We were so overwhelmed we could only focus on our own tasks just to get through each day. Carrie took on Mitchell's care and the children. I focused on my new job and making a living. This worked for the next five years, but our new life would eventually demand more. I would later see our time at Wright Patterson AFB as a transition period where Carrie and I made the decision to merge our separate but parallel paths.

Chapter 2
NO! Not my Son! – Mom

It was early fall of 1989, I was a wife and young mother of two. Craig and I had met in college, fell in love, and married the summer of 1982. Seven years later, we had our whole life ahead of us, dreaming of six children and a beautiful old house surrounded by a white picket fence. We were stationed at Wurtsmith AFB in Oscoda, Michigan, active in a local Baptist church, bought our first home, and were expecting baby number three. My planned-out life was right on track! At least that is what I thought. However, in all my planning, I failed to do one important thing. I failed to ask God what our future should look like. Sure, we were in church every Sunday morning, Sunday night, and Wednesday night (remember, I did say Baptist church). I was also in a Bible study with our pastor's wife, went to all the women's meetings, served in the nursery, and helped in AWANA. I was checking all the right boxes expected of a good Christian wife and mom. But God knew better and had a different plan for our future. He knew what we needed. That is when God introduced us to baby number three.

Craig was a pilot in the Air Force. Military life would not have been my first choice, but it was Craig's choice, so I went with it. My dad was also in the Air Force until I was sixteen years old, so I was very familiar with the lifestyle. Those who have never been in the military really miss some unique opportunities to stretch your life. Part of Craig's work schedule at that time was to be on alert, meaning that the military person lives near their plane (Craig flew the B-52) for a week and is not allowed to go home or leave the base. What happens is everything at home either breaks, cries, or gets sick – you know, all the stuff that happens when daddy is away. Maybe not a big deal, but it happens every three weeks. It was more than tiring.

During those years in the military, Craig and I met one of our few lifelong friends, Steve and Sharon Baum. I met Steve and Sharon along with their bundle of children at church while Craig was on alert. Steve and Sharon had just arrived at Wurtsmith AFB. We soon started up a friendship that has lasted over thirty years. I was intrigued because they had four children, and this was not far from my plan of having six. I was with Sharon at her house when I found out I was pregnant with Mitchell. Of course, I was at their house because, you guessed it, Craig was on alert, and I wanted to have someone there to be happy or sad depending on the test results. Sharon and I were so excited! We were both standing in her bathroom staring at the stick and waiting for the line to appear. It was positive, and we hugged and yelled with excitement. I then drove to the alert facility to let Craig know our happy news.

As with my other two pregnancies, morning sickness was my all-day friend. My oldest son, Taylor, learned to make peanut butter and jelly sandwiches for himself and his little sister. He would also bring me crackers as my head was in the toilet most of the day. Finally, after six months, I was feeling great again. It was sometime in the first three months of my morning sickness we moved from our tiny first home to the Wurtsmith AFB housing so we could have more room for our growing family.

The time for our newest family member to be born had arrived. Craig and I dropped our other two children off at Steve and Sharon's house and headed to the base hospital. Back in the late 1980s, doctors did not do ultrasounds to find out the sex of the baby. Therefore, it was not until Mitchell made his debut that we knew he was a boy. His delivery was very quick, and he was born in the labor room. Back then, the labor room and delivery room were not the same cozy space moms have today. Out he came, and I was so happy to have another boy to love. I really did not care what I had because I already had a boy and a girl. However, deep down, I had always wanted a house full of boys. We had already decided on a name – Mitchell Lee Minor. Mitchell was after Craig's roommate and great friend in college, and Lee was after a man and his family who had influenced Craig during his high school years. Mitchell was full term, weighing in at 8 pounds and 6 ounces with a high Activity, Pulse, Grimace, Appearance, and Respiration (Apgar) score. The doctor did mention that his head measured a bit small, but he did not mention it again. Mitchell was just perfect to us with a head full of dark hair and chubby cheeks. He reminded us of his sister when she was born. After my mandatory three-day hospital stay, we went home to begin life as a family of five. I had no idea what was in store for our lives. None. In this instance, our ignorance was bliss.

Mitchell's siblings reached their baby milestones at different ages. I just figured each child was different with its own time line to follow. For this reason, I was not concerned when Mitchell did not reach similar milestones. I just thought and said to myself, "Oh, my, he is just so laid back." I breast fed Mitchell as I had done with my other two. I did not know at the time that Mitchell did not have a good sucking reflex so finally, after four months, I decided I was not producing enough milk and switched him to a bottle. He still was not sucking well, so I got nipples with bigger holes. He did not like anything when I tried to spoon-feed him. His tongue would just spit it out. I thought he was just a fussy eater. He did not hold his head up either, and it was becoming obvious at six months old. I know what you moms are thinking as you read this: "Are you kidding me? She did not notice something was wrong with her son?" I can say with absolute resolve that no, I did not. Maybe deep down I was lying to myself somehow subconsciously not letting myself think about the possibilities. Every once and awhile Craig would bring it up, saying he thought something was wrong, and I would tell him to be quiet. I told Craig that Mitchell was just on his own schedule. They say hindsight is 20/20. I would agree. Looking back, I wonder how I could have been so blind, especially after having two other children. How could I not see that Mitchell was not developing normally? I had even studied special education in college, taking classes in developmental delays and mental retardation. What in the world was I thinking? Today, I know exactly what was wrong with my thinking. I was saying to myself that this kind of stuff does not happen to people like Craig and me, and certainly not to good Christian people. This kind of stuff does not happen to ME! I did not ask or want this! I wanted instead to help people with special needs children. I did not want to be one of those parents that needed the help. "Nope. Not me. Not my family. No, no, and no." I prayed that the Lord would let me ignore this just a little bit longer.

Anyone who knows my husband Craig knows that his logical brain would not let him ignore obvious evidence. No, he would not! Therefore, when I would not listen, he approached our family doctor who had delivered Mitchell.

We attended the same church, and Craig spoke with him one Sunday night at a potluck dinner. The doctor told Craig to have me schedule an appointment for the following week. I already had Mitchell's sixth-month checkup scheduled for that week, so I took him in to see his doctor as planned.

Mitchell's sixth month checkup was May 11, 1990, at the Wurtsmith AFB Medical Center. I got him ready as I did for any outing and met Sharon at her house to watch our other children. I arrived at the small hospital building on time, and Mitchell met with his doctor. His doctor asked questions about what he could do at home. My answer was the same for each question he asked: "No, he is not doing that yet." I emphasized the word *yet*, trying to hold onto my hope. After a while, I was getting a bit defensive as my face flushed red. I could feel the warmth. My mind was screaming, "Leave Mitchell alone! He is his own person and will do these things when he is ready! Let us go home!" After a few minutes of silence, Mitchell's doctor said he would like Mitchell to see another pediatrician; he would have his secretary set it up. My mind started talking back at me: "Why can't this doctor just tell me everything is ok? Why does Mitchell need to have another pediatrician to tell me he is ok?" I suddenly realized, "Oh, my goodness. Maybe, just maybe. Oh no, I can't go there," I thought. "I can't." Mitchell's doctor returned from setting up the next appointment and told me that Mitchell could be seen the following Friday in the Pediatric Clinic. His voice sounded different with a kind of a sadness to it. He was very kind and helped me gather all of Mitchell's things. He said when we left to keep in touch. Looking back, I am sure he knew. He must have known. He was a doctor after all, and I think he just did not want to be the one to tell me. Home I went.

It was Mother's Day weekend. Craig was on alert, so the children and I would be driving to eat with him on Sunday after church. I went about my normal day on Saturday; I do not really remember thinking much about the appointment until Sunday night. After I put the children to bed, the house was quiet, and I started thinking and thinking, "What if something was wrong? What would we do? No, there cannot be something wrong. There just cannot be! God, please do not let anything be wrong with my Mitchell, Please!" My plea was a prayer with God that evening. I have looked back at that prayer and have often wondered what God was thinking as he heard it. I would like to think God was gently saying, "Nothing is ever wrong with someone whom I have woven together. *Mitchell may not be as the world expects him to be, but he is what I meant him to be.*"

Monday morning I awoke with my eyes sore from crying the night before. After getting the children up and ready for the day, I decided to call the Pediatric Clinic office and ask if they could see Mitchell sooner than Friday. The nurse who answered told me there were no earlier appointments. I began to cry. Through my tears, I told her, "Mitchell's family doctor indicated Friday that maybe something was wrong with Mitchell and that I could not wait until Friday." I added that I did not want to wait until Friday to find that out. She very sweetly said to bring him on up, and she would work us in. I thanked her. I was relieved, but at the same time, extremely nervous. I thought that perhaps today, I would know something. I quickly called Craig and told him I was taking Mitchell to see the doctor, and then I called Sharon to ask her if she could watch Grace and Taylor. When Sharon agreed, I drove over to her house, only a block away. When

I entered, I noticed that Steve was home and Sharon looked like she was ready to go somewhere. I do not remember which one told me, but they had decided that Sharon was going with me. She said that I should not go by myself. I exclaimed that I was quite fine to go by myself. Steve and Sharon would hear nothing of it and insisted on going with me. (Remember, Craig was on alert so he could not go with me.) Looking back with this wonderful hindsight that I now have, God was taking care of me through Sharon, just like a good Father does.

I do not remember driving to the hospital or the waiting room. My only memory of that appointment was sitting in the exam room while waiting for the doctor, meeting with the doctor, and then leaving. Etched in my memory forever is the exam room. It was a small room with a brown exam table, two uncomfortable metal chairs with faded blue cushions, a sink, and rolling stool. Sharon and I sat and waited for only a bit before the tall doctor entered. He made pleasantries then got right down to business. I could tell this doctor did not excel in his bedside manner. I answered his questions about my pregnancy and about Mitchell's birth. It seemed like he was firing questions at me as fast as he could. He then asked me to place Mitchell on the exam table in just a diaper. I remember the doctor prodding, pulling, and stretching Mitchell. The doctor measured Mitchell's precious head while saying "Mmm" several times before looking up at me. I have never forgotten the doctor's brown eyes staring at me while blurting out, "Your son is going to be physically and mentally handicapped. Do you have any questions?"

Did I have any questions? This doctor had just pulled the rug out from under me; my heart was pounding, my throat was tightening up, my stomach felt sick, and I couldn't do anything but cry. I remember Sharon hugging me as the floodgates of my tears opened fully. I just sobbed uncontrollably. The doctor said he would come back after I had pulled myself together. That only made everything worse. I wanted to scream at him that he was incredibly insensitive.

I was angry with the doctor for delivering the news I did not want to hear, and I was angry over his direct and seemingly insensitive approach. I know better today that this doctor was not trying to be unkind. He was just relaying his knowledge to me in the best way he knew how. Over the years, I have wondered if there is a gentler way to tell bad news like this. As experience has shown me, there is a better way. Mitchell has had many wonderful doctors since then definitely scoring an A+ in bedside manner. Others, although very knowledgeable in their field of study, simply lacked any type of gentle spirit that accompanies a good bedside manner. I guess it all depends on the personality of the person. My message to all doctors is that a bedside manner does matter.

The tall doctor returned to our room and began to tell Sharon and me all about Air Force policies regarding a dependent with a special needs family member. The doctor said we would need to move to another Air Force base that was better able to help care for Mitchell. Move! Did he say, "Move?" I could not believe the doctor was telling me I would need to move and leave my church family and dear friends, friends now needed to help us navigate this unknown territory after learning the worst news a young mother could ever get about her child. I felt so overwhelmed, so scared, so mad, and very sad. "THIS WAS NOT IN MY PLAN! What was the Lord doing?" It was at that moment that I started down the dreaded "WHY ME" path. It is a very selfish path, and I am embarrassed to admit that I stayed on that path far too long. It is not healthy, wise, or God-honoring at all. Sadly, it took God several years to get me off this path. However, God loves me, and he was relentless and faithful to help me see it his way. He never gave up on me!

Somehow, Sharon and I made it back to her house where Steve was watching six children (their four and my two). Steve could tell we had been crying. Sharon filled Steve in. I would have told Steve the bad news, but I just could not bring myself to say any of those words aloud. I called Craig and told him we were on our way to tell him what the doctor had said. I do not remember who watched our children. Someone must have. Steve, Sharon, Mitchell, and I drove to the alert facility in silence. When we arrived, Craig was waiting in the parking lot, and he then got into the van. He looked at me with concern and worry in his eyes. He was waiting to hear about this dreaded doctor appointment. I once again could not say the words. I looked at Steve and said, "You tell him. I can't." Steve did not want to be the one tell a father his son was handicapped, but he was very kind-hearted and did that hard job for me. Tears started rolling down Craig's face. The tears had never stopped rolling down mine. I did not know so many tears could be stored in my tear ducts. All four of us just sat in the van crying and looking at our Mitchell. Craig was able to get a replacement quickly for himself to finish out his week of alert. Military people are just like that. They take care of one another and have each other's backs. His brothers and sisters in arms were concerned for our family, and it showed. Craig never sat alert again. His commanders made sure Craig had time to adjust to a new reality and care for his family. I was, and still am, very grateful for Craig's leadership during that time and the remainder of his years in the Air Force. I have often said that the Church as a whole could take lessons on caring for one another from the military. The military is a family, and the bond is strong.

Back home we were faced with the task of sharing Mitchell's and our family's new reality with family and friends. When you are military, you usually do not live near your biological family. For this reason, it is common for your church and military friends to become like family to you. During those first few days of adjusting to this news, our Oscoda Baptist family stepped in. Meals began to show up, friends sent cards, and people took our other children to have play dates with their children. No one from church called and asked if we wanted any of those things. Our church family saw each need and served us. If they had asked us, we would have certainly answered that we are just fine. However, we were far from fine, and those acts of kindness still bring joy to my heart. This taught me to never ask people if they need anything when it is obvious they do. Get close enough to discern the need, and go serve them in love.

One conversation I will never forget was when Denise, whom I did not know very well from church, came to console us and bring us dinner. I remember her bringing her handicapped son to the church nursery and laying him down in a crib for us to watch. His name was Dwayne. He was about ten years old with dark hair and dark eyes. Denise was familiar with the path that we had just started. I have always remembered her kind and very wise words to us that evening. She explained that finding out your child has a disability is very much like a death. I was shocked at the term *death*. However, as I continued to listen, her words made a lot of sense to my broken heart. She explained to Craig and me that we had been expecting a normal child. After seven months with Mitchell, we discovered what we thought was our normal child suddenly no longer existed. Figuratively, our normal child had died. She explained that we needed to go through the grieving process. Then, after that grieving, we would be ready to get to know our new son – the son we were not expecting. I listened to her because she spoke with authority. She had gone through that grieving process. She had learned from her own heartache and now was able to share what she knew with us. She was comforted then so she could comfort us now. Although I did not know Denise well, we now shared a special bond, one that all mothers of special needs children understand.

In the first few days after discovering Mitchell's condition, I needed to talk to another mother of a special needs child. This particular person was someone dear to my heart, my cousin Brenda Carter. Her precious son, Johnathon Matthew, was born many years earlier before I met Craig. Johnathon had hydrocephaly and spina bifida and lived only thirteen months. Johnathon left his mark on all my relatives. We are close-knit kin. Brenda must have sensed my need to talk with her, or God simply laid it on her heart to call me because the phone rang. We cried for a bit, and I asked her the question I had wanted to ask: When does it stop hurting? When will my heart stop aching for my Mitchell? When? That was my question. Brenda's response to me was not what I expected to hear as she knowingly exclaimed: "Never!"

Craig was my rock those first few days and continues to be my rock to this day. I just could not bring myself to say those words aloud that something was wrong with Mitchell. I tried calling my parents that first evening. I dialed, put on a brave front, and then handed the phone to Craig. Craig had no one to hand the phone to, so he accepted the hard task and then said those words repeatedly as we called all our family and friends. Our friends took care of letting our church family know, easing our burden. It was days before I could bring myself to say those words out loud, "Mitchell is handicapped." I did say them in my head though. I was talking to God about it all day long. "God, what in the world, what are you doing here? Why in the world did you do this to ME? Do you really know what you are doing?" God listened patiently to my whining. He let me be angry with him. He let me yell in my head at him. When he was ready, God would tell me the answers to my questions. Well, he was waiting for me to be ready to listen and accept his answers.

The days that followed are kind of a blur. During the next week, we met with a Chaplain and had several doctor appointments. Craig began the paperwork to transfer to another base with a larger hospital. One of the very first appointments was to x-ray Mitchell's head. During the initial pediatric appointment, the doctor never mentioned a diagnosis to me. As I sat in the radiology waiting room with Mitchell, I began to read over the paperwork that I was to give to the x-ray technician. It was then that I saw that word describing Mitchell's condition. I thought to myself where had I seen that word before? It dawned on me that I had read about this condition in my history of mental retardation class back in my college days. *Microcephaly.* My heart sank as tears welled up in my eyes. I remembered reading about mistreated individuals who had tiny heads. Their demeaning label was *pinhead.* Circuses put people with microcephaly on display because their heads and bodies were strikingly out of proportion. Microcephaly means small head or small brain and is a congenital brain defect, meaning it is present at birth. The brain does not develop to its full size as they get older. Developmental delays accompany the diagnosis and vary in severity. I began to wonder if this is what the doctor thought Mitchell had? If so, why had he not said that to me during that first appointment with him? This was my earliest lesson on dealing with doctors. Always ask your doctors questions and ask them until you get an answer.

A few days later, Craig and I took Mitchell to see a neurologist in Saginaw, Michigan, followed by an MRI and CAT scan of Mitchell's head. The results all verified the microcephaly diagnosis. Doctors found calcium deposits in Mitchell's brain, indicating brain damage occurred while his brain was developing. In addition, the outer layer of tissue covering Mitchell's brain (meninges) did not fully develop. As we sat and listened to the results of the MRI and CAT scans from the pediatric neurologist, my brain began to fog over. I felt as if he were speaking about some other family's son and not our son. My heart was pounding, and it felt like it was right in my throat. I tried to be brave. Today, I am not sure why I even tried. I cried and cried. Craig was once again the rock of the family. Before we left, the doctor made one more statement to us that we have never forgotten, and this affected us for years. He said that he thought our son may live to be five years old. My mind screamed to me – five years old! That was the age of Taylor at the time. That was not very long at all. What would these five years hold for us was all I was thinking as we walked with Mitchell to our car to drive two hours back home. I do not remember our drive back.

The Air Force worked with us to relocate to a base with a large regional hospital. Craig researched which bases had the larger hospitals and what help was available in different states. I was so glad Craig led our family through this chore. Craig is a very detailed person and a great planner. His skills came in handy those days. The Air Force narrowed down our choices to Lackland AFB in Texas, Andrews AFB in Maryland, and Wright Patterson AFB in Ohio. These three bases had the necessary medical facilities and a flying unit with aircraft Craig could fly. After looking into the available state programs for disabled persons for each location, Ohio was hands down the best fit. In addition, there was a pilot position open for Craig to fill at Wright-Patterson AFB. Before we could say, *Mitchell*, we were on our way to Wright Patterson AFB, Ohio. We now call Ohio home.

A TIME OF UNCERTAINTY
(July 1990 – October 1995)

Chapter 3
A Pilot's Death – Dad

Professionally, my next five years in the Air Force were incredible. While Carrie was attending endless doctor and therapy appointments and discovering with each visit Mitchell's new health complications, I became a workaholic. This is where I can posit a good excuse that I was trying to emotionally escape from our family troubles. The design of this kind of excuse would suggest that somehow I was not culpable for poor decisions because I was physiologically not aware that I was escaping from reality. Pure bunk! The inescapable truth was that I was selfish! It is no secret that men often choose professional success over their family responsibilities. I saw this firsthand in the military as many successful airmen outperformed their peers. A closer look at their success often revealed their coming in early, going home late, and working most weekends. I can sum up this kind of professional success very easily. They took the time that belonged to their spouse and family and converted that energy into winning at work.

In my estimation, many airmen who were balancing job and family lost favor leaving great leaders behind. Of course, this was not always the case. Some leaders saw through the smoke to right the scales. Lieutenant Colonel Jeffrey Riemer was one of those men. I worked for Jeff in those first few years at Wright Patterson AFB, and he taught me how to continually improve my character. I would need this later in the darker days to come. Jeff's words matched his deeds. Over the next four years, I began to view Jeff as a big brother. One time he organized a trip for several men to attend Promise Keepers in Indiana. As many are aware, Promise Keepers was big back in the early 1990s challenging men to keep their promises made to their spouse and family. The commitments I made during that weekend retreat began to gnaw at my conscience. This was the beginning of God's whispering into my ear that a change was necessary. It would be another two years before I accepted God's direction.

During this period of our lives, Carrie was on a quest to fix Mitchell. Early on, a specialist announced that Mitchell would likely not live past five years old. Let that sink in for a moment. Hearing this did something to Carrie. With an impish smile on my face, I say, "Never tell a red head nothing can be done." I could see Carrie's obsession to fix Mitchell was a little misplaced, but there is no stopping a Norse mama bear when it comes to her cubs.

For families with special needs children, the beginning years are less physically challenging. Friends and family, take note. When a young family presents with a special needs child, the sheer power of their youth helps the mom and dad push through many physical difficulties. Mitchell was very light and easy to pick up and care for in the first couple of years. Normal equipment like strollers still worked at the time. We did not understand this at first, but the burdens of caring for a special needs child typically increases over time – in our case, exponentially with each passing year. This is likely true for any family caring for the profoundly handicapped whether by birth, from a sudden accident, or for an aging parent. Some of the changes were insidious and some were punctuated chaos. Carrie's account of the many changes and her role in Mitchell's care is riveting. The tendency is for people watching from a distance to think a family has it all under control when nothing obvious stands out. I am telling you right now this is not true. We did not wake up one day and find it difficult to care for Mitchell. It sneaked up on us. Family and friends need to move in a little closer and start looking for the clues as the pressure mounts. All our stories of our serving Mitchell's ministry should help you to know where to look.

Our dear friends Mark and Cheryl Klimek stand out as one of the first of a few families that moved in a little closer. We met them when we attended Grand Heights Baptist Church right after moving to Ohio just outside Wright Patterson AFB in Fairborn. Mark and Cheryl are extraordinary people, and I consider Mark a mentor and a friend. Young men, listen carefully: *Always find older and wiser men to model your future self.* Everyone knows that people are not perfect, so do not get hung up on the little things. Some people have attributes that you know you are missing in spades. For dads beginning a similar journey, start looking for mentors sooner rather than later. When you are leading a family with a new special needs child, you must mature a little faster. Early on, I had my first two mentors. They were unaware of their new assignment. As I mentioned earlier, Jeff Riemer taught me how to shore up my character and keep my promises. Mark Klimek taught me how to subtly hang in there and make a difference in hurting people's lives. Later, Mark taught me a whole lot more because, as civilians not prone to moving around, he and Cheryl were able to continue building into our daily lives.

Our friends Steve and Sharon Baum never lived near us again. However, as lifelong friends often do, we found a way to get together at least twice a year. In times of need, we know that they are only a phone call away. I can count on one hand our closest friends that know us completely. In my estimation, Steve and Sharon lead that list.

Although it is important for family and friends to lean into an overwhelmed family, the overwhelmed family also has a responsibility to lean in as well. My military friend, Steve Davis, taught me this. Carrie and I were planning our move to Cedarville, just twenty miles east of Wright Patterson AFB, and Steve said to me, "Let me know when you move so I can help." He reminded me at least five times. The big day came and went, and I did not let Steve know as I had promised. It was a difficult move, and my pride kept me from asking anyone for help. Carrie literally shouldered the brunt of this bad decision. At church, the following week Steve came up alongside of me, put his left arm over my shoulder, and said, "Craig, I'm disappointed in you." I could see the disappointment in his face, and I knew he was not bluffing. He said that he had heard that I had moved and that I had robbed him of a blessing. My heart sank. He continued by reminding me that he was in charge of his yes and no and not me. His simple words changed me that day, and I apologized profusely; I appreciated his forgiveness. I learned a valuable lesson that day: Mitchell's ministry did not belong to just Carrie and me.

As Carrie and I worked separately but together to keep our lives on the same set of tracks, we learned a not-so-intuitive life lesson. We did not catch on until many years later. Carrie became this super-organized, 24/7 Mitchell caregiver. When I think of all the things she did and still does today, my head spins. Now anyone who knows Carrie, including herself, would never describe Carrie as super organized. It is amazing how many squirrels enter her field of view in a day. I must laugh because this literally happened. One day I was trying to have a serious conversation with Carrie, and she kept subtly glancing past my right ear. I was sure my eyes were not on my right ear. Frustrated, I finally looked over my shoulder and right outside the window was, you guessed it, a squirrel. We both burst out laughing. In contrast, no one who knows me would describe me as the model for emotional attentiveness. I would make the worst counselor because my advice would always be the same: Just stop doing what you are doing, and get over yourself. This a great attribute for a pilot but not so much for a husband or dad. Despite my serious shortfall, I somehow became Mitchell's comforter. Usually after work or on the weekends, I held Mitchell, quietly singing and humming to him, sometimes for hours. I always felt his little frame completely relax as if the entire stress of his day was absorbed by my chest. His relaxation was so complete that he would often clear a simmering seizure and fall into a deep, restful sleep. I always seemed intuitively to know when Mitchell was in pain, and I often prayed that God would allow me to share in his pain to ease his burden. At large church functions, people would tell me that when we parked Mitchell in his wheelchair in the corner of the banquet room, his eyes would follow me wherever I went. Carrie and I learned that in our weakness God was at his strongest. I have no doubt Mitchell's ministry was the work God prepared in advance for Carrie and me before he set the foundations of the world.

Early on, Mitchell taught me a lot about the kind of person I needed to be. With complete clarity, I remember an intensely personal teaching moment. I was sitting in the pew (right side six rows back) at Grace Baptist Church in Cedarville, Ohio. I was holding Mitchell during a special program. Standing on stage were about fifteen toddlers, all around Mitchell's age, singing

"Jesus Loves Me," complete with hand movements in the cutest way only toddlers can perform. Without warning, I choked up as a rush of sadness and tears seized me. I thought, "Mitchell should be on that stage." Instantly God took over my heart. In the unmistakable soft voice of the Spirit, God said to me, "Craig, I know how much you want Mitchell to walk and talk and do all the things you intended for him to do. I also know you love Mitchell unconditionally." With tears now visible, the Spirit's voice continued, "I want you to know how much I love you. You are so spiritually handicapped, and you will never do the things I intended for you to do in this world. I love you in that same way." For the first time in my life, I truly understood God's unconditional love for everyone and for me. This kind of love was no longer a definition but an understanding as a groan from my heart. Every time I recall this moment, tears come to my eyes, and I thank God for saving me!

My role as a dad and husband became very difficult, and I had to decide whether to pursue my own professional goals or to change them to reflect my new reality. The problem was our new reality was constantly changing. I cannot describe the anxiety I felt over this issue at the time. I started coming to work late every morning because Carrie simply could not do it all. Thankfully, I had the support of understanding bosses. A special thanks to men like Al Schoolcraft and Richard Archibald, real men of character, who protected my ability to balance family and work. In the morning at 4:00 AM, I got up with Mitchell to comfort him when he cried; it was like clockwork, and I sometimes held him until it was time to get ready for work. Carrie needed her rest in order to cover the doctor appointments while caring for our new baby son and making sure our other two children made it to school. I am not exactly sure when, but as Mitchell approached two years old, he started to become too heavy for Carrie to lift in or out of the bathtub. This became my job. Mitchell's dead weight made him difficult to maneuver, and he was slippery when wet. Mitchell's first wheelchair fitting was around this time.

By the time Mitchell was four years old, he had his first surgery to insert a feeding tube. Besides needing help physically to care for Mitchell, Carrie also needed emotional support that by now I was only sporadically providing as the fog began to lift over my selfish professional ambitions. Carrie long abandoned the dream for our lives she originally envisioned. It took me another two years finally to let go of mine.

As Mitchell was approaching five years old, I knew we were fast approaching a tipping point. As an Air Force pilot, I was constantly flying away on missions, frustrating the support Carrie needed from her husband. It was years later before the Air Force would begin its Exceptional Family Member Program (EFMP) to help airmen with a special needs family member to balance their family and work. The Army already had a program that would eventually be the benchmark for all the Department of Defense. During this era, officers were required to move to other locations to develop as leaders and remain promotable. We called this move a Permanent Change of Station (PCS). I was feeling the pressure to PCS, and I knew by this time that Mitchell required highly specialized doctors for his care. Because Mitchell is nonverbal, it took the doctors several months, and sometimes years, to figure out how to best care for him, about the length of time an officer was expected to move.

We discovered early on that the Air Force was not equipped to handle Mitchell's growing list of profound physical handicaps. The Air Force was already farming part of Mitchell's care out to specialized civilian doctors. However, it required much red tape to get the necessary approvals for civilian doctors to see Mitchell off base. Mitchell's care became disconnected and uncoordinated. The Air Force was great at taking care of airmen, somewhat good at taking care of spouses, a little less capable when it came to healthy children, and completely ill equipped to take care of children like Mitchell. We had no doubt that, if we stayed in the Air Force, Mitchell would not live very long. The problem was that moving simply was not an option for Mitchell's well-being, and not moving simply was not an option for making the living we were accustomed to.

From this time forward, Carrie and I had to make very tough decisions that no family should ever have to make. We did not have any family living nearby to help us share the load. We were far from our families and essentially bound to the local civilian doctors who finally understood how to care for Mitchell. So quietly and prayerfully we had to make the decision of whether to stay in the Air Force or leave. I did seek council from several senior military officers who were also my friends. After explaining my quandary, all agreed: leaving the Air Force was the decision they would likely make if they were in my shoes. These same men were grooming me for a very successful military career, so agreeing with my decision was not easy. It took Carrie and me over a year to decide.

Just before Mitchell's sixth birthday, I turned down a promotion to Major, resigned my commission, and left the Air Force. Carrie and I were at peace with the decision, knowing confidently that this was what God wanted us to do. However, we had no idea that we would wander in the dessert, and we were blissfully unaware of the coming hardships that would test the foundations of our relationship and faith. If we had known what was to come, I am confident we would have made the wrong decision.

Chapter 4
I Can Fix Mitchell – Mom

We packed up our belongings and headed to Wright Patterson AFB near Dayton, Ohio. As with most military moves, we did not know where we would be living when we arrived. We checked into base billeting, and they had a tiny apartment available until we found a place to live. We signed a lease to rent an old house (a dream of mine was always to live in an older home) in Fairborn. Our house would not be available for another six weeks. We were unable to stay in billeting the entire time before moving into our new rental. Therefore, we rented an apartment in Kettering with a month-to-month lease. We also found Grand Avenue Baptist Church, now called Grand Heights Baptist Church, in Fairborn. It was there that I met two of my dearest friends: Becky Hayes and Cheryl Klimek. We have been friends for over twenty-five years, and our children grew up together and remain friends today. Becky and Cheryl helped bring a sense of normalcy to my chaotic life. We would often meet for lunch, have Bible studies or just talk and let the children play. Our oldest son, Taylor, started kindergarten in Fairborn, and Grace and I started out on our *Fixing Mitchell* adventure.

During these early days of taking Mitchell and the other two children back and forth to doctor visits and therapy, I remember talking to God while I drove. I hate change to begin with, so moving so abruptly and learning about Mitchell's new condition did not sit well with me. I asked God, "Why did you send us here where I have no one to help me? Please tell me why." Of course, these conversations were through tears, and the radio was a little louder so Taylor and Grace could not hear me crying. Then one day, it is as if I heard God's still, small voice gently say to me, "I sent you here because I am all you and Craig need. Depend on me. After all, I am the Creator of the universe and the Creator of Mitchell. I will see your family through this." I cannot say that from that day forward I always trusted everything God did, but I do know that he gave me a deep, calm peace that we were not alone in the seemingly unplanned journey we were about to take.

Because Ohio was one of the first states to offer an early intervention program beginning at birth instead of age three, Craig set up our first visit to Four Oaks even before we arrived in Ohio. Craig and I went together to Mitchell's intake appointment in July. Of course, since we did not know anyone well enough to babysit them, Taylor and Grace tagged along. The Four Oaks early intervention center, located in Xenia, Ohio, was a service of the Greene County Board of Mental Retardation and Developmental Disability (MRDD). The Greene County Board of MRDD is now the Greene County Board of Developmental Disabilities (GCBDD). I was very nervous on the way to the center, not really knowing what to expect in an intake. The staff, some of the finest people I have come to know, quickly settled my nerves. I keep in touch with some of them to this day. During the intake meeting, we met the school administrator, who was a special education teacher, physical therapist, speech therapist, and occupational therapist. She was good at what she did! When they scheduled Mitchell for occupational therapy, I did wonder why in the world he would need any occupational therapy at such a young age. Mitchell would not be getting a job for years. That day I learned the difference between physical and occupational therapy. Physical therapy was the treatment of disease, injury or deformity by physical methods rather than by drugs or surgery. Whereas, occupational therapy was for those recuperating from physical or mental illness, encouraging rehabilitation by performing activities necessary in daily life.

Later in the intake meeting, the therapists sat with Mitchell on the floor, stretching his muscles, and moving his joints to assess his range of motion. The purpose was to write goals for him to accomplish in his Individual Education Plan (IEP). I remember how I felt on the parent side of an IEP versus writing an IEP. Being on the emotional side of an IEP was completely different from my writing goal driven IEPs for my college class assignments. Each therapist and Mitchell's teacher suggested goals from their field of expertise, and we just agreed with their recommendations. At the time, we did not know Mitchell's true potential, let alone what he might accomplish by the end of his first school year. While we were busy with the intake meeting, one of the staff members kept Taylor and Grace busy in another classroom. Four Oaks had a very family-friendly feel.

Mitchell's six years of attending Four Oaks was a blessing, and the love we felt and knowledge we gained was due to the wonderful staff. Four Oaks school has since grown into several schools throughout Greene County. Parents tell me the quality of the staff and care for the children continues to this day. Mitchell still receives services from the GCBDD, and we have been able to keep up with some of the key people from his days there.

I remember Mitchell's first day of school at Four Oaks. We had the choice of Mitchell riding a bus or me driving Mitchell to class. I drove him to school for over five years.

On the way that first day, I distinctly remember thinking, "Now, pull yourself together and don't cry when you see the really handicapped children." Well, on the way home, I had a very different conversation with myself. "Wow, I think I brought the really handicapped child to school today. I don't know why some of those children were even there." Later I discovered that to qualify for services a child only needs to be *at risk* of a delay. Some of the other children could crawl, walk, and talk. I knew that several of the children were from foster homes and were born from mothers who used drugs or alcohol during pregnancy. This made my heart ache for those sweet little children. I was also angry because the child's condition was preventable. I did not even drink a diet coke (which was my main addiction at the time) during my pregnancy. Not fair I thought. It also bothered me that many of the toddlers rode the bus all by themselves to and from school. I had to remind myself that God was in control of these little ones as well. I had to work through many emotions during my time at Four Oaks. I was young and still learning not to judge other moms' parenting choices or styles since I had not walked in their shoes. (Craig and I work very hard not to judge other parents with special needs children choosing a different path.) We chose not to place Mitchell in an institution. Instead, we chose to keep him at home. This worked well for us. However, other parents may decide differently. Again, we constantly remind each other that we have not walked in their shoes or know their story.

I also remember Mitchell's last day of school that first year. Mitchell had not reached one single goal written in his IEP. Not even one! I was very sad and a little angry. I thought that the therapists were writing each goal because they knew from their experience Mitchell would achieve the goal. Crawling and sitting independently was one of the goals that first year. I really thought Mitchell would be crawling and sitting by himself by the end of May. The therapists worked hard with Mitchell three days a week, and I continued his therapy at home. I did my part, and Mitchell rarely missed a day. Mitchell did not crawl or sit by himself, and he never has. My heart was just broken. When we met to set next year's goals, I wanted achievable goals. They continued to set goals year after year, and he never met even one. This broke my already broken heart more. Every year I slowly learned just how profoundly handicapped Mitchell really was, and every year less of my naïve hope remained.

During Mitchell's second year, an IEP equipment goal was to fit Mitchell with his first wheelchair. We met this goal the spring of that year. I had seen a picture of the chair and even helped pick it out. When it arrived, and Mitchell sat it for the first time, it looked so much more like a wheelchair than I was expecting. Mitchell looked handicapped in his wheelchair. He looked less handicapped tucked out of view in his stroller. Wow, that was a reality check for me. My son would be using a wheelchair for the rest of his life. That was a new idea I was not ready to embrace.

Shortly after getting the chair, I decided to take Taylor, Grace, and Mitchell to the Commissary on base to get groceries. Taylor was eight years old, Grace was six years old, and Mitchell was two years old and sporting his new shiny blue chair with big wheels. It was a disaster from the start with a shopping cart, wheelchair, and two high-energy and mobile children. Grace was too short to push the wheelchair or the cart. Grace could not see over the handles. Taylor was a typical boy and pushing anything would be a drag race. Having no other alternative, I pushed the wheelchair and pulled the shopping cart. As I turned a corner, I rather quickly ran over the foot of a nice man in his lovely blue uniform. I apologized profusely and turned two shades of red – easy to do with my pale skin. He was not upset at all and even asked if he could help me in any way. That evening I shared my story with Craig, and he asked me his name. I said, "I do not know his name; he never said, but I did notice he had two stars on his shoulder." Craig informed me that I had run over a two-star general's shoes with the wheelchair that day.

During that first year with the wheelchair, I was pushing Mitchell out to the van after leaving the base commissary while the bagger was following me with the groceries. I noticed a man in a wheelchair following us. The bagger placed the groceries in the van, and I was working to get Mitchell out of his chair and into his car seat when the man in the wheelchair started talking to me. He asked if I had ever thought of taking Mitchell to a faith healing service, informing me that his church had them regularly, and if I had enough faith, my son could be out of that chair. I was so hurt and mad at the same time. I tried to be as polite as I could and said that I was not interested. I continued to get Mitchell buckled and then went to the back of the van to put the wheelchair into the van. He kept talking to me, and I was fighting back tears. As he tried to hand me a pamphlet about the services I said, "My son is not sick; thank you anyway." How dare he ask me such a thing and say *if I had enough faith*! I was boiling inside by the time I started my van and pulled away. As I was driving home, it hit me that the man was in a wheelchair himself. Well, I thought, either his church has terrible healing services, or he does not have enough faith himself! I am sure he meant well and thought he was being helpful and kind. I did not take it that way at all. We probably both learned something that day.

Mitchell attended Four Oaks for five more years. During those years, I took Taylor, Grace, and eventually Levi. The first couple of years there was a room where siblings of the students would go play while moms worked with their special needs child. It was so helpful, and I so appreciated that service of their program. Later, the school integrated the siblings into the preschool classes and the kindergarten class. I really am glad that my children had an opportunity to learn and play with other children struggling with various learning and physical disabilities.

In January 1991, therapists fitted Mitchell's wrists with the first of many braces. Because of the severe spasticity in his wrist muscles, Mitchell had developed muscle contractures. A Wright Patterson AFB occupational therapist made Mitchell's first pair. He had never made a pair for small wrists before but did a great job. Mitchell did not and still does not like his hands touched so it was not an easy or fun process to get them made. It was a long and tiring day having his first pair made. On my way home I thought, "Oh great, one more thing to keep up with and not lose."

That April during one of Mitchell's physical therapy sessions, his therapist noticed Mitchell making some unusual eye movements. She mentioned to me that she thought they were seizures. I thought, "Seizures? No! Seizures were people falling to the ground and their limbs stiffening up. These cannot be seizures." I then started thinking, "Not seizures, too, Lord." I decided to trust her knowledge and made the call right away to get Mitchell seen by a neurologist.

Wright Patterson Hospital happened to have a pediatric neurologist on staff, and Mitchell's appointment was set rather quickly. During his first appointment, the doctor said that Mitchell's unusual eye twitches were in fact seizures. Mitchell's eye twitches were frequent, and he did not have a seizure-free day. Mitchell's EEGs showed that Mitchell was having seizures constantly. This was not good news. I learned years later from his neurologist at Nationwide Children's Hospital that Mitchell's seizure disorder was Lennox-Gastaut Syndrome (LGS). LGS is a rare, severe, and the most difficult type of seizure disorder to control. Mitchell's seizures became steadily worse, and Craig and I consider Mitchell's seizure control our hardest battle to fight to this day.

December 1991 was very emotional for Craig and me. After having Mitchell, we were questioning our plan to have six children. Mitchell by himself was like having three children, and of course, we were already a household of five. During this time, I had a miscarriage from an unplanned pregnancy. I was heartbroken nonetheless. However, at the same time, a little bit relieved. My mind began to ask questions again. "What if God decided to give us another special needs child?" Craig and I wrestled with that thought for weeks. I was scared and nervous but also felt deep down that our family was not complete yet. Could I trust God with this? Would I trust him that if he wanted us to have another special needs child, would I really accept that? Finally, after many conversations with God, I decided to trust him. I also felt in my heart that Mitchell was going to be the only special needs child in our family, but I did need to come to that point in my faith that I would trust God with the outcome of our next child. I guess deep down I did not have control over how Mitchell turned out, and I was not sure I could trust God not to do this to me again.

Since making the decision that God chooses the outcome and not me, I have had a difficult time when people say, "I don't care if it's a boy or a girl as long as it is healthy." It was especially heartbreaking when Mitchell was right next to me. It really hurt, and I took it personally. When someone says this to me, I typically respond with a smile, "Dear, you will love them no matter what." I know people just say phrases like this without really thinking. However, I can emphatically say that we were given that not-so-healthy baby, and we love Mitchell with all our heart. To the parents who choose to have a special needs child through adoption, you are my heroes! They take on this journey of love knowing the cost from the start. I have a dear friend, Kathleen, who adopted several special needs children, and I have always admired her bravery. She and I have prayed for each other's children for over twenty years now.

Soon after deciding to trust God with our baby number four, we found out we were expecting our caboose in the fall of 1992. Little did I know that this would be Mitchell's best friend. I have always struggled with trust issues, but Craig, on the other hand, did not need time to learn to trust God; he somehow resolved this in is heart long before we met.

That same year we bought a home in Cedarville, Ohio. We had found the town of Cedarville through our friendship with Mark and Cheryl Klimek and Becky Hayes. They lived in Cedarville, and I loved driving to visit them in this small town in the middle of cornfields. When Craig and I were looking to buy a home, we were looking for a good school district, and Cedarville won easily. On Father's Day weekend that year, we moved into our ranch style house on five areas with a creek out back. I did not love our house per se, but the yard was a child's dream place to play. We also made sure we stayed in Greene County to ensure we did not interrupt Mitchell's therapy at Four Oaks. It was next to our new home that we met our new neighbors and lifelong friends, Joe and Andrea Harkleroad and their four children. Joe and Andrea had three sons and one daughter. Our children forged friendships that last to this day. A few years later Becky and her family bought the house on the other side of us, and I now had friends for neighbors on both sides. It was wonderful having them close by and the children loved playing together during their entire childhood. That fall of 1992, Taylor started second grade, Grace started kindergarten, and Levi arrived in November.

Feeding Mitchell had always been a chore. He did not nurse or take a bottle well, and he never could drink from a cup. Spoon feedings were terrible. I worked on tongue exercises his speech therapist had showed me to try to get him to chew and swallow better. His food had to be pureed. Most of the time Mitchell would swallow some food the wrong way, choke, and aspirate, throwing up everything, and we would have to start all over again. Without fail, this would happen on his last bite. Feeding time was very frustrating, but I knew Mitchell was very hungry. Imagine trying to feed someone for over an hour three times a day. Some days it felt like all I did was feed Mitchell. During this time, Mitchell got aspiration pneumonia requiring hospitalization twice. One day at school, his speech therapist recommended that I ask his doctor about a feeding tube. Our G-tube journey began that day.

I remember talking with a couple of his doctors at the base hospital; neither doctor thought a feeding tube was a good idea. One doctor said he felt like we were giving up on Mitchell if we got him a feeding tube. I thought, "No, I am working hard to feed my son, and he is losing weight." The other doctor wanted to prescribe a medicine for Mitchell to make him hungry. This was the side effect of the medicine. I thought, "How absurd! It was clear he was having difficulty eating and not that he was rejecting food because he was not hungry." Finally, I took Craig with me to one of the doctor appointments. He pulled some military talk on them, and we were able to get an off-base consult with a gastrologist at Dayton Children's Hospital.

The Dayton Children's Hospital gastrologist asked us right away why we had not come in earlier to get Mitchell a feeding tube. We explained that Craig was military, and we had been desperately trying to get an off-base referral for quite some time now. He said he was prior Army and understood the politics of getting referrals. When we took Mitchell's shirt off the doctor took one look at Mitchell and said with slight disgust, "I have never recommended a feeding tube during a patient's first visit until now." By this time, Mitchell was skin and bones; you could count every bone in his body. Add to this the fact that Mitchell's tongue was sticking out of his mouth, and he was a complete quadriplegic. We felt immediately like bad parents even though the doctor did not intend to make us feel that way. It is that moment when you first feel guilty not knowing that you should have known all along.

Mitchell's next appointment was with a surgeon to determine the type of feeding tube for Mitchell and choose a surgery date. The doctors chose a Gastronomy Tube (G-Tube), which looks like a blow-up toy button placed right over his stomach. This type of feeding tube has worked great for Mitchell and is the only feeding tube system he has ever known. In November 1993, when Mitchell was four years old, he had his first and easiest surgery. We had no idea of all the surgeries Mitchell would eventually have. During the surgery, the doctor also did a Nissen Fundoplication to help prevent reflux and aspiration leading to pneumonia since Mitchell had this problem twice before. A Nissen Fundoplication simply made the sphincter entering the stomach smaller so that it was harder for any stomach contents to go backward up the esophagus to reach the lungs.

Surgery day began early – extremely early for me! We arrived at the hospital shortly after 5:00 in the morning. Craig laid Mitchell on the hospital gurney, and the staff began to prepare him for surgery. The nurses ran through their routine asking medical history questions, confirming his current medications, and setting up the intravenous (IV) bag. Mitchell was our first child to have a surgery of any type. Craig and I were both very nervous as the staff busied themselves with Mitchell. Occasionally, our eyes would meet, and we were both trying not to cry. I did very well until they came in, said the doctor was ready for Mitchell, and started to push the gurney out of the room. The nurse told us to go wait in the waiting area and that we would receive regular updates. I felt a pit in my stomach, and my throat tightened as I realized these strangers were taking my son away from us. The feeling of seeing the nurses roll your child away is one of the most helpless feelings a parent will ever experience. I could no longer hold back the tears that flooded down my cheeks. Craig also began to cry trying very hard to be strong for me. We walked to the waiting room and saw some familiar faces from our church. That felt so wonderful. Our deacon and a couple of friends had come to sit with us for awhile. That act may not seem very important, but if you have never sat in a waiting room by yourselves, you know how lonely this time can be, especially when it is your child. Let me tell you that it is one of the most blessed actions you can do for a family member, friend, or even for an acquaintance. It costs nothing but a little bit of time.

Halfway through the surgery a nurse came to give us an update. She let us know that everything was going as expected. Finally, the doctor came out to let us know that he was finished, and Mitchell was in recovery. The doctor told us that Mitchell would be going to the Pediatric Intensive Care Unit (PICU) just as a precaution. I thought, "Wow, PICU?" This was our first experience with a PICU. The care given to a child in a PICU setting is amazing. During this stay, Mitchell was never alone, and the staff was great at keeping his pain level under control. I had never really seen anyone right after a surgery. Mitchell was very pale, looking almost not alive, while lying in that hospital bed. This image was worse with all the tubes and machines tied to Mitchell. As I stood there, my heart broke, and I wondered if this would be worth it. I can truly say that it was. Before surgery, Mitchell's surgeon had said these wise words to us, "This will be a short term pain for a long-term gain." That Doctor was right! Several times after that, we had to decide to take the short-term pain to get the long-term gain, and it never got easier.

During the first eight weeks after surgery, the hole in Mitchell's abdomen had to heal before inserting the actual G-Tube. I am not a nurse for a very good reason: I do not do well with blood and wounds of any sort. I was very nervous that I would accidently pull out the temporary tube while I was cleaning the site and changing the bandage. They assured me this was very unlikely. Not only did I worry about myself doing it, but also, waiting at home, was a one-year-old little brother who loved to crawl all over his big brother Mitchell. How do we keep Levi from seeing this and pulling it out? It was no easy feat. Grace was a great help during this time. She would entertain Levi while I changed Mitchell's diapers or his clothes, so the tubing was never visible.

Even though the hospital staff assured me I was very unlikely to accidently pull it out, they gave me a straw to keep close just in case. They said I needed only to insert the straw into the hole so it would not close. Well, that did it for me. The first time I contemplated changing the bandage that had a clasp on it holding the tube in place, I caved. I just could not do it. Living in a small town does have its advantages. You know pretty much everyone. I knew Evie Chisolm, who worked as a nurse in a pediatric doctor's office in a town nearby. Evie lived in Cedarville and went to my church. I called her and explained my situation, and she told me to bring him over. Therefore, each week for six weeks, Grace and I took Mitchell over to her house, and she would change Mitchell's bandage around his tubing. She would also show me how to change the bandage in case I became brave enough. Finally, I was brave, and I changed it the last two weeks. I was so proud of myself. If we trust ourselves, we are all capable of doing what we think we cannot do. Trust – there is that word again and there I was learning it again.

Finally, after eight long weeks, Mitchell received his G-tube or *button* as we call it. We must change the button every three months or sooner if it is not working well. For the first few years, I took Mitchell to the hospital or doctor's office to replace the button. Finally, I asked the doctor if I could do this at home and if they would show me how. Replacing the button looked easy enough. The doctor gave me a lesson, and I have been replacing his button at home ever since. Mitchell's big brother and sister would eventually learn to change his button at home as well. Taylor was sixteen, and Grace was fourteen when Mitchell had a mishap with his button, and it broke off. I had inserted a straw, and we were waiting for UPS to deliver a new batch of buttons. I was not home when the package arrived. Taylor and Grace took the initiative and put the button in place after reading the instructions. I found out right away after they gave me a call. I was shocked but very proud of them. Our children grew up faster than most and learned to be responsible at an early age.

Feeding Mitchell with his feeding tube was a breeze. It was so fast – minutes versus an hour or more by mouth. I do remember the first time in public that I fed Mitchell using his feeding tube. I was so worried about offending someone. We were in a Wendy's restaurant, and I was trying to make sure no one could see. Why I was worried I have no idea; you cannot see anything gross. The button looks like a plug on a blow-up beach ball. The feeding tube attaches to a syringe and locks in place with a slight twist. Once in place, pouring the liquid food into his stomach was simple. It was so nice when Mitchell started to gain weight and get the nutrition he needed. Several months after Mitchell's surgery, Heather Harkleroad commented, "I cannot count Mitchell's ribs anymore." She was right, and we were enjoying this little victory. Grace was only six but wanted to learn how to feed Mitchell. I thought, why not. Grace caught on quickly, and she was well on her way to becoming an enormous source of help. Today, several of

Mitchell's nieces know how to feed Mitchell, clean around his button, and apply cream and gauze. I absolutely love watching the next generation learning to serve!

YEARS OF ADVERSITY
(November 1995 – December 2000)

Chapter 5
Our Darkest Days – Dad

The next seven years were the darkest of my life. I hesitate to share because it might be a discouragement to someone beginning the same journey. However, during this time of our lives, miraculous things happened, and we learned to trust in God. Well, maybe trust God significantly *more* than we had before. I try to think of how I might have led my family differently during this time, but even today, I cannot envision a scenario that would have significantly changed the outcome. As I organize my thoughts, my chest tightens and anxiety wells up from deep within my gut. Please know that what I am sharing is difficult to articulate despite my stoic nature.

In general, Carrie and I fought life on two fronts. This time, however, we did it together. Thinking back, we really did not have an option if we were to survive as a family. Our children did not have a choice either. This was a time of pure survival, and it went on for a long time. I do not remember being unhappy, but I do remember from time-to-time the stress being so overwhelming that all I could do was curl up and cry. I do not ever remember Carrie and me crying together. I am not sure why. We are both doggedly stubborn. Neither of us would never give up without a fight and willingly let the other know we did not have it all under control – clearly a good trait applied poorly. Carrie, however, might know differently. She has a memory like a steel trap. It is her blessing and her curse. On the other hand, I have a memory like a steel sieve. I see only a blessing here as I need only to ask Carrie what really happened.

The first and obvious front of our two-front war was serving Mitchell while raising a family. The second front was making a living in a way that medical insurance would cover Mitchell. We had to do both in a way in which we would not go bankrupt. The best way to communicate this part of our lives is to tell the story as it unfolded. The battle line for this war was the front and back door. Our home was the safe place, and Carrie and I made sure the battle did not get through the door.

Before I left the Air Force, we had started a picture framing company, and my plan was to make a self-employed living so that I could be close to home and have the flexibility to help care for Mitchell. We were making enough money to make a living, but I knew it would be tight. I thought if we got in trouble, I could work as a government contractor. I knew I could also work odd jobs as a finish carpenter to make up the difference. As a condition of leaving, the Air Force required me to resign my commission and pay back a large portion of my pilot bonus. I had accepted this bonus a few years back with a commitment to continue flying. I was certain, given our special circumstance, the Air Force would forgive the debt. Nope – they set up a payment plan. We did not plan for this in our budget, but now I had already turned down a promotion to major. We were firmly committed to starting our new way of life. Also, the requirement to resign my commission cut off any option of joining the United States Air Force Reserves. The Air Force cut off my potential for retreat. Once out of the Air Force, my only option was forward.

When I had made the decision to leave the Air Force, it was right on the heels of decommissioning the 4950th Test Wing at Wright Patterson AFB. The Air Force sent the aircraft and their missions, including the NT-39A that I piloted, to the 412th Test Wing at Edwards AFB in California. Leadership gave me the choice to follow the aircraft and PCS to California. The adventurous side of me wanted to make the move, but for starters, Edwards AFB and the civilian community completely lacked the necessary medical facilities. Clearly, this was not a viable option. In addition, senior leadership said that they would sponsor my application to test pilot school. I had to turn this rare opportunity down as well. After the 4950th Test Wing's mission moved to California, there were no aircraft left for me to fly at Wright Patterson AFB. This all happened a little over a year before I left the Air Force. I will never know whether I would have been required to move to another flying job, which was the purpose of the bonus. I could have taken my chances and fought a PCS to remain in Dayton. The Air Force may have allowed me to stay at Wright Patterson and work a desk job. Again, I will never know. Despite all the what-ifs, there was still the pesky notion that we had diligently prayed about this decision and had the peace that we were in God's will.

No one knew the complexities and the issues surrounding our decision to leave the military. No one asked. What I sketched above is only the major highlights. Many other small things factored into our decision. Six months later, when we began to have our first of many financial difficulties, I suddenly found myself completely alone wearing a scarlet letter that looked like a dollar sign. Of course, this was how I felt and not the result of a community communique. In general, when someone is having financial difficulties, people assume the condition is the consequence of poor decisions and demonstrates that they are not in the will of God. The reasoning probably went something like this: If he had not left the Air Force, he wouldn't now be in financial trouble. Although this kind of reasoning hangs on a true statement, we owe it to anyone overwhelmed not to stop there. This statement is equally true: but for God giving that family a handicapped child, they wouldn't be in financial trouble. I do not know if our friends thought this, but the silence was deafening.

When we let our church know about our financial trouble, our Pastor stopped at our frame shop wanting to make sure I was not suicidal. He explained that people in my position often make that decision. I assured our Pastor that I was not suicidal. Convinced, we prayed, and he left. I remember Carrie and I simply staring at each other in disbelief. I wanted to say, "I hadn't thought of that but thanks for the idea." All joking aside, friends and family should watch and ask about suicidal thoughts, but you probably should not lead off with this question. We did not take offense, and this was our first clue that people were not necessarily going to understand our financial predicament. Sadly, I probably would not have either.

The lesson here: We all need to show genuine concern, ask questions, and listen intently to those dealing with adversity. You may not be able to walk a mile in the other person's shoes, but you can walk with them for one of the miles. Many people do not do this, I fear, because they are afraid that God might ask them to help. In addition, I think we sometimes fool ourselves into thinking the other friend has got it covered. In general, saying nothing can be as harmful as saying the wrong thing. More often than not, money is not the solution. Time is your most valuable possession. Invest your time first before you ever reach for your wallet.

Meeting our new financial trouble head-on, Carrie and I worked in our self-employed business together. In our new post Air Force life, we both worked harder than we had ever before. I replaced my workaholic lifestyle for a slave lifestyle. I worked more hours a day than I thought possible, bringing in poverty level wages. Before we settled into this work routine, I did try to get a job as a government support contractor. I was qualified but quickly discovered through my contacts that I was essentially black listed. This was an unofficial practice where companies avoided families with high medical bills. Mitchell was having $100,000 surgeries every other year, and his steady state medical costs were in the thousands per month. We had achieved our goal of not moving and keeping me close by. However, at what cost? At this point, we had no other choice. What we had to do next to survive and keep Mitchell medically insured is the stuff of nightmares.

Upon leaving the Air Force, we were able to buy expensive Civilian Health and Medical Program of the Uniformed Services (CHAMPUS) family medical insurance. We needed only to keep up with the high premiums. Six months after leaving the Air Force, CHAMPUS cancelled our health insurance after we missed one payment. We knew the rules, and it was our fault. We could have kept the insurance for another year. It was a simple mistake with devastating consequences, or so we thought. In retrospect, this only took what was inevitable and moved it up one year. Based on Mitchell's future surgeries, the timing was likely a blessing. However, overwhelmed does not even touch the emotions we were feeling at the time. Carrie sobbed; I was frozen. This incident does not even make the top ten list of our most overwhelming events to come.

At this point, we had no choice but to apply for state help. Fortunately, we qualified for the help immediately due to our poverty status. The entire family, including Mitchell with his increasing medical costs, was covered. We tried food stamps for one month, but that turned out to be too difficult for our already bruised egos. It was at this point the full weight of our predicament hit us. In order to keep this insurance, we could never earn a self-employed income over a poverty level. We already knew that we could not work for another company to get medical insurance. Even if we could afford it, Mitchell's preexisting condition made buying insurance impossible. Before we could stabilize ourselves in our new reality, we took on additional credit card debt that only made things worse. Over the next five years, we made every business decision to keep us right at the highest income still considered poverty. I became a small business and personal tax expert, guarding our monthly gains. Making things worse, we now lived in a home which we really could not afford. All we could really afford was a small trailer, which was not enough space for taking care of Mitchell or for a family of five. If we rented a smaller house, the savings would be marginal per month. In addition, we were so busy trying to survive and take care of Mitchell, we literally did not have enough time to look for a place, let alone move.

So, hemmed in, we maneuvered between not earning too little so we could pay our bills and not earning too much in order to keep insured. If we could suddenly become very successful in one fell swoop, I dreamed of paying cash for our entire medical expenses. I tried a couple of times but finally resigned myself to the fact this was our lot in life until Mitchell passed. During this period of our lives, I worked an average of eight to nine hours a day, seven days a week. I kept this up for roughly five years until I could give no more. I crashed.

Shortly after leaving the Air Force in October 1995, Mitchell's first major surgery marked the beginning of our time of trials that lasted until 2002. This was a long stretch of peak adversity. We aged twenty years in those seven years, depleting all the energy of our youth. Every major surgery during this time was a near miss for Mitchell, accompanied by a formidable family financial crisis. I cannot explain why both happened at the same time. Blessedly, the gap between Mitchell's surgeries was just enough time for us to catch our breath and adjust to our new reality before doctors could perform the next reality-altering surgery.

Our daughter Grace was already eight years old and, by this time, was a seasoned servant helping care for Mitchell. The medical things she did for Mitchell at this young age were well beyond her years. Like Carrie and me, God planned in advance Grace's role in serving Mitchell's ministry. It was obvious then and is obvious now. Levi was three years old at the time and loved to climb all over Mitchell, forming a brotherly friendship. Levi's antics and attention were a great distraction for Mitchell as he navigated very painful days. I do not know how much Mitchell understood then or even now. Mitchell has a situation awareness of those around him and, as such, clearly recognizes certain family and friends. Mitchell's response to different people is very subtle and is not discernible to the casual observer. As noted earlier, Mitchell is nonverbal. He can't tell us where it hurts and doesn't understand the words *yes* or *no*. If Mitchell did understand this concept, he would have had the ability to use his face to signal his understanding. Therapists tried for years to teach Mitchell this simple concept, but with no success.

Leading up to this first hip surgery, Mitchell's new civilian doctor told us that Mitchell's hips were out of socket. We were having difficulty changing Mitchell's diapers because his legs would not open correctly, and we could tell that he was uncomfortable. I remember looking at the x-rays and saying to the doctor, "How can that be? The Air Force doctors never told us about this." After the doctor received copies of Mitchell's Wright Patterson AFB hip x-rays, he showed us that, indeed, his hips had been out of socket for at least a year. Carrie and I looked at each other, finishing each other's thought. Good thing for Mitchell we were no longer in the military! This discovery immediately led not only to Mitchell's first major surgery, but also to his first brush with death. I remember Sharon Baum made a special trip to sit with Carrie during Mitchell's first major surgery. Carrie recounts our family's incredible experience with emotional acuity as we came to grips with our new financial reality in the first year after the Air Force.

We were never alone during this period. Our next-door neighbors, the Harkleroads, had already been building into our lives. We moved in next to Joe and Andrea the summer of 1992 while still in the military. Mitchell was only two years old. Our children grew up with their children. By the time of Mitchell's surgery, we had been friends for four years. Thinking back, we must have been quite the odd family. With a grin, I can say unequivocally that we still are. We also had the love and support of Danny and Jackie Pyles, who also had a parcel of children that played and grew up with our children. Danny and Jackie did not live right next door, but a short hike over a creek, fences, and fields put us at their back door. Abigail (Abbey) Pyles, now Abbey Goins, later moved in to our home for roughly six years, helping us care for Mitchell while she was going to classes. We now challenge Danny and Jackie for some daughter rights. Both the Pyles and Harkleroads raised amazing children. We all attended Grace Baptist Church together in Cedarville, and we knew that we were in the prayers of many dear saints. Our friendships endure to this day, and we are better people for it.

I would be remiss not to thank Mark and Pat Tompkins. Mark is a talented carpenter and a godly man. He brought me alongside, and we worked carpentry jobs together during these bleak years. I slowed him down, but he made sure I made income to survive. Pat became a state caregiver for Mitchell many years later. She took care of Mitchell as if he were her own son. They gave up part of their lives to serve our family so that we could serve Mitchell. I believe that they understood our predicament because Pat had a Downs Syndrome brother. Amazing people!

By the time Mitchell was eight years old, his back had already begun to rotate and curve to the left. He wore a back brace for a while, but the brace did little to stop the scoliosis that went from 10 degrees to 70 degrees in one year. The muscles in one-half of his little body were tighter than the other half, drawing his entire frame into an unnatural position. The impact to his lungs and internal organs led to an immediate surgery. This surgery was intense, installing a metal rod the entire length of his body. Standing by helplessly as your child goes through that much pain does something to a parent. Again, Carrie tells the story in a way that will leave you emotionally drained.

In the year leading up to Mitchell's second surgery, I was tired. I was not depressed. I was physically exhausted. I remember we packed up the family to spend a couple of weeks with Steve and Sharon. Steve and Sharon now lived in Missouri near Whiteman AFB. This was a place of respite for us. When we got to Steve and Sharon's house, I went to bed and slept for an entire week. I regained consciousness briefly for food and the bathroom. People often ask, "Can you actually sleep for a whole week?" My answer is yes, and I have witnesses. When I finally woke up, I felt refreshed. I understood then that my work tempo was ultimately not sustainable. I also resolved to make a change. I did not have the foggiest idea how to do that, so I did the only thing that I had power to do. I prayed.

God answered my prayers, but I was not prepared for the answer. Immediately following Mitchell's surgery, I began losing the energy to work long hours in order to make the money to pay the bills. We had lived on a financial precipice now for four years. I tried several different business schemes to include a couple more custom frame shops in the area and a coffee shop in downtown Cedarville.

Of course, we always had the option to go bankrupt, but I fought this with every fiber of my being. Going bankrupt was the easy way out, and I refused even to consider it. Now, the house payment was two months behind, and other bills were slipping to thirty plus days. Few people knew how long and how hard I worked. I remember one time I was replacing a roof for a customer in the summer. The temperature outside was 90 degrees, and I had a 104-degree temperature. I was shivering and wore a winter coat to keep warm and was able to finish the job. We desperately needed the money. I completed the job, brought home the check, and collapsed for three days.

Families with a special needs child are subject to hidden complexities that are unique to our trying to make a living. In general, a normal family in financial trouble can achieve dual incomes by having the other spouse work. They can even work different shifts. For a family with a special needs child, this is impossible. The equivalent of one spouse must work day and night to care for a single, special needs child in the home, obviously, without pay. This was the reality back then until new laws would correct this problem roughly four years later. In addition, family expenses are simply greater with a special needs child at home. Food costs are more when living out of hospitals, as are the higher travel costs from going back and forth during seemingly endless hospital and doctor appointments. Vehicle purchase costs are significantly more because wheelchairs do not fit in small economical cars. Big vans get poor gas mileage. Weekly medical road trips increase vehicle wear, leading to more frequent servicing and maintenance costs. Home energy costs are also higher because of breathing problems and poor circulation. You simply cannot open the windows or put more blankets on the bed. Essentially, your home becomes a hospital setting. As financial pressures increase, your bills can routinely cycle in and out of thirty days late, seriously affecting your credit rating. Low credit scores lead to higher car insurance costs. When you start getting in trouble, credit card companies immediately increase your interest rates. This leads to higher monthly payments. If you can finance a car, the interest rates are double. The list goes on and on, and we experienced all of this and more.

In quiet counsel, a social worker let Carrie and me know that if we were to divorce, Mitchell and our children could get the help we needed. Of course, under this scenario I could not live at home. Some would also suggest turning Mitchell over to the state. We heard this same message many times. Not once did Carrie and I give any serious thought to either of these life approaches. I remember trying to explain this to family and friends, and they simply could not wrap their heads around it. I think people simply could not believe something like this could be true. I would not believe it had I not lived it! Remembering the trap we were in seems surreal to me today. However, I must remind myself that God allowed it, so it must have been important to his purpose. I would rather be in God's will in poverty than out of His will in wealth. Of course, in His will in wealth would be good as well.

One friend, a financial expert, graciously stepped into the ring to help me sort out our immediate financial crisis. I am not sure David Rost fully understood the web of our circumstances and its origin, but he came alongside to analyze our finances and work a solution. Dave completely assessed my self-employed expenses and revenue, including our personal bills. I gave Dave complete access to all my financial records. He helped me devise and implement a get-well plan that would keep us in our home and avoid bankruptcy. I settled my credit card debts for roughly fifty cents on the dollar. The credit card debts were only a little less than when we left the Air Force four years ago. The twenty-five percent interest rates kept us in bondage. We have never carried monthly credit card debt again.

Of course, I needed cash to pay off the credit cards at a discounted rate. For starters, I had a few thousand dollars from a recent carpentry job. Next, I decided to auction off all our household personal property to come up with the rest of the cash. Carrie was not happy. Other than our house and run-down cars, this was all we had left in the world. Our dignity was already gone. This was the most humiliating thing Carrie and I ever had to do. This was particularly rough on Carrie, and I noticed by her countenance that she had lost confidence in my ability to take care of the family. It would take years to regain her trust. How could I blame her! Here we were publicly auctioning off all our belongings in our front yard. The entire community was picking through our personal belongings, laughing and enjoying a beautiful day while celebrating great deals. Meanwhile, Mitchell was inside the house recovering from his third surgery. I felt like a complete failure, and I am sure that many shared my sentiment. Inside, my heart would absorb the entire scene, and I was never the same again. The once proud B-52 Aircraft Commander was now a common beggar.

I am eternally grateful to Dave for his sacrifice and the carpentry work he contracted for me to do in the year to follow. David and Barbara Rost paid me well to work on their home and treated me with great respect. I do not know who it was, but someone caught up our house payment during those confusing days – something I did not notice until a couple months later. In addition, our friends got together, bought several pieces of our furniture at the auction, and gave them back to us. I was particularly fond of an antique oak hall tree. I am staring at it right now next to our back door. That hall tree is a reminder of the year I had no more to give and had to hand it all over to God. Carrie's friends gave back an old china cabinet given to her by Deane Wright. The auction ended, and Bart Sheridan and his dad, the auctioneers of Sheridan and Associates, gave their fee for conducting the auction back to Carrie and me. Bart and Sandy Sheridan remain dear friends to this day.

Carrie and I express our love for all our friends who ministered to us that auction day. In the end, the get-well plan was a success, and we kept our almost empty home. God was good to us that day and provided exactly enough to balance the checkbook and pay off our debts.

Four years ago, our pastor asked me a serious question in our frame shop when our financial troubles had first begun. I had no jokes left this day. Today was the day someone needed to ask me that question. As an eternal optimist, I never thought I would ever wonder if the world might be better without me in it. This was the lowest point in my life, and it lasted a day. I told Carrie but quickly laughed it away. Thankfully, I snapped out of it the next day. It scared me, and once again I focused on making just enough money to pay my bills and not too much to keep the state medical coverage to avoid bankruptcy. However, this time we had no credit card debt and no Air Force debt.

After our financial near miss and Mitchell's difficult surgery, I put all my energy into searching for a change. I continued to pray and asked God to show me the way. We were approaching the year 2000, and Mitchell was now ten years old. He was losing his baby face, and his contorted body and hands drew the attention of every passerby. Children gawked as parents desperately tried to divert their attention from Mitchell. I remember our daughter, Grace, staring those children down with a glare that would break glass. We did not blame God for our circumstances. I think we understood then, as we do now, that God loves us and understanding the reason was simply above our pay grade. I remember we celebrated the beginning of the New Year with Mark and Cheryl Klimek. Just before the clock struck midnight, I reflected on my high school days when I pondered what my life would be like in the year 2000. I snickered to myself and kissed Carrie.

The year 2000 was a good year as Mitchell continued to heal. I started full-time work at Cedarville University in June. I was already a part-time adjunct faculty member, teaching chemistry laboratories. By this time, because of our businesses in town, Carrie and I both had many friends at Cedarville University. When I first searched for a full-time job at Cedarville University, obviously, there were no pilot or leader wannabe jobs, and I ignored that Mitchell's medical costs might be an impediment. I reasoned that Cedarville University surely would not practice screening applicants for high family medical bills. Not a Christian organization.

I found online that Cedarville University did have an opening for a finish carpenter in the cabinet shop. I applied for the position and then pleaded my case with the lead carpenters. I can only imagine what these good men thought. I was clearly over qualified when it came to my education and Air Force background, and my carpentry skills clearly did not match the quality of their carpentry skills. Nonetheless, in order to assess the quality of my work, these men gave me a project to complete. I think I built a custom oak window box. Growing up I worked as a finish carpenter through high school and college. I had also picked up some current cabinetry skills through our custom framing business and working carpentry jobs with Mark Tompkins and for David Rost. It was my more recent carpentry experience, the last five years, which made applying for this job even plausible. When I turned in the oak window box, I held my breath. Finally, a call said I got the job. I was shocked. The pay was not much, but it came with the most precious thing we needed: health insurance. Soon after, a doctor asked Carrie, "Who hired your husband?" The doctor was aware of the unspoken custom of businesses not hiring people with a special needs family member. Carrie proudly announced: Cedarville University. Carrie said the doctor was visibly surprised, and I must admit that I was, too.

I worked for Cedarville University a little over five years, proudly earning my five-year pin. My leaders and peers invested in my family and me even though I was not a good fit or nearly as talented. Honestly, I believe it was a bad business decision to hire someone like me. Everyone I worked with was gracious, and I am a better person today for the undeserving investment and friendships. When I started at Cedarville University, I oversaw the cabinet shop. When I left, I was an office manager.

During my time at Cedarville University, I was struggling to find my identity. I was always trying to regain the respect I had lost when I was an Air Force pilot. In this unattainable quest, I remember one time I made a complete fool of myself. After a recent promotion to office manager, my first office with a door came with the job. Up to this point, I wore the standard issue uniform shirts with my blue jeans. I strolled into my new office with some very fine threads. I also had some nice framed diplomas and aircraft models from my flying days to put in my office. It took me about a week to realize that I had offended everyone around me. No one said a word. I realized some of the emotional baggage surfaced when circumstances completely upended my life. I was suffering from an identity crisis. In my wounded mind, I had given up literally everything, and I wanted others to know that I was worth so much more. It was the wrong forum and the wrong time. What looked like arrogance was really a self-worth struggle. It would take me a few more years, after I left Cedarville University, to accept my new status. It is difficult to shake the angst of unrealized potential. I understand now that my plan is never as good as God's plan for my life. We are in our final journey with Mitchell, and I am still working to get the remnants of a proper perspective out of my mind and into my heart.

Cedarville University helped me get a Master's in Business Administration and Finance. More likely than not, this was to help me with wherever I might work in the future. I knew there was no permanent place for me at Cedarville University. In my final year, Rod Johnson, the Associate Vice President of Operations, graciously let me know that there was no foreseeable growth potential left for me at Cedarville University. Rod suggested that if I were looking for more that I should move on. He then assured me that I was welcome to stay at Cedarville University as long as I wanted. He was respectful and honest, and I appreciated his candor. I started looking for a new job the next day. My work at Cedarville was a time of healing. The people and mission at Cedarville University, then and today, are amazing.

When I started working at Cedarville University, Carrie and I did not know that in the fall of the following year, Mitchell would have another major surgery and another brush with death. But for now we were in the eye of the storm and life was calm. It was around this time I could tell that my family was war weary. I came up with a plan. Leading up to Christmas 2000, I scraped together roughly three thousand dollars to take the family to Disney (World) in Florida. My in-laws, Ernest and Hilda Taylor, joined us, and they graciously paid for our lodging on Disney property at the Shades of Green. This was our first real vacation, and we discovered, much to our surprise, that Mitchell was our ticket to the front of the line. We hit pay dirt! They took one look at Mitchell and treated us like royalty. They thought we were on a Make-A-Wish vacation. We had never heard of Make-A-Wish. We stopped trying to explain and went with it. We had so much fun, and for the first time, I was able to sit down with our other children and really listen to them. I was amazed at how much I did not know was going on in their lives.

I learned a valuable lesson that Christmas, and I made sure we went on a major vacation every year after that. My friend Jeff Cunningham went out of his way to set me up with inexpensive timeshare weeks in Orlando. We vacationed every early spring for the next twenty years. I also made some other changes. I made sure my children saw me at every school and sports event. As a family, we had some exceedingly tough times, but we countered those tough times with love. Carrie and I invested deeply into all our children.

Raising a profoundly handicapped child will not only put a strain on your wallet, but it will also put an enormous strain on your marriage, children, and friendships. The percentage of divorce goes up when a family has a special needs child. I do not know why this is true, but the more stress your family is under, the more your family will reject your leadership. Somehow, you must keep trying to find a way to lead your family. Do not take it personally. This also happens outside your home. When you struggle financially, people will reject your leadership. In general, people will never invest the time to discern whether your circumstances are more God's design versus your own. Even if you convince one or two people, you will not have the energy to swing the minds of an entire community. My advice is to let it go. You are responsible for leading, and followers are responsible for following. When they do not follow, they need you to lead the most. I admit leadership can be a very lonely calling. This is especially difficult for men because they measure their self-worth by the respect they receive from others. Win God's respect first and wait for your spouse, children, and friends to catch up.

Nothing kills romance more than having a child at home constantly in and out of some stage of dying. I wish I could give you the magic words to solve this conundrum. I can tell you it does get better over time if you lead your spouse in love. I found it was the little things that made it work. Every morning before I left for work, I kissed Carrie and told her that I loved her. Some mornings I did not mean the words as I should have, but Carrie did not know. I can count on one hand when I did not kiss Carrie goodbye because my anger beat me. Anger is nothing more than a tool to control other people. We simply use anger to signal to others that if you want a peaceful relationship with me, you need to see it or do it my way. Wrong, wrong, and wrong. Rid anger from your life because it has no place in any relationship. We all know there is room for righteous anger. However, I am certain that when any of us feels this special kind of anger, the Spirit will overwhelm us with affirmation. I have not felt this yet in my lifetime.

To shore up Carrie's and my intimacy and friendship, twice a year I planned a nearby weekend getaway. This was not as easy as you might think. Carrie had a very difficult time leaving Mitchell's side. My solution was ingenious but simple. I quietly arranged for our friends and our children to take care of Mitchell without Carrie's knowledge. Grace was in on it, secretly packing Carrie's overnight bag. When I got home from work, everybody showed up, and Grace handed Carrie her overnight bag. The car was running in the driveway. Pretending to object every time, Carrie got in the car, and we had a great time. Once we were away from the tangible stresses, Carrie and I were able to dream of a better future. I also learned, in those brief getaways, how I might lead our family toward better days.

When adversity consumes your wife, keep your marriage bed pure! The pressure to do otherwise can be difficult enough, but it is tenfold worse when any crisis requires you to step back into the number two position. This goes back to the covenant I made with Carrie and before God – "for better or for worse." My first step to navigate this issue was to ask God very directly and, on my knees, to never let me get anywhere near the position where I had to make a choice. I knew that if I got that far, I was likely going to make the wrong choice. I prayed this prayer, and I meant it. I am confident that everyone reading this knows that the chances of falling are greater when dancing on the edge of a cliff. We also know exactly when we decide to walk over to the cliff to peek over the edge. When you start heading to the cliff's edge, whether in real life or your thought life, ask God to help you turn around. It is best never to take the first step. However, you always have the second-best option of turning around before you get there. Bottom line: your will power is never enough. To be successful, you must take God with you. Secondly, when struggling in any area of your marriage, talk with your spouse if you are able. You both have a stake in the relationship. Pray together and love together. Finally, a friend can also help you stay accountable. During some of my most difficult times, Steve Baum was my confidant.

About this time in our lives, I began a new tradition that continues to this day. I took Grace out on a daddy-daughter date just before Christmas. This proved to be a great way to spend time with my daughter and to get to know my wife's needs better. Only four days separate Christmas and Carrie's birthday. Up until this time, I bought Carrie the worst Christmas and birthday presents imaginable. Sweaters five sizes too small and colors that did not match Carrie. I did not know she wore fall or autumn colors (I still do not know what that means). I also bought Carrie cleaning appliances to make her feel special. I discovered that all I had to do was feed Grace some restaurant food, and it unlocked the Rosetta stone of knowledge revealing Carrie's deepest gift desires. From then on, my gifting became the stuff of legends. As a bonus, I was able to build into my daughter's life. Today, my daughter-in-law Sarah is now part of this special trip. Although their culinary tastes are expensive, it is worth every penny!

I did these things because I decided early on that I needed to protect Carrie. I knew she was up to her eyeballs in work and stress and that I had to take a backseat in her life. I know anyone who has a child can appreciate this imagery. Everyone agrees how difficult it is for a new mother in the first two years of a child's life. The mother never gets enough sleep and initially looks forward to a time when their baby sleeps through the night and then looks forward to a diaper-free life. In general, the husband steps back into the serving mode as the new mom heals and gets into a new rhythm. Now imagine this never ending for twenty-eight years! Let that sink in.

I think back to the early- to mid-90s when I decided to abandon my selfish, professional dreams. I looked at Carrie then and thought, "I am not treating her like I should, and I am being selfish." I also told Carrie that I would stop immediately and never do this again. I ended by asking Carrie for her forgiveness, and she acquiesced. It was another ten years before she believed that I meant what I said, only because I was true to my word. I see Carrie's and my relationship very simply: Carrie and I are just one person. This is what God sees. If I mistreat Carrie, I mistreat myself. I am far from perfect. However, I learned early that I could not have the right relationship with God unless I came to him with Carrie.

Whether you have a special child at home or not, the best relationships work on one simple principle: each person focuses on serving and meeting the needs and wants of the other person. That is all it takes for any relationship to work whether in a marriage, between friends, or with God. When one side of the relationship (one person) starts to protect or insist that their wants and needs be met, then the relationship falters. When both parties act like this, then there really is no relationship. We have a God who focuses completely on us. What does God need and want from you?

During this brief calm in the eye of the storm, we began to see the eye wall approaching. In the year and a half leading up to 2001, Mitchell's seizures began to get more and more out of control. In 1991, Mitchell began to have subtle seizures. His seizures may have started earlier, but we did not know what we were looking at until his physical therapist pointed out the tiny eye movements. As time progressed, his seizures were more prominent until one day his seizures became explosive, effectively locking up all his muscles. When this happened, his eyes rolled back into his head, and his arms and legs shot out with violent tremors. Mitchell made a loud and continuous high-pitched noise and was unable to draw in a breath. He turned blue. In addition to these big seizures, he would constantly have involuntary eye movements and face twitches. What started out ten years before as barely perceptible seizures was now full-blown Lennox-Gastaut syndrome (LGS). LGS is life threatening and is a rare and severe kind of epilepsy. Children with LGS have several different kinds of seizures, and they have them often. These seizures are the most difficult to control.

Doctors medicated Mitchell with one seizure control medicine and kept increasing the dose until Mitchell's seizures were gone, and he was completely incoherent. Mitchell would simply stare into space and did not react much to his environment. His new condition was soul crushing. We had lost our little boy – no more smiles and no more deep communication through eye contact. Mitchell was gone. Mitchell's neurologist said that this was Mitchell's new life. Carrie was not satisfied with this answer, and based on what happened next, God did not think so either. Carrie was sitting in a waiting room for another appointment and came across an article in a magazine about a special ketogenic diet showing promise in seizure control. When I got home that night, Carrie immediately told me about the article. I did not think much of it, but, thankfully, Carrie was persistent. Shortly after reading the article, Carrie asked Mitchell's regular doctor if she would refer Mitchell to the specialist named in the article. Soon Carrie had an initial consult with this doctor at Nationwide Children's Hospital. This diet was controversial back then and a last-resort recommendation. The neurologists tried many different seizure control medicines before they announced that Mitchell was a candidate for the ketogenic diet. This process took a year and a half. Finally, the doctors said that Mitchell could start on the ketogenic diet and that it would require a week's stay at Nationwide Children's Hospital. The diet was a complex mix of ingredients that started with a canned liquid. The concoction was high in fat and low in carbohydrates. Within days, Mitchell's seizures were significantly fewer, requiring only a small amount of seizure medicines to close the gap. Mitchell was back! Well, almost back. Mitchell would never again be as vibrant and responsive as he was before LGS.

We were elated! Mitchell's floor nurse began the next step of coordinating with our health insurance company to pay for the special ingredients so we could continue the ketogenic diet at home. The doctor said Mitchell could not leave the hospital until this was complete. We were shocked when the nurse came back and told us our health insurance company denied this service. Over the course of two days, the nurse talked to multiple representatives but with no success. The health insurance claimed the ingredients were food, and they did not cover food. We could not believe what we were hearing. If I had remained self-employed, living on the ragged edge of bankruptcy, then Medicaid would cover the food ingredients. Now here we were with health insurance, and the expectation was for us to buy this expensive food, which would have surely bankrupted us. I vaguely remember the cost of the ingredients being more than a thousand dollars per month. Once again, the quiet advice was Mitchell could get everything he needed if Carrie and I would only divorce. We were dumbfounded. I thought, "Will this nightmare never end?"

In a panic, I called the Cedarville University Human Resources (HR) Department and explained our quandary. The next day the HR director called and said that they had talked with the health insurance company without success. The director exclaimed, however, that the University would find a way to pay this expense directly. Did I mention that Cedarville University is incredible! Shortly after this conversation, however, I received the most amazing call. It was then we discovered that God was directly intervening to fix this problem and fix it for good.

When the phone rang, it was a representative with the Greene County Board of Mental Retardation and

Developmental Disabilities (MRDD). (The name today is Department of Developmental Disabilities (DODD).) The lady began to explain what Carrie and I already knew at the time. Two years earlier Carrie put Mitchell on a list to receive the Individual Option (I/O) Waiver. Mitchell was currently around number seven hundred on a list at least twice that long. This was a first-come, first-serve queue and moving up on this list meant that someone above you had to die. A morbid approach, we thought, wishing others would die so we could get their services. We were never hopeful that Mitchell would receive these services since his ranking climbed by only a hundred in the last two years. As such, I never bothered to understand what it meant to receive this waiver. She then went on to explain that the Governor received authorization to sort the list based on need. I got up out of my chair at this point. The next thing she said sent chills down my spine, and I started to choke up. She added that after the Governor's new sort, Mitchell moved to the top of the list and could receive 100% medical health coverage without regard to our household income, in-home support from care providers up to eighty hours per week, and funds to modify our house and car to better take care of Mitchell. She continued nonchalantly, "Would you be interested in receiving these service benefits?" Stuttering I said, "Yes, absolutely yes."

In my excitement, I tried to tell the lady about the incredible timing and that Mitchell was lying in the hospital right now needing a special food. I think I was talking too fast in all my excitement. She interrupted me and said that Carrie and I needed only to come down to her office and fill out the paperwork. When I told Carrie and the floor nurse, we all stared at each other in complete disbelief. Then we praised

God for His direct intervention at the last possible moment. I have discovered that God uses this last-minute approach a lot. Later, I cried privately knowing that this would change our lives completely. No longer would having a profoundly handicapped child be a financial penalty. We could earn dual incomes if we wanted. We could have some freedom while paid caregivers took care of Mitchell in our own home. We could get the long overdue home and vehicle lifts that we desperately needed. I cried and cried.

We completed the paperwork, and the hospital sent Mitchell home with enough food to last until the mail delivered his prescribed ingredients to our home. By August, our friend Pat Tomkins would be Mitchell's first caregiver. As Pat began to care for Mitchell, his orthopedic doctor and surgeon noticed that Mitchell's hip was not rotating correctly. X-rays confirmed that Mitchell's right hip was out of socket again. Mitchell was very uncomfortable. Because Mitchell is nonverbal, he could never tell us if he was in pain or not. The orthopedic surgeon recommended another hip surgery. This was going to be hip surgery number two and overall surgery number five. We did not know at the time that this would be Mitchell's last but most difficult surgery. If it were not for Carrie's persistence and the prayers of an untold number of saints, our journey with Mitchell would have ended that week. Of course, God had other plans, and Mitchell's ministry would not end here.

The scene was very familiar on surgery day. We had done these three times before. We brought Mitchell in early, and it was not long before the nurses took us back to prepare Mitchell for surgery. The nurses put Mitchell in a familiar light blue hospital gown, completing his attire with an intravenous bag of fluid. As usual, Carrie and I flitted nervously around Mitchell's bed touching him and talking to him as you would a baby about to experience something they would not understand. Mitchell would be twelve next month. The nurses announced it was time to wheel Mitchell back, and we prayed over Mitchell for the tenth time. Carrie and I were fighting back tears, and I remember wiping a couple of tears away that had escaped despite my best efforts. Carrie was less successful. Watching your child roll down the hall toward surgery is emotionally indescribable. It is kind of like watching your child get on their very first school bus times one thousand. As with all of Mitchell's surgeries, we knew the risks. Each time we would dread the surgeon's post-surgery consult.

We waited too long for the surgery to end. Our church deacon came and prayed with us, and a few phone calls took our minds off the moment. It was two hours past the expected four-hour surgery when a nurse appeared at the desk. We could see the nursing staff talking to each other and taking quick glances our way. Finally, the nurse came toward us and said the surgeon was on his way. They were not fooling us! We watched other families meet with the nursing staff after a surgery all day long. Occasionally, we would see families meet directly with their surgeons resulting in the family letting out a gasp or covering their mouths. If the news were more serious, then the surgeon sat down. Carrie and I hoped Mitchell's surgeon would remain standing. We braced ourselves for the impact.

Mitchell's surgeon sat down, and his voice and countenance were noticeably different than I had ever seen before. This surgeon was usually all about business when it came to the parents, but I did not care because he was the best at what he did. He was the kind of doctor where his confidence entered the room before he did. I liked him. This time he had a sheepish look. He immediately said that Mitchell was in recovery and that he had experienced some difficulties. He explained that he accidently dropped Mitchell's femur and that it hit the surgery table. He went on to say that when the femur hit the table, multiple spiral fractures went down his bone and that he had to cage the femur before pinning it to his hip. He added that Mitchell's bones were unusually brittle and that normally a bone would not fracture like that.

Perhaps the surgeon thought we might get angry. All I really heard was that Mitchell was in recovery and that he had made it through his surgery. Three years earlier Mitchell had his entire back filleted open and a rod put in place and tied to his vertebrae. In this moment, a cage on his femur seemed trivial. All I wanted to do was to get to Mitchell's side. Unknown to Carrie and me at the time, the next three weeks would wring every emotion from our being.

Before long, we were with Mitchell in the recovery room and then his regular room. Mitchell did not wake up. We knew something was wrong, and the nursing staff was treating us like overreacting parents. Carrie and I were getting angry and anxious. The nurses said that this was normal for profoundly handicapped children like Mitchell. We explained repeatedly that this was not Mitchell's normal. I am sure this was true from their experience, but we knew better. We were seasoned parents of a profoundly handicapped child, and this was major surgery number four. Carrie and I cannot explain our connection with Mitchell, let alone communicate this connection to others.

Once again, I warn the world, "Do not tell a red-headed, Norse mama bear that nothing can be done." Carrie went into action, and I was paralyzed and in her way. Carrie kept telling the nurses that Mitchell needed to see a neurologist right away. I do not understand the politics and protocols of different specialists, but for whatever reason, the staff rejected Carrie's request. Carrie finally went to the charge nurse and said, "What do I have to do to get a neurologist to see Mitchell?" The nurse said, "You need to start yelling at me and make a scene. I will then get a neurologist to see Mitchell after I call the guards and you are hauled away." Carrie said, "Let me tell my husband what I'm about to do so he isn't surprised when the guards escort me out." Carrie walked up to me, and I happened to be on the phone with Mitchell's primary care doctor. I was explaining Mitchell's condition to his primary care doctor and that the attending doctors were ignoring Carrie's request. Carrie had left a message earlier with Mitchell's primary care doctor, and she was calling back when I answered. Carrie took over the conversation and then things began to happen.

The next thing I knew the nursing station received a call from Mitchell's primary care doctor who ordered an immediate neurology consult. Mitchell's neurology team was already a part of Nationwide Children's Hospital having worked to get Mitchell on the ketogenic diet the last two years. Mitchell was six months into this very controversial diet. Most doctors snickered when we mentioned Mitchell was on this diet despite the 90% reduction in his seizures. The neurology team knew Mitchell well and acted quickly. Mitchell was still unresponsive a day and a half after surgery, and the neurologist immediately ordered blood tests.

Within short order, they whisked Mitchell away to ICU. Mitchell had chemical pancreatitis, and his liver and pancreas were shutting down. Mitchell was near death. The root cause was his very caustic, seizure medicine used in tandem with the ketogenic diet. Mitchell's pancreas and liver were already at the tipping point before surgery. This issue went undetected before the surgery. The stress of surgery sent his body over the cliff. Doctors took Mitchell off this medicine immediately.

Over the next several days in ICU, the doctors did more tests. I do not know how many people have ever been with a loved one in ICU, but the mood is somber and serious. Even the air and light seem to be at attention, and you can feel a reverence. Time seems to stand still in this special part of the hospital. During this time, Mitchell's liver numbers continued to climb sharply. Finally, Mitchell's doctor came in the room with very bad news. He said that Mitchell was suffering from chemical pancreatitis, and, if he survived, it would take days for his numbers to go down. The doctor was clearly not hopeful. Mitchell was unconscious. I was holding his hand, numb from head to toe. I was not ready for Mitchell to leave us. My very personality, identity, and part of my soul were now entwined with this little boy. I knew that Mitchell had suffered so much up to this point and that going home to be with our Lord was best for him. Carrie and I sobbed in silence, then with all the energy we had left, we got on the phone and engaged everyone we knew to pray for Mitchell.

The prayers that went up for Mitchell that night formed a tsunami of love. We learned that our friends in turn called every friend and every church they knew. Prayers for Mitchell circled the globe. Carrie and I took turns sitting with Mitchell every few hours. There was a small room with a bed just around the corner where we could take short naps. Carrie's naps were always shorter than mine. When it came to the details of caring for Mitchell, Carrie always did most of the heavy lifting. During the night and into the next morning, the nurses continued to check Mitchell's liver numbers. The doctor came in the next morning with a perplexed look on his face. He kept looking at the sheet of paper and said that Mitchell's liver numbers are going down fast. By this time, Mitchell was opening his eyes with a disgusted look on his face. Mitchell was on his way back! A week later Mitchell left ICU for a regular room.

Eventually, Mitchell came home, and this was his last surgery. As I write this, nearly sixteen years later, the emotions are just as tangible today as they were then. I can practically taste the anxiety. Those six years were marked by four major surgeries, lack of equipment to care for Mitchell, time being absorbed by Mitchell's care, preventing respite, and an impossible financial catch-22 that left us scraping to hold onto whatever we had left. Even the word *stressful* falls short in describing the heavy weight that was on Carrie's and my shoulder, not to mention our children. Had it not been for our faith I am certain there would have been a completely different outcome. While we were going through this time of adversity, we incrementally disconnected from the real world. All our friends our age were struggling to raise their own families and deal with their own issues.

We could tell that people did not know how to help. Worse, we did not know how to tell people where we needed help. Our heads were down, fighting for our survival, and we did not have the energy to turn our head left or right to let people know we were drowning. In general, people looking in are very critical. I am not sure why this is true. I remember when I was sobbing over our circumstances with a friend he said, "It doesn't sound like you have peace in your life." He continued to ask if I had any unresolved sin in my life. I remember searching my heart that moment and saying while sobbing, "Nothing stands out." I walked away from that conversation devastated. I know my friend did not intend for this to happen, but it caused me to realize that people saw our circumstances through the lenses of their own normal or societal experience: When someone is going through financial trouble, it is because of making bad financial decisions. When someone is going through terrible suffering, then it is because of doing something to upset God. When someone is completely unglued from the stress of their circumstances, it is because of unresolved sin or losing their godly perspective. The list for this kind of reasoning goes on and on, and family, friends, and acquaintances said all these things and more – some directly and some in veiled conversation. The only way for anyone to avoid this shallow logic is to dig into the other person's circumstances – not part way, but all the way. In the end, facts should displace conjecture as you take off your glasses and put on theirs. This requires withholding judgments and conclusions until you have had time to assess, pray, and consult wiser people. If you do this then you move from being a bystander to an advocate. That is what Carrie and I were missing during this tumultuous time.

Life after Mitchell's surgery, ketogenic diet, and I/O waiver put our family on a completely new trajectory. We started 2002 with a new spring in our step. Mitchell was healing, and so was the rest of the family. We had two teenagers in the house, and the next fifteen years became our time of just living.

Chapter 6
At Death's Door – Mom

The year 1995 brought about big changes to our family and taught us some very valuable lessons. After much prayer, discussion and angst, Craig and I made the decision to do what we knew was best for Mitchell and our family. We decided to leave the Air Force life. We knew we were leaving job security and good pay for an unknown path and paycheck. Through our decision process, God revealed to me a couple of important truths: first, my husband's paycheck is not really from the Air Force or any company. Our paycheck is from God. Second, I do not think others can know what is truly best for another person or family just because they might have made another decision. Why? Because you cannot possess all the facts, and the Spirit of God is not likely to get your permission first. I know many of our friends and family could not get past the fact that we gave up a good paying job. However, if that good paying job is not what God has planned for you at the time, then it is not a good job. Craig and I work very hard not to judge others. We are not their Holy Spirit, so to speak. During that time, I hated telling people of our plan because I hate, and I mean hate, confrontation. I hated having to try to explain our decision to people repeatedly – people who did not know all the facts or thought our facts were not true because they decided they were not true. Sadly, I think family and friends made their decision whether to help us based on this singular issue. The stress on our family was already overwhelming without having this discouragement heaped on us. Sadly, this caused me great stress, and I took that stress out on the only person I felt I could: on my dear husband. Today, I have a softer view of our experience. I understand now that God was stretching our community.

Leaving the Air Force meant that for the first time I could choose our doctors. This was so freeing. I spoke with my friend, Evie Chisholm, and asked about the doctors with whom she worked. Evie highly recommended and educated me about a program in Ohio called The Bureau for Children with Medical Handicaps (BCMH). BCMH helps pay for medical expenses of children like Mitchell. Evie's doctor's office accepted payment from BCMH, so it was perfect. While, BCMH did not cover all expenses, we were thankful that they did cover some. Thus began our relationship with Star Pediatrics in Xenia, Ohio, with Doctors Nancy Hesz and Thaddeus Tripplett. I felt at ease the moment we met. I really liked their caring approach and collaboration with me regarding decisions for Mitchell. Although Doctor Hesz was Mitchell's primary care doctor, Doctor Tripplett would step in seamlessly when she was not available. I also took our other three children to see these caring doctors. Mitchell remained under their care until he was twenty-one. This is when Mitchell began having high blood pressure issues. Doctor Hesz thought a non-pediatrician could better care for Mitchell given his new adult issue. Doctor Hesz always wanted what was best for Mitchell. Doctor Pinkerton, a local family doctor, stepped up to the challenge. I remember our last appointment with Doctor Hesz because it was like saying good-bye to a friend. We both cried as she assured me that I could always call her if needed. We now consider Doctor Hesz and Doctor Tripplett friends of the family and are exceedingly grateful for the care and love they showed our entire family.

It is always emotional when your child goes off to kindergarten. It is especially hard when your child has special needs. It is almost unbearable when your child also has medical issues. I met with the kindergarten teacher and the principle of Cedar Cliff Elementary school that summer to work on Mitchell's Individual Education Plan (IEP). I always dreaded those meetings to set Mitchell's goals. At the time, Cedar Cliff Elementary did not have a multi-handicapped class. I did not mind because kindergarten was only a half-day program. I was more interested in Mitchell enjoying himself. In addition, and more importantly, I knew Mitchell would teach his classmates more than his teacher could ever teach him. Honestly, the thought of Mitchell influencing the lives of other special children was wonderful.

I drove Mitchell to school his first day and wheeled him into his classroom. I remember wanting to stay awhile, but I did not. The aide in his class, Mrs. Ankeney, came over and rolled him to his spot in the classroom. I cried on my way home. When I got home, the house felt weird with just Levi. That was one of the longest half-days of school. After his first kindergarten day, Mitchell rode the long bus to and from school. One of our family's jokes became that Mitchell did not ride the short bus since most schools use short buses to transport special needs children. You can count on our family to find the humor in any circumstance. At the end of his first school year, Mitchell's kindergarten teacher said that she had not quite known what to think of having Mitchell in her class and how it would all work. She beamed saying, "It was a joy to have Mitchell because he made a real impact on one of the other boys in the class." Evidently this boy was repeating kindergarten and was having a hard time making friends. Well, that little boy decided to become Mitchell's friend, pushing his wheelchair wherever he needed to go and helping Mitchell do his work. She commented on how the boy's self-confidence grew that year. I say, "Well done, Mitchell!" Clearly, Mitchell had a successful school year, and I was beginning to see Mitchell's purpose: his ministry.

Mitchell attended Cedar Cliff Elementary School until the fifth grade. After that year, we opted for home instruction. We did not realize this was an option, or we would have chosen this sooner. Because of Mitchell's medical issues, attending school was not what was best for his health. Mitchell would catch many illnesses, resulting in his missing an enormous amount of school. One day, a letter came in the mail threatening to send a truancy officer to our home. "What a sense of humor," we thought. We politely suggested to the school that sending a truancy officer to the home of a profoundly handicapped student might be a public relations faux pas.

I do not think Mitchell enjoyed going to school. He would cry often, and the staff could not comfort him. The teachers would call Taylor or Grace from their classroom (usually Grace) to calm their brother. If that did not work, Craig or I received a phone call to come check on him. Usually we just took him home. Once he was home, he was just fine. I sometimes wonder if he had figured that system out.

During this time, Mitchell needed to have his vision and hearing checked by specialists in Dayton, Ohio. It is no easy feat to test the vision or hearing of someone nonverbal. I was wondering as I drove with Mitchell and Levi to the test center how this might be done. The Specialist did Mitchell's eye test by looking into his eyes with a special lens. He was very kind, and I could tell he felt very comfortable being around special needs children. When the eye specialist was finished, he assured me that Mitchell's vision was wonderful. What a blessing! Mitchell enjoyed watching his movies very much. "A little gift from God," I thought to myself.

Next came the hearing test. Administering this test was not easy. Mitchell, Levi, and I were in a soundproof room and the testing technicians were in an adjacent room behind a window. Using their equipment, sounds came from different sides of the room. In theory, Mitchell was supposed to turn his head or eyes to look for the sound. After several tries, Mitchell would not respond. I knew Mitchell could hear, so I was wondering what was happening. Then Levi, being a bored little four-year-old brother started making noise. Right away Mitchell moved his eyes to find Levi. The technicians noticed this movement and asked if Levi could come stand with them and talk to Mitchell. Levi was not shy and went right away. They had Levi talk to Mitchell instead of their making sounds. Mitchell looked toward the direction of Levi's voice each time. Mitchell still looks for any of our family when he hears our voice. This is especially true when he hears his dad's voice. When Craig comes home from work, Mitchell hears his dad's voice coming from another room and starts making loud noises. Craig thought Mitchell was always this loud until Pat explained: she said it only happened after Craig walked in the door. Mitchell is a daddy's boy, and Craig is his comforter. Of course, the hearing and eye specialists told us what we already knew. Mitchell had excellent vision and hearing. My pride swelled after Mitchell did well on both his tests.

We were never much of a television family. Not much of network television family. Previously, we had always loved to watch old movies on VHS. Our family has seen almost every

Disney movie ever made. It may be because watching television was an activity we could all do together, no matter what age or ability. By this time in our lives, family night was routine in our home. This night consisted of watching our newly purchased movie and eating snacks. We looked forward to every Friday night. Mitchell loved watching television. He had a TV in his room to watch during the day. The inside of his room was visible from the living room. Without fail, Mitchell's brothers and sister would stop and snuggle with Mitchell while he was watching TV and then run off to wherever they were going. Because Mitchell liked television so much, Craig decided to buy a cable subscription. One night we accidently left a cable television show on all night. The next morning, Craig and I sat up quickly in bed. Startled we both asked, "Is Mitchell alive?" Craig was the first to reach Mitchell. He was lying peacefully awake watching cartoons. Before that night, Mitchell cried in the middle of the night without fail. Those years were so tiring. Craig would get up and rock Mitchell to sleep nearly every night to protect my rest. I appreciated Craig's act of love. However, a mom just cannot fall back asleep when her baby cries. We had tried everything we could think of to get Mitchell to sleep through the night. One night I even thought of taping his pacifier to his cheeks so he could suck it all night. Of course, we were desperate and decided not to employ this plan for safety reasons. Instead, I hatched a plan to exploit the fact that Grace was a hard sleeper and did not move at all once she fell asleep. I would put Grace to bed next to Mitchell with her forehead pressed up against his pacifier. Presto, the pacifier would not fall out. Tired parents can be very creative. I took pictures of this special moment, and it is one of my all-time favorite pictures of them together.

Installing cable revealed to us that Mitchell woke up scared – kind of pitiful if you think about it. Mitchell would wake up in a dark, silent room, unable to move and all alone. For years after this, we kept cartoons on all night for Mitchell until I discovered that you could not trust any channel after certain hours of the night. To solve this problem, we bought a DVD player with automatic repeat. Running twenty-four seven, a DVD player would only last a year in our house.

Now that Mitchell is older, we play music all night and leave a light on in his closet. My routine before going to bed each night is to kiss Mitchell while he is wide-awake, say goodnight, tell his guardian angels they have the night shift, and head off to bed. It is a nice feeling.

While on the subject of guardian angels. God's Word describes their duties. When Mitchell was about five years old, Levi had been playing in Mitchell's room most of the day, and toys covered every square inch of the floor. It was time for bed, and I decided not to have Levi clean up his mess. Instead, I cleared a spot in front of the television stand, so I could set up Mitchell's nighttime movie selection. I tucked Mitchell in and headed to bed, stepping over toys on the way to the door. Mitchell cannot move any part of his body except his neck and make facial expressions. He simply lies there unable to roll in any direction. When we put Mitchell in a spot, he will be there when we return. Period. The next morning, I walked into Mitchell's room, and he was lying on the floor in front of the television stand about five feet from his bed! Not only was he lying there, he had a pillow under his head, and his blanket on top of him. I know what you are thinking: Craig or one of the children made Mitchell comfortable after he fell three feet down and five feet over from his bed. A discovery by anyone in the night would have been a three-alarm fire. Everyone vehemently denied just covering him up and leaving him. Only a seizure could have possibly made Mitchell roll off the bed. It was amazing that the toys were cleared away from the spot where he was lying with a pillow under his head and a blanket. Mitchell did not even have any rug burns. I say it was Mitchell's guardian angel doing his job. I believe Mitchell had a seizure, fell off his bed, was caught by his hard-working angel, and placed comfortably on the floor. Why not put him back in bed! I say it was to teach me to make sure he was closer to the wall next time. Another time, Mitchell fell asleep on the couch. He was sleeping soundly, and we did not want to wake him. The next morning, he was not on the couch; he was on the floor by the couch. His head was now in the opposite direction than we had left him, and, you guessed it, he had a pillow under his head and a blanket covering him. Both times, he had no injuries, and he never cried. We say Mitchell has the best guardian angels. I look forward to thanking them one day for a job well done!

Mitchell was in for a rough year. In the fall leading up to 1996, Mitchell had an appointment with his new orthopedic doctor at Dayton Children's Hospital. Mitchell's x-rays showed that both of his hips were out of socket. My medical ignorance was on full display during this visit. I proceeded to ask the doctor, "Would you like me to lay Mitchell on the table so you can pop his hips back in?" The look on his face was priceless; I knew immediately I had said something wrong." The doctor looked at me quizzically and said, "No, Mitchell will need surgery to put them back in." "Oh no," I said, "Not another surgery." After a few follow up appointments, we learned that not only were his hips out, but his hip sockets had not formed deep enough to hold the ball of his femur. The surgery would not be simple. The doctor explained that he needed to pin Mitchell's hips and that he would be in a body cast for at least eight weeks. The doctor scheduled the surgery for early spring.

Surgery day rolled around, and we made the dreaded drive to the hospital early in the morning. Of course, we had no idea how this surgery would mark the beginning of the most stressful seven years of our lives. My friend Sharon had come from Missouri to be with us during this surgery. We arrived at the hospital, went to the surgery center, and waited for the nurses to call Mitchell back. Before long, Craig and I were rolling Mitchell back to the surgery prepping area. The staff and nurses at Dayton Children's Hospital were amazing, preparing Mitchell for surgery and preparing Craig and me for what was to come next. The nurses let us help change Mitchell into his hospital gown since we were much more familiar with his little body and how rigid it was. Getting Mitchell's clothes on and off was beginning to be a chore. Changing his diapers was especially hard because his hips were out of socket. Keeping him clean was just as difficult. I kept remembering what Mitchell's surgeon had told us before his first G-Tube surgery, "Short-term pain for Mitchell's long-term gain." When the time came to let the nurses take Mitchell away, both Craig and I teared up. It never gets easier sending your child off to surgery, no matter their age. We constantly kissed, hugged, and reassured Mitchell, and then he was gone.

We knew the routine and waited in the waiting area for the nurse's mid-surgery report and then the final report from the surgeon. Finally, Mitchell's surgeon came out to tell us how well everything had gone. Next, he said that he did not need to send Mitchell to ICU, but rather he would send Mitchell straight to a regular room after a short stay in the recovery room. This was good news because Mitchell went to ICU after his first surgery to place his G-Tube and do the Nissen fundoplication. The original plan was to put Mitchell in ICU after this surgery. In retrospect, this was a bad idea. Nonetheless, Craig and I were pleased to hear this news and went back to see Mitchell in recovery. It was extremely difficult to see that huge body cast on Mitchell. He looked very uncomfortable. Mitchell was lying flat on his back and was casted from the middle of his chest to his toes and had a bar attached at each knee holding his legs apart. The doctor left an opening around his diaper area so we could change him and left a hole to access his G-Tube. His little toes were sticking out. In recovery, Mitchell woke up looking visibly upset, and then off we went to his room.

I stayed the night with Mitchell, and Craig brought Sharon back the next day to keep me company. Days can get very long in the hospital with a sick or recovering child.

After Sharon and I settled in for the day, I remember what happened next as if it were yesterday. It is etched in my brain forever. I was sitting on one side of Mitchell's bed, and Sharon was sitting on the other side. With Mitchell between us, we had to look over his cast to see each other. Mitchell was on a rotation schedule to help the cast dry evenly. One position had Mitchell lying on his stomach. Because of Mitchell's rigidness, we never put him on his stomach at home, but the staff assured us this was necessary for the cast to dry correctly. Sharon and I were both cross-stitching and talking to each other while Mitchell was in this new position with his face toward Sharon. Sharon got a concerned look on her face and said, "Carrie, come here quick. Look at Mitchell. He looks kind of blue." I jumped up and ran around to Sharon's side of the bed.

I was stunned; Mitchell's lips were extremely blue, and his chest was not moving. I quickly went into momma bear mode, as Craig likes to say, and pushed the call button and yelled, "Mitchell has turned blue and isn't breathing!" I tried to turn him over myself, but he was too heavy in that cast. Nurses came running in, and suddenly I heard a loud automated CODE BLUE announcement over the intercom stating Mitchell's room number. The nurses and I got Mitchell turned over as fear began to swallow me up. One of the nurses grabbed the blue manual breathing pump hanging over his bed and put it over his face and nose. She began to pump while oxygen was flowing. In less than a minute, the crash cart team arrived, and someone pushed me towards the door and said that I had to leave. "Had to leave? No way!" I thought and placed my foot in the doorframe as she closed the door. My foot left enough space for me to see what was going on. I watched what I thought was my son dying. My heart was heavy, and then it started breaking into pieces. I heard no one speak in the room. Each person knew his job and anticipated what the other was doing. In those days, one of my favorite shows was *911*. I remember saying in my head that this is like watching a *911* episode in person. I watched the doctor give Mitchell a shot as they got the paddles ready. The moment was surreal, as I stood there frozen with fear. "Oh God," I pleaded, "Please don't let Mitchell die." "Please God," I begged repeatedly. Tears were running down my face, as snot ran down my quivering lip and chin. I did not care. All I knew was that I was watching my son die. There are no words to explain what a mom feels in this moment. The emotional distress cuts through your physical body and enters your soul.

I felt Sharon's hand on my shoulder. I thanked God for sending Sharon. A friend from church who worked at the hospital heard the CODE BLUE and room number. She knew right away it was Mitchell and came to check on us. She called our church, and someone from church contacted Craig. I was so thankful that God had placed all the right friends at the hospital that day. Finally, I heard the most glorious sound. Mitchell was crying! The only time I was ever happy to hear Mitchell cry.

The doctor asked someone to get the mom. I was already at the bedside and thanking them all for saving Mitchell. I have never hugged a doctor so tightly. I remember he just said, "We are all just doing our job." By this time, Mitchell's surgeon had arrived and said, "Let's transfer Mitchell to ICU for a few days." I agreed and added, "And let's not turn him over on his stomach again while he is in that cast." After Mitchell's near-death episode, I placed a sign over Mitchell's hospital bed, during the remainder of that hospital stay, stating in bold letters, "DO NOT TURN ME ONTO MY STOMACH!"

Mitchell had respiratory failure that day due to a combination of morphine slowing his respiratory rate and the weight of his cast preventing his lungs from expanding. His allergy list in his medical records now even says he is allergic to morphine; we never wanted to take a chance with that drug again. I am ever thankful to the Lord for having Sharon come stay with us during that surgery. She was sitting exactly where she needed to be in order to see Mitchell's distress. Had she not been there, Mitchell would have quietly slipped unnoticed into eternity. I know God placed Sharon there that day because Mitchell's ministry was just getting started.

Mitchell's eighth and ninth birthdays passed with nothing too unusual to report. We continued our routine appointments, seeing each specialist and trying to keep his seizures in check and his allergies down and his back from curving off the charts. During this time, I had researched different hospital options (since I finally had a break and could!) and discovered that Columbus Children's Hospital, now Nationwide Children's Hospital in Columbus, had a wonderful Cerebral Palsy Clinic. I had Mitchell's orthopedic records transferred to Nationwide Children's Hospital, and he began seeing an orthopedic surgeon, Doctor John Kean. He also began seeing Doctor Michelle Miller in physical medicine. It was our first introduction to the practice of physical medicine. Physical medicine focuses on enhancing and restoring functional ability and quality of life for those with physical impairments or disabilities affecting the brain, spinal cord, nerves, bones, joints, ligaments, muscles, and tendons. I also really liked that Mitchell could see several different doctors or therapists in one visit. This took a lot of stress off my caring for Mitchell given his many disparate medical issues. In addition, the multi-discipline approach of focusing on quality of life was very appealing to Craig and me.

It was around this time that I realized there was no fixing Mitchell. I finally admitted to myself that Mitchell was not broken. *God had made Mitchell exactly as he was supposed to be.* God formed Mitchell in my womb, and God simply does not make mistakes. God had big plans for Mitchell as our stories reveal.

God also answered my personal question of why me? Remember I had asked this question of God when Mitchell was first diagnosed. Why did he force this hardship on our lives? I had no say in the matter. God revealed to me through his Word, sermons, friends, and prayer that he had chosen us and made us specifically for this task. Of course, God knew.

He was waiting for me to be still long enough to listen to his calling. This was the beginning of my being able to thank God for giving us a perfect little boy – a boy who would teach us much about ourselves and about him, a boy that would teach our family and friends about him, a boy that would teach everyone who reads this book about him. These lessons would have been impossible to learn from my plan for my life. I am exceedingly thankful that God loves all of us enough to give us the life we need and not the life we want.

It was at one of the Cerebral Palsy Clinic appointments that Doctor Kean first mentioned that Mitchell's scoliosis was getting out of hand. The first treatment would be a brace for Mitchell's back. An orthopedic brace facility near Nationwide Children's Hospital made Mitchell's back brace, or as we jokingly called it, a taco shell. Grace and I took Mitchell to his first brace fitting. "Oh my," I thought, "This thing was going to be a pain to get on and off and a pain for Mitchell to have to endure." The taco shell was hard plastic in the shape of his body and fit like a glove around his mid-section from his underarms to his hips. It was open in the back and had straps to tighten and Velcro to keep it closed around his body. They cut a circle out of the front to access his G-Tube.

It was springtime when Mitchell wore his back brace for the first time, and the summer proved unbearably hot for Mitchell in this hard-plastic contraption. A thin t-shirt just fit between his skin and the shell. After a year in the brace, Doctor Kean shook his head and said, "He did not like to do a back fusion surgery on someone so young." The brace did little to stop Mitchell's progressive scoliosis. His spine was rotating and curving at the same time, and he went from ten degrees to nearly seventy degrees in that year. The curving of his spine was affecting the function of his right lung, preventing Mitchell from taking a full breath. Mitchell's back was like a boomerang. Once again, Mitchell's uneven cerebral palsy muscles were in control of his body. It was the same process that pulled his hips out of socket resulting in his second major surgery roughly two years before. Mitchell's body and muscles were his own worst enemy. Doctor Kean explained that fusing Mitchell's back at such a young age would affect the growth of his trunk. Bottom line, he would not grow much more. I thought this might be a blessing in disguise since Craig and I were having a very difficult time lifting Mitchell. Doctor Kean's staff scheduled Mitchell's back surgery for the fall of 1999.

Mitchell was now ten, and in a month, he would have his back surgery. I remember thinking Mitchell had lived double his predicted life expectancy. I also remember when he turned five thinking he must be nearing the end of his life. Recently, Doctor Lucas, one of Mitchell's current physicians at Nationwide Children's Hospital, asked me, "How long was I told Mitchell would live when he was younger?" I asked her, "How did you know that I was told a time?" She said, "Because I knew that when Mitchell was young, it was common practice to give a time estimate on one's life when diagnosed." Curious, I asked her what she would have told me. She replied, "Now doctors are taught to never tell parents a life expectancy for their child." Giving us an expiration date created an unnecessary fear, a fear we dared not speak aloud. Our children would internalize this fear as well. We now know that God's perfect love casts out all fear. This was something we would all learn much later in our journey with Mitchell. However, just prior to Mitchell's back surgery, we were at the pinnacle of our adversity and attention was inward and not outward.

Today, Mitchell is twenty-eight years old. As these words roll through my mind, and I cannot help but shout, "Amazing!" Over the years, many would suggest Mitchell's longevity is due to his family's love and care they observed first hand. I think they are right. Our love toward Mitchell was tangible and contagious.

Craig's love was an example for us all. Craig held Mitchell in his arms much as you would hold a baby to comfort them. Mitchell's body seemed to melt into Craig's arms, and Mitchell would completely relax. Craig did this in our home, during church, and whenever Mitchell would subtly signal his desire to be comforted. Mitchell still does this today. Somehow Craig instinctively saw when Mitchell needed a tender embrace. Many people over the years have commented on how they witnessed this act of love by his dad. They often say it spoke to their heart and at times brought tears to their eyes. Mitchell is heavier now, but Craig still sits and holds Mitchell the same way while reclining in a rocker in Mitchell's room. Mitchell still melts in his dad's arms.

I show my love for Mitchell by taking care of his physical needs as you would a baby. Mitchell is nonverbal, so I always tried to put myself in his skin and figure out what he needed or what would be best for him. I love his smile when I am attending to him. That precious smile and contagious laugh makes every diaper change a joyous adventure.

Taylor showed his love by helping his dad keep food on the table. Sacrificing his childhood, Taylor was always there with a smile. His jovial personality brought levity to a family in distress. In addition, Taylor never missed an opportunity to talk and touch Mitchell whenever he passed by. Mitchell loved his big brother, and Taylor made sure Mitchell felt his love in return.

Grace showed her love by helping me attend to Mitchell's physical needs and by being by Mitchell's side whenever she could. She played with him when they were both little, and as they grew older that play developed into a friendship. I can see now where Mitchell provided Grace with a sense of purpose while giving her confidence along the way. Grace was like a second mother to Mitchell and was always willing to accompany us on Mitchell's doctor appointments. During high school, her teachers were very willing to grant Grace early dismissals to attend to Mitchell.

Levi showed his love much like Craig, physically comforting Mitchell. He would come home from school, throw his book bag down, and lean against Mitchell while they both watched television, until they both fell asleep. As Levi grew older, he continued to dote over Mitchell. When we took Mitchell to each of Levi's football games and wrestling matches, people routinely saw this brawny, athletic guy lean over and kiss his handicapped brother. Mitchell was never an embarrassment to any of our children. Mitchell has taught everyone in our family to love well, and we all continue to love on Mitchell to this day. Of course, our family has grown through marriage and birth. This contagious love keeps on going.

We arrived very early at NCH surgical center the morning of Mitchell's surgery for Mitchell's first surgery at Nationwide Children's Hospital. A very friendly, professional staff met us. We were very nervous, but the staff put us at ease. Doctor Kean met with us and explained again how he would be straightening Mitchell's back as much as possible and placing a metal rod along his spine to hold his back straight. Doctor Kean was aware of Mitchell's complications after his last surgery and agreed not to give Mitchell morphine. As a precaution, he also decided to send Mitchell to ICU after surgery. Craig and I were happy with this decision. In addition, Mitchell would not be in a cast after this surgery. Some people from our church came and prayed with us while we were in the waiting room. Once again, God's people brought a sense of comfort to us. We sat and waited for our mid-surgery report and the doctor's final surgery summary. Although surgery went well, Doctor Kean was not able to straighten Mitchell's spine as much as he had hoped. Mitchell's tight muscles had already done their harm. We were pleased with Doctor Kean's results. Mitchell went to recover in his ICU room and had a week's stay in the hospital. After getting Mitchell home, Craig and I decided to put Mitchell's bed in the living room while he healed. Because Mitchell's room was at the other end of the house, this made my steps to check on Mitchell less.

While Mitchell was healing, our financial troubles finally caught up with us. This was a very hard time when we made the difficult decision to auction off our belongings to give us a fighting chance of not losing our home. I had buried these feelings in a box deep inside me. When I started thinking back on those moments, I realized that I did not want to share my feelings because I was embarrassed. Pride caused me to hide these memories away. I have tears welling up in my eyes as I write about that dreadful day. For a woman, selling off all your household belongings is inconceivable. For a man it would be like selling off all your tools. This is what Craig had to do. I remember people asking why in the world we were selling our belongings. It was so stressful to try to explain and to have to explain repeatedly. One of my friends was not supportive at all and said some very unkind remarks about Craig to me. The insinuation was that Craig could do more and that he should not be putting me in this position. I knew others thought this. Ever since Craig left the Air Force, he endured these kinds of lonely attacks. Sadly, I started believing this myself for a while. However, I knew better. I knew how extremely hard Craig had been working and the trap we were in to cover Mitchell's medical costs. I have a husband who loved me, kissed me goodbye every morning, brought me coffee every morning in bed, was much more patient with me than I was with him, and was working over ten hours a day in those tough days. However, no one seemed interested in the truth. I think sometimes when people see someone going through long-term financial trouble, they latch onto the simplest justification of why they are not going to help in order to feel better about not helping. My message to anyone watching a family going through a long-term adversity is not to formulate your own opinion. Assume that you do not have all the facts. Having lived a life of adversity that most readers will never experience, I know that most of the time I did not need their thoughts, probing questions, or money; I just needed a hug.

During all this adversity, God brought blessings to us. We have several friends who gave us some nice items of theirs to add to our auction. We had not asked them to do this; they simply wanted to help. In addition, I have a group of dear friends who found out which items we were most sad about parting with, and these wonderful women bought them back for us. I remember coming home after everyone had left (I did not want to be there during the auction) and finding in my kitchen an antique oak coat rack for Craig and an antique cabinet for me. Their kindness left me in tears. We still have both pieces of furniture today, and they are even more precious to us because of the auction. The auction company that we had hired, Sheridan and Associates, gave us back their portion of the proceeds. Their kindness was unexpected, and we are grateful for their investment in our family. Finally, the obvious good that came from the auction is that we cleared the debts denying us financial stability. We also kept our home, which we desperately needed to best care for Mitchell at the time.

Looking back, I can now thank God for our long stretch of financial hardship. It taught me to trust God in a different way, to be more frugal, and to be sensitive to others in a similar situation. Our children have fond memories of our *poor* days, as they affectionately call them. Our family learned to appreciate what we have in both poverty and wealth. Our house is no longer empty. God filled our home with new furniture and with new memories. God knew what was best for us!

After our successful auction, Mitchell continued to heal from his back surgery. However, the storm clouds were gathering as another medical issue began to take shape. Mitchell's seizures were increasing. To counteract his increasing seizures, the doctors increased his seizure medicine until Mitchell was nearly a zombie. He was always tired looking, had lost the joyful look in his eyes, and did not smile as he used to. I complained to the neurologist, but he stated that this was now life for my son. I did not like this answer, so I decided it was time to shop around for a new pediatric neurologist. Sitting in a waiting area waiting on repairs to Mitchell's wheelchair, I picked up an issue of *Exceptional Parent Magazine*. There I read an article I thought might be the answer to Mitchell's seizures. The article was about a diet to control seizures. Not only that, this ketogenic diet was for the very type of seizures Mitchell experienced. My heart started to pound, and I could not wait to get home to show Craig the article. (I have a confession to make: I stole that magazine from the waiting area that day.)

The next day when I started researching this diet, I found out that this was not just some random diet, but research from John Hopkins Hospital validated the results. Next, I searched for a place where Mitchell could see someone about the diet. My next discovery made me almost leap out of my chair: Nationwide Children's Hospital. Mitchell's hospital! I could not believe it – right in our back yard! This was a God moment. I contacted Mitchell's primary care doctor, Doctor Hesz, and asked if she would send a consult to the Pediatric Neurology Department at Nationwide Children's Hospital. She agreed. Two months later, our ketogenic journey began.

In 1999, Mitchell met his first neurologist at the hospital. Things moved very slowly. I wanted to get Mitchell on this diet immediately. During Mitchell's first appointment, I learned that there was a process. The ketogenic diet was the last resort in seizure control. Therefore, the doctors had to eliminate all the other possibilities available for seizure control. Patience has never been my strongest attribute, but I was getting plenty of practice as an advocate for a special needs son.

Before starting the diet, the neurologists tried various combinations of anti-epileptic drugs (AED). In the beginning, when the staff asked which drugs had been tried on Mitchell, the doctor was puzzled when I said only one AED had ever been given to Mitchell. I remember she commented on the quantity of seizures Mitchell was having during the appointment. She believed it was an extreme amount. At that time, Mitchell was having seizures almost constantly. I told her that Mitchell's last neurologist had said that this was going to be life for my son. This new doctor looked at me and with confidence said, "This will not be life for your son. We will work with him until we have his seizures under control." My heart smiled. I knew God had sent Mitchell to the right place.

Over the next two years, the neurologist tried several different AED combinations on Mitchell followed by EEGs to check the drug's effectiveness. Along the way, Mitchell's seizure diagnosis became Lennox-Gastaut Syndrome (LGS), a rare childhood epileptic disorder, only appearing in two to five percent of children. LGS is very hard to control. As usual, when Mitchell gets a diagnosis, it's always the worst one.

Finally, at the end of the year 2000, the ketogenic team decided Mitchell was a great candidate for the diet. The staff gave me a book to read on the subject and scheduled Mitchell to check in to Nationwide Children's Hospital the following March. During Mitchell's hospital stay, he would begin a controlled start to the diet. Craig and I both were praying that this diet would be a miracle for Mitchell. I have learned through Mitchell's seizure journey that *seizure free* is not a term we can use for Mitchell. Although Mitchell does have some seizure-free days, *seizure control* is always the realistic goal.

In March, Mitchell's admission to the hospital was uneventful. Seizure control through the ketogenic diet requires strict controls. Some compare it to an Adkins diet, but that is not a fair comparison. Doctor supervision is necessary for the ketogenic diet. Please do not try this diet at home. During his hospital stay, the doctors eliminated sugar and carbohydrates from Mitchell's diet while introducing low amounts of carbohydrates. Protein and fat intake are high with this diet and make up most of the formula. A dietician worked to figure out the right ratio of carbohydrates, fat, and protein.

Next, the dietician determined Mitchell's necessary daily caloric intake and how much extra water he could have per day. The diet requires measuring everything to the gram. The doctors constantly checked Mitchell's blood sugar levels and urine ketone levels to determine when Mitchell reached the right level of ketosis. To this day, we check Mitchell's ketone levels in his urine weekly to make sure he is on track.

God once again showed his faithfulness to Mitchell and our family, providing the means to pay for Mitchell's new diet. During that time, I was not worried about how we might pay for this diet. I knew that Craig was doing all he could to make this happen and that God would be faithful since he had brought this diet to Mitchell. Mitchell had been teaching me lessons about God that I needed to learn. We should never be anxious and always pray our troubles to God because God still does miracles today in the lives of his people. When I look back over Mitchell's life, God proved himself to us repeatedly.

After returning home from a successful start of the ketogenic diet, Mitchell's new routine began. Weighing each ingredient in Mitchell's new formula to the gram was tedious. I am not a detailed person, but I became one regarding Mitchell's food. Thanks to the I/O Waiver, the cost of Mitchell's food ingredients was covered. This was such a weight off our shoulders. Within days we began to see fewer seizures from Mitchell. Not only did Mitchell get no sugar in his food, but also, I had to become a label reader. Anything you put on your skin or in your mouth may contain sugar. Your skin will absorb sugar!

The ketogenic diet book became like a user's manual for Mitchell's diet. The book listed ingredients to avoid. I discovered I needed to be very careful because a product could

Mitchell's Memoir

have sugar even if the word *sugar* was not in the ingredient list or called by a different name. Toothpastes, lotions, sunscreens, soaps, and shampoos all had to be sugar-free. Today it is second nature for our family to read a label before buying something for Mitchell or before applying it to his skin. We had to change all of Mitchell's current medicines to the form containing the least amount of sugar. Not all doctors at that time were convinced that the ketogenic diet really worked and some would question my request to change to a sugar and carbohydrate-free version. The glares I got sometimes were comical. One doctor from another hospital laughed and said, "Does that silly diet even work?" I informed him that it did and that it worked quite well with Mitchell, eliminating 90% of his seizures. An impressive statistic!

As part of the I/O Waiver, Mitchell received sixty hours of a Home Personal Care service person. This person could be from a health agency or an independent provider (IP). To become an IP, a person must complete an application through the Ohio Department of Developmental Disabilities (DD) and work with the local Board of DD in their county. This is a State of Ohio program, not a national one. Craig and I did not like the thought of hiring through an agency and having someone we did not know caring for Mitchell in our home. Now I would be able to leave the house, by myself, to do simple things most take for granted. I could now shop for groceries or take our other children places. I was very excited about this new freedom.

I do not remember when Pat Tompkins' name jumped in my head, but I know God put it there. I had met Pat a few years earlier through a mutual friend, and we became friends because we both loved the Lord and had a special needs family member. David was Pat's Downs Syndrome brother. I asked Pat what her first memory of Mitchell was. Pat said, "We were at a park sitting on bleachers together, and she noticed me with Mitchell." Pat went on to say, "You looked very tired, so I offered to hold Mitchell in order to give you a break." As she held Mitchell, she thought that he was adorable and so sweet. I say it was love at first sight. When I learned of the IP option from Mitchell's caseworker, Julie, at the Greene County Board of DD, I knew that Pat would be perfect for this. We knew Pat and trusted her, two important things when selecting a caregiver for a family member, even though I am sure she selected us first.

It was difficult for others to learn how to care for Mitchell, but I could teach them. Craig and I had known Mitchell since birth, and we learned gradually to adjust to his new diagnoses, medicines, and ways to position his body to avoid bedsores. For Pat, she would need to learn this all at once. She was willing, and I felt such a peace that she was to join our care-giving team for Mitchell. Pat began her paperwork and took the classes the state required to become a caregiver. Caregivers must renew their status every three years and are considered self-employed. They must follow the State's guidelines. Pat would be required to keep extensive records regarding Mitchell's care. Each year I met with Mitchell's caseworker, Julie, to come up with his Individual Service Plan (ISP). Starting in August 2001 Pat served our family and Mitchell faithfully for fourteen years. During those years, she became family and a dear friend to us rather than just a caregiver. We had many chats over the years, and I always could count on her for wise advice.

God brought another person into our lives who would later become a caregiver for Mitchell. We had known Abbey

Pyles and her family since we had moved to Cedarville. She had known Mitchell since he was three years old. Abbey had just turned 18 years old, the required age to become a provider. I remember telling Abbey's mom, Jackie, about the new I/O Waiver opportunity to have caregivers in our home. Jackie mentioned it to Abbey, and she contacted us right away. As with Pat, we already knew Abbey and thought she would be a great fit. She was available the opposite times of Pat's hours, which was evenings and weekends. Craig and I were both very excited over the thought of having Abbey take care of Mitchell in our home. We were looking forward to a little break. For thirteen years, we took care of all of Mitchell's 24/7 physical needs. In our estimation, our family did a great job. However, we were very weary. Craig and I appreciated the added helping hands. Abbey, just like Pat, needed to learn all about Mitchell. She too was a quick learner and was such a blessing to our family. Abbey was even able to take a couple of vacations with our family to Florida. Having another adult caregiver for Mitchell while we were on vacation gave Craig and me the rare opportunity to have a date and to spend some extra time with our other children. Those vacation times were true vacations for the entire family.

My parents, Ernest and Hilda Taylor, love Mitchell dearly. After I became a grandparent, I understood how they must have felt towards Mitchell. My parents lived in Virginia until the fall of 2004 when they moved to be near us. After they moved close, dad gave Grace a break from accompanying me to all of Mitchell's appointments. Even before they moved close by, dad would come about once a year and help me with Mitchell. He came one time so I could go stay with Sharon in Missouri for a few days while she recovered from a major surgery. He watched Taylor, Grace, and Levi while Craig worked. We always knew if we needed him to come stay with us or to help that he was only a phone call away. That was such a great feeling. Dad could do diaper duty, mix his food, take him to appointments, and just be a grandpa at times.

When Mitchell had his major surgeries, both of my parents would come and watch the other three children so Craig and I both could be at the hospital as much as Craig's workload would allow. If Craig had to be at work, Mom would sit with me to keep me company and make sure I was eating as I should. It really was not until they moved here that they fully understood the amount of care and time Mitchell required.

As Mitchell has grown older, more care, time, and energy are required. My parents are now in their eighties. Dad is battling stage-four colon cancer, and he and Mom are still only a phone call away. He comes and sits with Mitchell when Craig and I both need to be somewhere in the evenings. On weekends, Dad will sit with Mitchell when Sarah or Grace are unavailable during the day. Mom goes to appointments with Mitchell and me when Grace is unavailable. Craig and I will always be extremely grateful for their love and service to our family.

In late summer of 2001, Mitchell's orthopedic doctor noticed that Mitchell's right femur had once again pulled out of his hip socket. Doctor Kean told me he that had seen hips come out again in his patients with high spasticity in their muscles, such as in Mitchell's case. Doctor Kean recommended surgery. During this surgery, Doctor Kean also wanted to perform muscle and tendon releases on both hips to make it easier to change Mitchell's diaper and to try to prevent another hip surgery in the future. "Here we go again," I began thinking. "Hasn't this poor boy endured enough, Lord?" No amount of wishing this situation away was going to work. Reluctantly, I scheduled Mitchell's surgery that day before we left the doctor's office. The next available surgery date would be in September.

September came quickly as did Mitchell's surgery day. Of course, surgeries are always early in the morning, so off we went to Nationwide Children's Hospital before the sun was up. Craig and I hated the thought of another surgery that involved a body cast. It had been five years since Mitchell's last hip surgery and his Code Blue episode, which was still fresh in my memory. We arrived at Nationwide Children's Hospital and knew the routine. The nurses prepped Mitchell, and the surgeon was ready. Once again, we had tears in our eyes as they rolled Mitchell down that seemingly endless hallway to surgery. I remember that waiting room well. It was a rather large room with several groupings of chairs and couches.

A volunteer sat at the desk by the entrance and kept families informed of surgery progress. We were expecting a four-hour surgery. We watched as nurses came and went giving families updates about their little person's surgery. The volunteer gave us an update mid-way through the surgery. She let us know everything was going well as expected. She also let us know that the doctor would be in when the surgery was complete. Two more hours went by; he should be in here any minute. We were getting anxious, but neither Craig nor I wanted to let on that we were getting concerned. Another hour went by. Surely, he started the next surgery and just forgot to come speak with us. By this time, Craig and I were asking each other what was taking Doctor Kean so long to come tell us he was finished. Another hour crept by. We were pacing the waiting room when the door opened and the doctor walked in. The expression on his face was one I had not seen on him before; he looked sad. My heart started to beat a little faster. He walked over to us and sat down right next to me. I wondered why he was sitting down. Craig and I were both looking into his eyes, waiting for words to come out of his mouth.

After a little clearing of his throat and a deep breath, he said, "There was a bit of a problem during surgery. Mitchell is just fine; he is in recovery. During surgery his femur bone slipped out of my hand and fell on the operating table, and when it hit the table, it spiral fractured down the length of his bone. Normally bones will not do that. Mitchell's bones should not have been that brittle. I am so sorry." I thought for a minute that he was going to cry. He continued telling us that he had to wrap a cage around Mitchell's femur and place several pins in it to hold it together and that is why it had taken so long.

I started to cry. I always seem to cry. I was only thinking of it causing more pain to an already painful surgery. Craig stated, "Surely it was not on purpose." Doctor Kean seemed shocked at the question and replied, "Certainly not; it was an accident." I think Craig was trying to reassure Doctor Kean that we were not the type of people to sue. Neither of us were angry with Doctor Kean. It was a blessing to discover how brittle Mitchell's bones were in order to fix this problem later. It would have been worse to find this out while we were moving him around at home. I was only sad that something else had happened to our Mitchell.

Doctor Kean sent Mitchell to recovery and then to his hospital room. ICU was my preference, but the medical staff felt that the regular floor was adequate for his recovery of a few days. When Craig and I met Mitchell in his room, our nightmare began. Looking back, no one could have predicted what would happen next. I do not blame anyone of the staff; I only would like to stress to the medical profession, please listen to parents and family members more. Parents of profoundly handicapped children are far more in tune to what is normal for their child.

Mitchell was always sleepy after a surgery just as any person would be. After the first three surgeries, Mitchell would open his heavy eyes and give us a little smile whenever we spoke or touched him. Something was very different this time. Craig, Grace, and I would try everything to get Mitchell to respond. Mitchell just laid there completely unconscious. We mentioned our concern to the nurses and residents. The programmed response was, "This is normal for children like Mitchell to have a harder time waking up after anesthesia." We knew better and tried to explain that this was not Mitchell's normal and that we thought something was wrong.

Next, I asked if they could contact his neurologist. None of them felt this was necessary. After a day, Craig and I were getting very concerned. I could sense in my spirit that I needed to act. My message to other parents who might find themselves in a similar situation is this: you need to listen to that still, small voice inside because you do know your child best. Do not be timid in advocating for your child when talking to professionals. We are Mitchell's voice because he does not have one of his own! I have always felt a responsibility to represent Mitchell well and to be his voice to the world, especially the medical world.

Finally, I had had enough. At one point the next day, I walked to the neurology floor to ask them to come see Mitchell. The staff tried to explain hospital politics. The neurology staff said I would need to have the attending doctor ask for a consult. "I am his mom, and I am asking for a consult," I said with a desperate sound in my voice. I knew in my heart that something was not right, but the specialists who could help fix it were not listening to me. I do not think I have ever felt so frustrated, and my anger level began to climb. Then I thought of fighting this battle from outside the hospital. I called Mitchell's pediatrician, Doctor Hesz. I reached the Star Pediatrics office and explained the situation, and the nurse promised she would have Doctor Hesz call me back.

In the meantime, I could not just sit back at Mitchell's bedside and do nothing. I told Craig and Grace I would be back. I went to the nurses' station. Experience told me that nurses always seem to have the answers to getting things done. I had seen nurses navigate around hospital politics before because they knew the system. I politely asked the nurse what I could do to get a neurologist to see Mitchell. I could see the compassion in her eyes. She thought for a minute and then said to me, "If you stand there and make a scene and yell at me to get a neurologist, I could call one for you. But afterwards I would have to call security to remove you from the floor." I liked how she thought. She had a sort of smile on her face, a devious smile that communicated that she knew how to work the system. I told her I would be right back to make a scene after I explained to my husband and daughter what I was about to do. I did not want them to see me dragged out by security without knowing what was going on.

When I got back to the room, Craig was on the phone with Doctor Hesz. Doctor Hesz was returning my call. "Thank you, Lord," I thought. I spoke with her, and she said that she would call the hospital and get a neurologist right away. I was so relieved. Craig, Grace, and I sat back and quietly waited for the action to begin.

About fifteen minutes later, Doctor Tsao, the lead doctor on Mitchell's neurology team, was in Mitchell's room. "Yes!" I said under my breath. Doctor Tsao looked over Mitchell and immediately put an order for blood work and an order to transfer Mitchell to the ICU. Doctor Tsao had always been a great doctor for Mitchell. After this hospital stay, he became Mitchell's hero! Shortly after arriving in ICU, we learned that Mitchell's blood work showed that his liver numbers were extremely high, and the liver was not working properly. The doctor did not know why, but Doctor Kean continued to follow Mitchell regarding his post-surgery responsibilities. However, he gladly turned Mitchell's ICU care over to Doctor Tsao. Grace and I both remember Doctor Tsao standing by Mitchell's bed saying, in a thick Chinese accent, "Mitchell is very complicated – very complicated." We watched Mitchell's liver numbers continue to climb into the night and next day.

The tension and anxiety that slowly builds when you are waiting for the doctors to figure it out is agonizing. It is a helpless feeling to watch your child lie there in an ICU bed and be able to do absolutely nothing for him. Nothing. In hindsight, this was not true. Craig and I had the power of prayer at our disposal. We paced and prayed. If you had heard my prayers, it would sound a lot like begging and pleading. God knows a mother's heart, and I knew he understood my feelings. Craig contacted our church, family, and close friends to pray that the doctors would figure this out.

Mitchell looked so vulnerable, lying there unresponsive and in that terrible body cast. I hate body casts to this day. His body was fighting hard, but his statistics indicated that his body was losing the battle. Mitchell began to retain fluid, and his body visibly started to swell. I sat in the hard wooden rocking chair throughout the day just watching Mitchell and praying. Craig paced back and forth. Sharon Baum was there from Missouri to help us during this surgery. My parents had come from Virginia to care for the other children. Everyone was in the waiting room. Only two visitors could sit with Mitchell in ICU at a time – a rule strictly enforced and for good reason. Visitors had to wash their hands and put on a paper gown before coming back since it was still unknown what Mitchell was fighting.

Each time I walked out to the waiting area to get a break, I would see a new face of a friend who had come to encourage us. Each face brought tremendous encouragement to my broken, worried heart. Hugs are great medicine for worried parents, and I needed plenty of them. Even Mitchell's aide from school came to check on him. Our deacon from church came, and our family in Virginia were calling and checking on Mitchell and telling us of their prayers for him. I cannot emphasize enough how important it is for God's people to visit the sick. When you do this, you are visiting the Lord himself. Never underestimate the value of your time in this endeavor!

I remember at one point sitting in that rocker, looking over at four doctors as they were discussing what possibly could be causing Mitchell's decline and thinking, "OK, there is a lot of brainpower there with four of you; can't you figure this out?"

In my heart, I heard God's still small voice saying, "Don't worry; I know what is wrong and will let them know when it's time." Yes, God did know. I was trying so hard to trust God with Mitchell's life – to trust God's plan and his timing. If God handed me a grade that day, it would not have been an A, or even a B or C. I was really struggling with trusting God at that moment. I was physically and mentally tired. I wanted to sleep but was afraid to. I was afraid of what God's plan might be, a plan that I might not like. I remember thinking, "After all of God's faithfulness in our lives, and especially in Mitchell's life, why did I doubt what God was doing?" Looking back I was just plain stubborn. God gave me this stubbornness to advocate for Mitchell not resist his will for my life.

Sometime during our third day in ICU, Doctor Tsao came in and said he was going to take Mitchell off one of his seizure medications. It was the medicine that Mitchell had been on the longest. He said he had an idea and wanted to try it. Late that afternoon, while Mitchell continued to lay there unconscious, one of the doctors came in to speak to Craig and me. His countenance was somber, and his voice was quiet. He told us that unless they discovered the underpinning cause of Mitchell's liver failure soon, Mitchell was not going to win this fight. My heart leaped in to my throat and tears started pouring down my face. "This just cannot be happening again," I screamed in my mind. All I could do was pick up where I left off in my begging prayers. "God, please! You cannot take Mitchell yet; I am not ready." Suddenly, I thought aloud, "Wait a minute. I am talking to God. God created everything, and he certainly could take Mitchell home if he wanted to. That reality hit me like a ton of bricks, and I wrestled with this thought for a while. Then, I changed my prayer. "God you certainly can take Mitchell home at any time, but if you take him home now, I cannot get through this without your strength." In that moment, when you first accept the fact that your child will likely die, your attention turns one hundred percent to God. The only thing that stands between you and the life of your child is a single decision by our Creator. I made my case, and now it was time to trust his sovereign judgment.

That night Mitchell had a male nurse. He was a quiet and no-nonsense kind of guy. He was a bit older than I was, and I misjudged him immediately. I thought, "This guy is not going to be gentle with my Mitchell." But I was wrong. He was one of the kindest and most gentle nurses Mitchell has ever had. As he was getting ready to change Mitchell's diaper, I got up to help him. He turned me away and said, "Get some rest; caring for Mitchell is my job tonight," adding, "Mitchell and I will be just fine." He even gave me a pillow to use. I have never forgotten that nurse's kindness. I did get a little sleep while keeping a watchful eye on Mitchell, despite the uncomfortable, wood rocking chair and the ICU no-sleeping rule. I had the opportunity to tell this gifted nurse how his kindness ministered to Mitchell and me that evening. We would meet him again, years later, during another ICU trip. I thank God for providing nurses to serve families through medical crises. I pray blessings on every one of them!

The next morning, the doctors said Mitchell's liver numbers were coming down fast, and we noticed Mitchell stirring from his slumber. The doctors announced that Mitchell was suffering with chemical pancreatitis because of his seizure medication. My heart cried my thanks to God. I thought, "Finally, we have a diagnosis." The staff told us that in general liver numbers would take days to come down because it was normally a slow process. But it was not so, with all the people praying for Mitchell. By the next day, his numbers had fallen by half, and then again by half the following day. Mitchell was waking up! Our Mitchell was back! The doctors were amazed and eventually sent Mitchell packing to another part of the hospital.

The nursing staff transferred Mitchell to the Neurology Department floor to finish his recovery from surgery and chemical pancreatitis. The staff was excited to receive him. He was in the hospital for a total of fourteen days. ICU claimed ten of those days.

After we were home for a few days, I was able to reflect on Mitchell's latest hospital stay. Again, I came to see that God was showing me that I could trust him totally. It was only after I gave Mitchell back to God that he gave Mitchell back to us. God nailed this lesson to my heart. I am thankful we have a God who works intimately in our lives even when we doubt his goodness.

When we arrived home from the hospital, Taylor and Grace's church youth group organized meals for us. It was a tremendous help and blessing. I commonly hear that church members do not organize and serve meals to families when there is someone at the home to prepare a meal. Craig has always told me that maybe this is what happens when people with the gift of administration and not the gift of helps run a meal program. I boldly suggest that the purpose of taking meals should be about encouragement. Bringing meals to a family is a powerful way for his people to engage and minister to people going through adversity. The act of making a meal is a time to reflect and pray for the family. The act of delivering a meal is the opportunity to encourage and pray with them. Hugs are not bad either. Someone might be tempted to say that people can do all this without bringing a meal. Although technically true, I can count on one hand the number of people who came to our home just to encourage, pray, and give us hugs. I run out of fingers and toes where this happened as part of someone's coordinating meals.

Mitchell remained in his body cast for twelve weeks because of his broken femur complication. Trust me when I say that a body cast is extremely difficult to keep clean, especially when wearing diapers. In addition, changing a person in a body cast is a two-person job, and sometimes even a three-person job. The twelve weeks Mitchell was in that body cast went by slowly for the entire family.

Doctor Kean continued to follow Mitchell for another six years. He was a very kind and caring doctor. Craig and I were thankful God put him in charge of Mitchell's orthopedic surgeries. At the end of those six years, he finally graduated Mitchell from his department. He knew there was nothing else he could do for Mitchell professionally. Doctor Kean did say, however, that if Mitchell ever required an orthopedic surgeon, he would be happy to see him again.

As I end my story on our years of adversity, I leave you with one simple thought: Nothing happens in your life without God's approval. He has a good purpose for every adversity. Learn to trust God early. Finally, be a stubborn advocate for someone going through adversity, and let God be a stubborn advocate for you.

FINDING PEACE
IN THE STORM
(January 2001 – Present)

Chapter 7
Reviving the Pilot – Dad

The first year after Mitchell's last surgery was a time of healing. The year before, Mitchell miraculously moved to the top of the I/O Waiver list to receive state and federal services that completely removed the barriers to making a living and fully caring for Mitchell. As if that were not enough, Mitchell began a controversial ketogenic diet, reducing his severe seizures by 90% and bringing him out of a two-year stupor to once again smile and interact with his family. Mitchell also had his right hip pinned again, eliminating his discomfort and allowing us to move his hip so we could change his diaper. Finally, God miraculously and overnight healed Mitchell from chemical pancreatitis, answering the prayers of many saints.

For the first time since 1995, Carrie and I could see a clear path toward healing our family. No more working as a merchant to make a living. No more working night and weekend side jobs just so we could eat and pay the bills. No more working without medical coverage for the entire family. No more fear of bankruptcy. The list of my *no mores* was long. Very long. As I write this, I pause to praise God through tears.

Taylor was now a junior in high school, sixteen years old, and bore the brunt of this very difficult time. His selflessness and hard work by my side, working side jobs, kept the family from certain financial ruin. I could not have done it without him. Our daughter, Grace, turned fifteen, and her emotional link to Mitchell was like that of a parent. By this time, Grace was more mature compared to her peers, having developed a servant's heart at an early age. Levi was only nine years old.

However, by this time Levi had traded places to become Mitchell's older brother, including him in every aspect of his play life. Finally, Carrie and I were war weary, and we had a lot to do to heal our neglected marriage.

I see this time as a snapshot in my head – a moment of calm with no looming cloud – a time where we spent our evenings going to every sporting event. I mean every single sporting event! Football and volleyball in the fall, basketball in the winter, and track and field in the spring. Buying all those sporting tickets was a small fortune, but the investment in our children was worth every penny! We all smiled more, laughed more, and loved more. I was proud of my family for having weathered such a time of trial. Looking back, the stress tore our emotions to shreds, but our love kept putting us back together.

If there were something like Posttraumatic Stress Syndrome (PTSD) for families dealing with unimaginable levels of stress for a prolonged period, our family would be a case study. I know our faith is what really got us through. I also know that we all had deep emotional wounds that would eventually need attention. Over the next fifteen years, these wounds tore open in unexpected ways – some gradually, some explosively. However, for now life was simpler, and we would deal with these issues another day.

Two years ago, we had learned of the Make-A-Wish Foundation. We applied for a wish, and The Columbus Make-A-Wish Foundation granted Mitchell a big screen television with surround sound speakers. The television was a rear projection system, and the viewing area was the size of a six-person tabletop. Taylor and I went to work making Mitchell's closet opening the exact size of the projector television.

Within a few days, we rolled the heavy projector television into position, and our Friday family-night movies came to life. Our Make-A-Wish brought us all together when we needed it the most. Carrie and I are forever grateful to the Make-A-Wish Foundation for making our family's dream for Mitchell come true when reality was closer to a nightmare.

In addition, we received another incredible gift that year: a new green Ford E-150 van. Just the year before, Mitchell's I/O waiver would pay for a vehicle wheelchair lift. However, we had only one problem: we had an old, run-down, white minivan that could not fit a lift. Our minivan was barely large enough to fit a family of six traveling with extra medical equipment. With brute force, we used to hoist Mitchell's bulky and heavy wheelchair into the back of the van. We had been doing this for ten years now, and we were beginning to have back trouble.

Carrie's routine for getting Mitchell and his wheelchair in and out of our white minivan was quite the spectacle. Carrie would snap-lift the roughly eighty-pound wheelchair. Then, while the wheelchair was midair, at the apex of its upward trajectory, Carrie would slam her leg against the wheels of the chair to send it flying into the trunk space. Carrie wore pants to hide bruises all up and down her left leg. By this time, Mitchell was also heavy. Putting Mitchell in the minivan seat required a similar move. Carrie would dead lift Mitchell, then spin, and fall into the vehicle with Mitchell, all the while trying to avoid slamming his head against the door-opening header. Getting Mitchell out of the minivan required brute strength. Of course, Carrie would never perform these acrobatic maneuvers when I was around. Unfortunately, I was gone making us a living while Carrie was traveling with Mitchell to a couple of doctor appointments a week.

A small group of our friends were the first to notice that we were having trouble getting Mitchell in and out of our minivan. Up to this point, Carrie's family was only around a couple of weeks a year and were unaware of the incredible difficulties that plagued our daily lives. My family was not part of our lives either and did not have the means to help even if they had wanted to. Our small group of friends began an initiative to gather donations to buy Mitchell a van. The Greene County MRDD suggested we put a lift in a new van because funds to move the lift to another vehicle would only be available every five years. The idea was to have a van that would last at least five years. The problem was a new van was completely out of reach because of our credit rating, having nearly gone bankrupt three years before. To overcome our bad credit would require a much larger than normal down payment. Even if we had an acceptable down payment, our interest rate would be double the normal. At the time, buying a used van with enough life was also financially out of reach. We lived paycheck to paycheck. Our run-down minivan probably had another year in it.

Before long, a church benevolence committee was involved so that the donations could be a tax write-off. One of the donors involved was a Ford Automotive Company retiree who could give away a couple of deep discounts per year to friends and family. This made a new van more affordable. Carrie and I were very excited about the prospect of receiving a van and humbled by the idea we could be benefactors of such a large gift. The recommended vehicle included minimal amenities, but it was new and large enough for a motorized rear lift. We selected an interior with four captain's seats making it easy to reach Mitchell since his wheelchair lift would place him in the back of the extra-long van. The price tag was around $35,000. I did not make that much in a year. In over a month's time, donations quickly came in, and the church benevolence committee brought me in to present the gift.

What happened next, I hesitate to share because Carrie and I do not want to leave anyone with the impression that we were not grateful for such a sacrificial gift to help us care for Mitchell and lighten our burden. However, when we decided to write this book, we felt called to put it all out there. It is one of our desires that our stories, *Mitchell's Memoir*, will challenge family and friends to assess when their service is helpful, harmful, or missing.

When I met with the church benevolence committee, I felt like a child going to the principal's office. I had a pit in my stomach, and I was trying hard to appear upbeat and humble. I did not want to come across as if I expected a gift in any way. I felt uncomfortable meeting with the committee because, beforehand, someone came to me and let me know that I was not going to receive all the money I needed to buy the van. I do not think the committee wanted me to hear this news at the same moment they would give me a check. The person told me that the committee felt, "I needed to have skin in the game." Immediately, I felt that unmistakable collapse of my spirit as my heart swelled in my chest. I was used to this feeling by now in our lives. I hid my feelings and simply said, "I understand. Carrie and I are very thankful for the gift." I continued to espouse how this gift was really going to help our quality of life caring for Mitchell. When I walked away, I thought to myself, "Skin in the game? Not only do I have skin in the game but I also have bone and muscle" as my thoughts went to Mitchell lying in bed. Choked up by now I thought,

"How could they say that? These people would go home to their normal families." Somehow, I had missed the transition from this being a project where people were organizing to help us to a project where we were soliciting help to get a van. I remember thinking that it was not a bad approach to have us chip in. I only wish someone had asked if we could afford to finance part of it. I would have said that I could because we had the room in our finances, and I would have wanted to volunteer my skin for the game. However, what if our finances were such I could not afford any monthly payment. I guess, in the end, I felt disrespected.

The committee's next request felt like a sucker punch. When they handed me the check, they asked me to try to repay the church benevolent fund, if or when I could. I wanted to walk away right then and say no thanks. "We did not ask for the help," I thought. However, we desperately needed a van, and I knew how hard it was for Carrie to take Mitchell anywhere. The bruises on Carrie's leg and her back pain were constant reminders of this fact. Knowing that we would be gifted a van lifted a heavy weight off my shoulders. When they nonchalantly asked me to pay it back, the weight returned. What I thought would be a gift became a debt, a gift I am still donating for today. Of course, some reading this might remind me I was under no obligation to return the money. Although technically true, the problem was that I said I would. Keeping my word was as important to me then as it is now. Think about it. There are very few instances where you cannot ever pay back money to someone. In my poorest state, I could afford twenty-five dollars a month. The point is that once you give your word to try to do something, you create an obligation. When an obligation concerns money, it is quite simply a debt. I met the benevolence committee debt free and left in debt – a debt I gave blood, sweat, and tears to remove after auctioning off most of our personal belongings. My anxiety and joy fought fiercely for control. I remember deciding to let my anxiety go and focus on the joy. The van was an absolute blessing, and it eased our daily burdens tenfold.

Before I leave this subject, I add one more thought to ponder. When we give our time or money to God's purposes, it is an act of worship. God never needs our money to accomplish his plan. The innocent request to pay back the benevolence committee created an unintentional consequence: a crisis of what will be my future reason (frame of mind) when I send money to the church fund? Do we send money to the benevolence fund to pay back a debt, or do we donate to the benevolence fund to worship our Creator? Obviously, there is no real choice here. All our money is God's money, and we chose the latter. The takeaway is that communities need to take special care when giving time or money to people in the middle of adversity. When you give, there are many unseen emotional bruises that are tender to the touch. Also, treat the gift of large sums of money the same as you would the gift of a casserole. All that should ever accompany a gift is love – the same way God gives us his gifts.

I did not tell Carrie about what happened until recently. It would have crushed her spirit. Let me be clear! The van was a blessing, getting us through a seven-year transition time where we would eventually be able to buy our own vehicles again. We are profoundly grateful! Profoundly! I share our experience to expose our thoughts and feelings, and we leave it to God to teach his people.

Although going through awkward moments like this is tough, it is better never to take careless words by others personally. I can confidently say that they know not what they do! There is a difference between someone purposefully harming you and thoughtlessly harming you. Do not react to these two types of people the same. If it is on purpose, duck; if not, overlook the offense. In both cases, love them.

My advice to family and friends is to be on guard as to what you say and do. Do not do this because you feel like you need to walk on eggshells. Rather, do so because you love them and do not want to add the slightest ounce to their already exceedingly heavy load. Remind yourself constantly that their heavy load is both physical and emotional.

When you give, let go completely of the gift. Once a gift leaves your hand, the next destination of the gift is between the new owner and God. Period! If you cannot let go completely, then I recommend you keep it. Also, try hard not to use a proxy for all your gifts. People going through adversity need to see your face and feel your touch. I can tell you that the middle of adversity is a lonely place.

When I hand deliver a gift, I try hard not to ask flippantly, "If you need anything just let me know." This usually rolls off my tongue without my thinking. Most people will never tell you what they need – including me. It is just plain awkward to start listing everything you need to someone who asks this question in passing. Instead, deduce from their immediate circumstance where they might be falling short. This is not hard to do. For example, if they are going back and forth to the hospital every day, you can be assured they need gas money. If you really do not know, find someone who is close to them to fill you in on their needs or find someone who has been through something similar.

Be very careful about giving advice to someone in the middle of adversity. I apply some simple principles. First, I never (mostly never) give unsolicited advice unless what they plan to do is illegal, immoral, or against God's Word. Next, if someone in the middle of adversity asks for advice, I immediately imagine a bright red, flashing warning sign in my mind. This reminds me to be exceedingly careful about what I say next. Think thoroughly through your response before offering any advice. Once it leaves the tongue, you cannot easily reverse its impact. Finally, tailor your advice to account for their life and background. The longer they have gone through their adversity, the more challenging this will be. In some cases, you will be completely ill equipped to offer any advice. In this instance, connect them with someone who can. I try to find someone who has the same wear patterns in their shoes.

Whenever possible, look for opportunities to edify and build up. Someone going through adversity needs encouragement. Make it your goal to leave them feeling good about themselves. Show genuine concern, and listen more than you speak. The simple question I ask myself is, "Am I loving my neighbor as myself?" I know exactly how I like to be treated. Remember the most valuable thing you can give is your time. When you bring a dinner, ask if you can eat with them. If they are in the hospital waiting room, sit with them. If they cannot get to church, bring the church to them. Especially, do these things if God has put the adverse family squarely in your life.

Around the time our friends and family generously gave us a new van, I began to shift my attention towards planning for our retirement. This would become my singular financial resolve and would shape every job and business decision I would make for the next fifteen years. Clearly, Mitchell was fragile, and we had no idea when God would take him home. If I waited until he died to reenter the technical workforce, I knew I would likely not have enough headroom to build a retirement. If I waited much longer to build a retirement, I knew Carrie and I could only rely on Social Security. Unfortunately, our Social Security wages were purposefully low during our seven years of poverty. This is one of the unfortunate realities of earning a poverty wage. If you are not creating wealth now, you cannot expect to have any wealth when you retire. Again, my focus was on Carrie's future well-being. I knew I could earn a wage if something happened to Carrie. The problem was that if something happened to me, Carrie would have nothing. I could not ignore this potential outcome.

With a clear and singular focus, I began my quest. Carrie did not understand my reasons or my resolve. Carrie's strength is living in the now, a strength finely tuned from raising a family and taking care of Mitchell while under duress no mom should ever endure. I am proud of Carrie for it. However, talk to Carrie about the future; her eyes glaze over as she focuses on something far off in her mind. My strength, on the other hand, is planning. I see the future almost as well as Carrie sees today. Together we have all time covered since the past is behind us. For now, I knew I would have to start out on my own. I began taking long strides forward.

I had no clear idea of how to achieve my new goal, so I did the only thing that worked for me in the past – increase my education. You do not need to be a rocket scientist to know, in general, the higher your education, the higher your potential wages. Of course, this is not always true. People can strike oil. However, if my past was any indication of my future results, I was only going to improve my living one pickaxe swing at a time. My work philosophy remains simple: prepare for opportunity. It is a simple axiom I adopted somewhere around eighth grade. I also learned early on that you should always choose a long-term goal and start heading in that direction. If you do anything that is not consistent with that direction, then you are wasting your time and signaling to others that you are not serious about your goal. Put simply, if your goal is to head to Texas from Ohio, and I see you go north to Michigan, I know you are not serious about your goal. Equally important is movement toward your goal. It is much easier to make course corrections toward a goal while you are in motion. It is also a lot easier for God to nudge you toward a better goal. Always remain sensitive to the gentle guidance of the Spirit with every stride forward. I have noticed that God layers many other goals for your life in parallel with your own goals. This is where God's preparation meets his opportunities for you.

I was starting my second year at Cedarville University when I applied to Wright State University's Masters in Business Administration (MBA) program. I took the Graduate Management Admission Test (GMAT), and my score was so low that I thought the only program I was going to be eligible for was the special needs program. Fortunately, my money was more valuable than my brains. Before my MBA coursework could begin, I needed to take a couple of undergraduate courses in economics, both macroeconomics and microeconomics. While working full-time at Cedarville University, I could take one free course a semester. In addition, Cedarville University had a generous education reimbursement program that would pay for most of my MBA. Did I mention that Cedarville University is an awesome institution with incredible people?! I took my economic course work under Bert Wheeler. Bert is a brilliant professor and a next-door neighbor. With Bert's help I now consider myself an alumnus of Cedarville University – alumnus with a little a. Over the next two years I worked, went to school, and came home to my family every night.

By 2004, Taylor was ready to graduate from high school. Taylor was five years old when Mitchell was born. I remember the day when I first met Taylor. Carrie had a very difficult labor that ended in an emergency C-section twenty-eight hours after labor began. Going into labor, Carrie and I had his name all picked out: Mitchell. Mitchell is the name I wanted, but Carrie always wanted our first son's name to be Taylor. After I saw the labor Carrie went through, I told the nurses before Carrie woke up that his name was Taylor. As I held my son in my hands, I cried, like I am doing now as I write this. As you have probably figured out by now, I cry easily. My stoicism is all a front.

Taylor was eleven years old when I left the Air Force. I remember taking Taylor with me on a road trip to Florida in the last few months leading up to my leaving the Air Force. My trip was a temporary duty to the Air Force flight test community in Destin, Florida. Carrie and I decided it would be a good thing for Taylor to have some dad-son time. We knew the demands on a first-born, and we knew that Mitchell absorbed a lot of our time. This meant Taylor received less of our time. I decided to take Taylor on a deep-sea fishing trip.

Our journey and time together were epic. Somewhere in Georgia, we stopped for the night and decided to go see the new Disney film about Goofy taking his son fishing. We laughed so hard we cried. I mean belly laughed. To this day, I cannot recall a time before or after that I laughed that hard and for that long. That movie struck a chord. We had a great time, and the fishing trip was an amazing experience.

From then on, Taylor would work by my side doing side jobs so we could survive. He worked hard during those difficult years with Mitchell, losing part of his childhood along the way. In no time at all, Taylor was suddenly eighteen years old and was graduating from high school. To make matters more emotional, he decided to join the Marines. After graduation, he was off to boot camp. We were proud of his decision and knew that he would likely go to Iraq after graduating from boot camp. Sure enough, he was off to Iraq. Carrie and I prayed for Taylor every night until he came home safe. When Taylor came home in the fall of 2004, we could breathe again, and we were proud of our warrior. Taylor had some near misses with the enemy, but God protected him. He left for Iraq a boy, and when he returned, he was a man. From then on, Taylor began his own journey, and I lost part of my best friend. It was an okay loss and the right kind of loss all parents experience when letting their child go. Eleven months after returning from Iraq, Taylor married Amanda, and I was Taylor's best man in his wedding. What an honor! We also welcomed Amanda into our family. I felt like I knew Amanda because I had been praying for her since Taylor was a toddler. I love them both dearly, and I continue to pray for them daily.

During my latter days working at Cedarville University, I began to hatch a plan to leverage my MBA to do something impossible. If this was going to work, I knew it was going take more than my will. God would need to open some big doors.

I decided to contact an Air Force Reserve recruiter. Now that Mitchell was medically stable and we had the I/O Waiver providing in-home support, I could justify a local Air Force

Reserve military career. I could remain near home to help with Mitchell, and I could pick up my career close to where I left off. Essentially, my ten years of prior active duty service would count toward my retirement. I would only need to work another ten years to pull a military retirement. This would be a long shot.

First, I would need someone on the inside to help sponsor my endeavor. I called Jeff Riemer, my friend and former boss. By this time Jeff was a two-star general. I told Jeff of my plan, and he was all for it. Jeff wrote a very nice letter of recommendation. I thought that I should look in a mirror and meet this person Jeff had recommended. Brigadier General Robert (Bob) Wright also gave me a good recommendation. Bob and his wife Deane are two of our closest friends. Second, I would need to meet the Air Force fitness goals. Given my age, this would require a little more effort. The fitness requirements included a timed mile and one half run, sit-ups, push-ups, and maximum waist measurement. In six months, I lost roughly twenty-five pounds, and I was running three to five miles a day. I cut my hair, shaved my beard, and walked into the Air Force Recruiter's office.

Prepared, I needed only the opportunity. My recruiter, Master Sergeant Tom Trice, listened to my story, and he became my biggest advocate. When you tell people the story of Mitchell and our family, they usually sit back in their chair with an amazed look on their face. I could tell Tom wanted to help us improve our life. He warned, however, that this would be an uphill battle. He said I needed the Air Force to approve two waivers before my package could meet a selection committee. I was over the age limit, and I had to prove that Mitchell was no longer a hardship that would interfere with my service. Before long the Air Force would approve both my waivers. My past military accomplishments were above par. This, in combination with my recommendations, newly minted MBA, and fitness scores convinced the Air Force to waive my age. Mitchell's I/O Waiver, providing in-home help, proved to the Air Force that Mitchell was no longer a hardship that could hinder my service or prevent a deployment. The final step was to convince a selection committee. We then began to wait and wait and wait.

Meanwhile, Mitchell was doing well until some doctor had the bright idea of taking Mitchell off the ketogenic diet. As the story goes, the ketogenic diet is hard on your internal organs and not recommended for any longer than two years. Mitchell was nearing the two-year mark, and the doctors would slowly begin to wean him off the ketogenic food and reintroduce sugar-laced food supplements like diabetic Ensure. I thought to myself that this does not make sense. The doctors tried all the seizure control medicines with no success, and the diet was knocking his seizures down to next to nothing. To me, the risks of massive seizures far outweighed the risk of the ketogenic diet. What did I know? I often wonder if Medicaid was opposing the cost of the diet. According to Carrie, some children's seizures did not return after taking them off the ketogenic diet. I was skeptical, but I knew they needed to try.

As Mitchell came off the ketogenic diet, his seizures began to increase until one day he had a massive seizure. When you watch your child having a seizure, it is a helpless feeling. It was late in the afternoon when a distress call came from someone in the family. I was home in minutes, arriving shortly after Carrie. Pat and Grace were helping get Mitchell in his wheelchair when I walked into his room. Mitchell was alternating between a massive seizure and a rapid succession of mini seizures. The mini seizures were already larger than his worst seizures while on the ketogenic diet. Mitchell would catch his breath in between each massive seizure. He made eye contact with me, and I could tell he was scared.

Tensions were high as everyone wondered if we should call 911 or drive Mitchell directly to Nationwide Children's Hospital in Columbus forty-five minutes away. Carrie made the right call and off to Columbus we went. Mitchell was white as a ghost, and we knew he was in serious trouble. I pulled up in front of the emergency room in thirty-five minutes. We were in the door and back in a room in one fluid motion. Doctors and nurses descended on Mitchell.

I could see Grace crying, and Carrie was in mama bear-mode. Carrie told the doctor that Mitchell needed a medicine right away. Evidently, Carrie knew this medicine worked well in the past. The doctor dismissed Carrie's request and injected Mitchell with an emergency seizure control medicine. When this medicine hit Mitchell's vein, he immediately lurched into the biggest seizure I have ever witnessed. Mitchell's arms shot high above his head. I thought they might come out of socket. His head rolled back to his right, and his eyes completely disappeared in his head. All I could see where the whites of his eyes. I was a spectator at this point, and time seemed to freeze. Mitchell did not cycle out of this seizure. His face became blue as every muscle in his body was one hundred percent locked up. I knew he was not breathing, and I began to tear up. To me Mitchell was dying a horrible death right in front of our eyes. Fear crawled up my back as this went on for several minutes. Again, Carrie called out some medicine name. This time, the doctor injected the medicine Carrie recommended, and Mitchell immediately went limp. The emergency ended as abruptly as it began. Then, Carrie, Grace, and I went limp as our emotional exhaustion drained from our physical bodies.

This massive seizure happened a little short of two years after Mitchell started the diet. His major emergency was right on cue. For the last ten years, Mitchell seemed to have a major near-death moment every other year. The neurologist put Mitchell back on the ketogenic diet. This probably had something to do with Carrie's firm demand to do so. Fifteen years later, he is still on the diet. With his seizures back in control, life returned to normal. Our normal.

Over the next year and a half, I received many status calls from my Air Force recruiter. Finally, in the fall, Tom called me with the bad news. He said he did everything he could. He was more disappointed than I was. I knew going in it was a long shot. By this time, I had left Cedarville University, and I was working for Ryan Homes as a Project Manager. I really loved this job, and I knew that if I had not become an Air Force pilot, many years before, I would have chosen construction management as my life career. Four months into my job at Ryan Homes, I got an unexpected call from Tom.

I could hear the excitement in his voice. Tom kept going on and on about my name suddenly appearing on a list signed by the Secretary of The Air Force. He paused for a moment and said, "You are in! All you need to do is the oath of office. I cannot believe it; you are in!"

I am not sure exactly what happened since the last time I talked with Tom months earlier. I had heard six months before that Major General Jeff Riemer assigned a Chief Master Sergeant at the Pentagon to work my package. I can only assume the Chief made it work. That is what Chief Master

Sergeants of the Air Force do; they make things happen. I also knew I had a big brother who came to my rescue. Carrie and I are eternally grateful to Jeff for the investment he made in our lives. I do not think he has any idea the impact he made. You would not be reading this book today had it not been for Jeff's singular act of caring.

I called Jeff and asked if he would administer my oath of office. He graciously agreed and flew up from Florida to do the ceremony. Surrounded by my family and close friends, I repeated the oath of office. Jeff had the oath memorized, and I simply followed his lead. January 26, 2006, I accepted my commission to become the newest Captain in the United States Air Force Reserve. I like to say I was instantly the oldest Captain in the Air Force, as many of my friends would jest over the next couple of years. Not really, but I was half-grey, ten years behind my peers, picking up where I left off as an acquisition manager, and on a path toward a retirement. I was too old to fly again, but that was okay with me.

I recall my story of returning to the Air Force in order to share with you the joy I felt being able to have a normal work life leading to a better income and a retirement. In three short years after receiving the I/O Waiver, I was finally able to work like any normal family man. While Carrie was focusing on improving Mitchell's day-to-day care, I was able to focus on making a living and securing our future. Together, Carrie and I were a team.

As Mitchell's medical and our household financial issues began to calm down, Carrie and I were finally able to lift our heads up out of the foxhole and reconnect with our family, friends, and community. When we did, we had no idea the carnage we had left in our wake as we were fighting our two-front war over a ten-year period. We discovered most everyone had a perception of our life choices that was significantly different from the truth. Experience has taught me that when people do not know the truth, they will make one up. I like to say these non-truths are misperceptions where human nature does not typically fill in the blanks with a positive answer. In general, successful people manage both perception and truth. However, while you are in the middle of adversity, you have no time to manage either. Normally this is not a problem for short-term adversities. You simply wait until the crisis is over to correct any misleading thoughts. During long-term adversity, however, this day generally does not come soon enough, if at all. Misperceptions in and of themselves are not destructive. It is not until people treat you in ways consistent with their misperception that it can become harmful. Do this while family members are under emotional distress, with no time to defend themselves, and it begins to look and feel as if you are kicking them while they are down. This is exactly how we felt.

Our first encounter was innocent enough. Carrie and I finally had enough free time to serve others and our community. We decided to start small and volunteered to run a live nativity during a special evening in our town. Working with someone in charge, we were receiving inordinate amounts of oversight for a very simple task. I finally spoke up and asked why. He simply said, "I was told to watch you carefully because you do not follow through." I had no idea this was how anyone thought of me. I felt completely crushed! What my friend was saying is that I did not finish what I started. I was unreliable. After some reflection, I knew what he was saying had some basis in truth. Misperceptions always do. However, the sentence would have been more correct if he had said that I was told to watch you carefully because your life is overwhelmed serving your family and Mitchell. Instead, the statement spoke of a character flaw as if it were a fact. The truth was I would overcommit out of fear of not making enough money while self-employed. I was in trouble and needed help. The bottom line is that I was deliberately making bad choices out of fear and not because I did not respect commitments. In addition, casual observers saw me leave the Air Force and five years later sell my businesses to work at Cedarville University. In their minds I was a quitter. Family and friends began to treat me with quiet contempt. I knew there was no way I was going to change people's minds, so I decided, that it was time to sell our house and move out of Cedarville.

It is difficult to express my thoughts and feelings over this. In general, I know it is harder to become successful when surrounded by people who do not believe in you or who are overly critical. I believe most people would agree with this statement. I knew my real story and my real potential. Therefore, I decided to believe in myself and not accept a narrative I knew was not true. I also decided that I could not expect family and friends to understand the complex circumstance that brought Carrie and me to this point. It was enough for me to know that God understood. I do not mean to imply it had no emotional impact on my psyche. However, I knew that dwelling on it would distract me from my goal.

Through this, I did learn how much power people have over others to either edify or tear down. I also learned that when someone is silent (not edifying), it is a passive way to tear down. It has made me more careful in my own speech and actions. I have decided that unless someone is doing something immoral, illegal, or against God's word, I will edify and build up. What I personally think a person should be doing is nothing more than my opinion, an opinion that may or may not be true. I even go so far as not to hold a judgment or opinion against another person. It is amazing all the nonverbal clues we give to people whom we do not personally agree with. Moreover, I cannot know all the nuances behind someone's decision, and God is likely not going to keep me updated on whether he approves or disapproves of their decisions. The bottom line is that I do not have time nor am I equipped to be anybody's Holy Spirit.

By spring of 2006, I moved Carrie, Levi, Mitchell and me to Beavercreek, approximately thirty minutes west of Cedarville. I sold our home in Cedarville and used the profits to clean out all our remaining debt. I bought a new home through my employer, Ryan Homes, to capitalize on a huge employee discount. We custom built the home with a special room to care for Mitchell complete with a ceiling lift and bathtub in his room. Carrie and I also wanted to give Levi the opportunity to play football at a large high school.

Our next noteworthy encounter was a run-in with church policy. Carrie and I signed up to be youth leaders, and we were initially welcomed with open arms. Our plan was to take Mitchell with us since Grace was part of the youth group. We did not receive an email invite to attend the final meeting before starting as volunteers. When I approached the pastor, he said that we could not be youth leaders because we did not attend church regularly. They did not seem to understand that if I leave the house, then Carrie must stay with Mitchell. If Carrie leaves the house, then I must stay with Mitchell. Unless the church arranges for someone to stay with Mitchell, only one of us can go to church at a time. In this instance, there was no place to put Mitchell if we did take him to church. In addition, this issue was during the time Mitchell was in and out of surgeries. Sometimes Mitchell is so sick we both need to care for him. We will miss at least fifty percent of church. Carrie and I both understand the value of church attendance. However, a policy not allowing a family to serve in a church because they are caring for a profoundly handicapped child at home does not even sound right. Again, I knew there was no way I was going to change people's minds, so I decided that it was time to change churches. We began attending Faircreek Church in Fairborn, Ohio, a year ahead of moving to Beavercreek. Our new home would only be five minutes from our new church.

The issue of our not being able to go to places together is very significant. We do not think that people appreciate how life limiting this is. Carrie and I can never spontaneously leave and get something to eat. We cannot take walks together or just go to a movie. Anywhere Carrie and I want to go together requires planning. We save our silver bullets of convincing someone to watch Mitchell for major events. We used to look with envy on couples who could pick up and go anywhere over the weekend. This emotional hardship is profound. Very profound.

People need to spend time talking with families saddled with long-term adversity. Many churches and communities would do well to learn how to better connect and minister to families like ours. It is easy to lose track of these precious shut-ins as the years keep rolling by. I cannot remember when an elder just stopped by to visit and pray with Mitchell. It is also easy to forget the constant pressure that is on the parents. The tendency is to start treating these families as if they are just any normal family. Carrie and I are here to tell you they are not. We are not.

To help family and friends continually connect with special families, Carrie and I suggest designating someone from the adverse family's community to be an advocate. Do not let the adverse family organize this. What I mean by community is whatever group of people most interact with the family. A church, neighborhood, relatives, or work place are some examples of a community that could organize to see to the needs of a family in long-term adversity. Having one or two trusted people who know all the complexities and everything that is going on with the family can verify the needs. This does some very helpful things. First, the family in the middle of adversity needs only to tell the story once. A family going through adversity generally does not have time to explain everything repeatedly each time a casserole arrives. Second, the advocate can observe and verify the needs and get the right people to come alongside and help. For example, the adverse family may need a financial expert to help get back on track, a repair and maintenance team to improve accessibility to the home, or counselors to deal with emotional and spiritual issues. The advocate can determine where the federal, state, and local programs fall short of the actual need. The sky is the limit. This topic could be its own book. Essentially, be sure to put an advocate between the family and the community for the benefit of both.

You may have noticed that both misperception examples resulted from our struggle to serve others. Well, God made a way. As is the custom with God, he chose a better way than I would have selected. I did not go willingly, but the Spirit made it clear to me to be still and follow. Shortly after my commissioning in the Air Force Reserves, Grace introduced our family to Harry and Echo VanderWal. This became a life-changing path for our family. I remember Grace coming home and proudly announcing that she had volunteered the family to help Harry and Echo prepare for their first missions trip to Swaziland. My very first thought was, "Who names their child Echo?" Grace explained that Harry and Echo went on a scouting mission to Swaziland and were now responding to God's leading to begin a mobile medical mission to the rural peoples of Swaziland.

I was upset. I could not believe Grace volunteered our family – volunteered me! Because I am the kind of person that honors commitments, and I did not want to look bad, I went. I arrived at Harry and Echo's house still in uniform from working my very first days in the Air Force Reserves. Carrie, Grace, and Levi were already hard at work cataloging eyeglasses and folding many clothes. Mitchell was observing from his wheelchair. There were piles of stuff everywhere. My first thought was, "Where is all the help?" It did not take me long to realize that we were all the help. I met Echo first and then Harry. My next thought was, "Wow, they are different." Echo was high energy, bold, and direct and "could have been a battlefield general," I mused. Echo kept everyone productive while working twice as fast as anyone else. Harry, on the other hand, was calm as a summer's breeze. Chaos surrounded him, and he glided right through the chaos as if chaos knew to part and let him pass. In orbit around Harry and Echo were three little four-year old boys: Luke, Zebadiah, and Jacob. There was also a one-year-old, Zion. Zion had a pacifier glued to his mouth and was trying to keep up with his older brothers. Grace had told me about these high-energy triplets and the baby of the family. My final thought before getting my work assignment from Echo was, "I like this family."

This was the beginning of Mitchell's Ministry intersecting with The Luke Commission (TLC) ministry. What connected both was Grace. A connection made by Mitchell as Grace recalls in her story. This was also the start of our family's serving among God's people in TLC. God has taken TLC to unimaginable levels of success by blessing its mobile hospital outreach. The TLC outreach ministry began during the peak of the HIV/AIDS epidemic, where Swaziland (now called Eswatini) had the highest HIV rate in the world. As a result, one-fifth of the country's children were orphans. Clearly, a culture in crisis. (To discover more about this incredible ministry go to https://www.lukecomission.org).

In those beginning days of TLC, Harry and Echo asked me to serve as the president of their first TLC board of directors while I worked to process and pack supplies for future shipments to Swaziland. Of course, Grace recommended this. I did not do much because Harry and Echo's vision was light years in the future. However, I think I was a good sounding board in those early years. Carrie was already serving by organizing, cleaning, and measuring the prescription strength of thousands of used eyeglasses. Harry and Echo have no idea what a blessing it was for Carrie and me to serve in any capacity. What Harry and Echo did not know was that they were serving us by giving us a place to serve God's people.

In 2007, life with Mitchell became routine, and he would be eighteen later that year. I never imagined Mitchell making it to eighteen. I remember thinking then there was no way he was going to make it to twenty. In addition, Grace left on her second TLC mission trip. My goal of creating a retirement fund was also taking shape as I began to consider ways to maximize my military pay. While working full-time in the Air Force, my monthly paycheck was well over double what I was making at Ryan Homes. Therefore, finding ways to work for the Air Force was a good idea. Of course, the more I worked on active duty, the larger my retirement paycheck would be when I was sixty years old. I decided to jump into Air Force life with both feet and volunteered for a short tour deployment to Iraq.

In May 2007, I left for Iraq only weeks after my first grandchild Emma was born. My deployment took me to the United States Embassy in Iraq. Saddam Hussein's Baghdad palace became the US Embassy and was located in the Green Zone bordering the Tigris River. As the Air Operations Officer and Deputy Commander, I was responsible for the airborne protection and air travel of the top seven Iraqi leaders. I worked with amazing warriors, and we keep in contact to this day. I remember my commander, Lieutenant Colonel Dave Martinson, pinning on my rank to Major after administering the oath of office. This took place on top of Saddam Hussein's old palace, and I became the long-anticipated Major Minor – a title and name guaranteed to elicit a smile.

The first day I arrived at the embassy I was standing in the processing line. I noticed a large wet spot from a water hose, which stood out on the sidewalk because the desert is bone dry. Someone told us a missile attack had killed a contractor as he pointed to the scorched damage to the face of the embassy building. I never knew who it was, but I prayed for their family. The reality of war settled on me in that moment.

My time in Iraq had its moments. I remember having to travel to Baghdad International Airport on a special assignment to pick up a general officer from southern Kuwait and escort him to the embassy. Before traveling along Route Irish to Baghdad International Airport to catch a flight south, the convoy leader told me if we came under attack to let them do the fighting. He told me to keep my weapon holstered and help if they were losing. I appreciated these brave soldiers, and I discovered later that they simply did not want me to shoot them in the back. I was in the Green Zone during the surge offensive. Every day missiles and mortar would land around the embassy. Hearing the high pitch and hissing of missiles going over your head is a humbling experience. Typically, you could take immediate cover in designated concrete blast protection shelters placed strategically along the walking paths. Sometimes, I was not close enough. In those instances, I would lie as flat as I could in a gutter and pray.

Our hooch (sleeping quarters), which I shared with Captain Robert Davis, was a short walk from the embassy. This was nothing more than a flimsy metal trailer. As I lay in bed in the evenings, I remember hearing AC-130 gunship fire and machine gun fire on the other side of the Tigris River. This was the background noise as I memorized small parts of Colossians chapter 3 each night. By the time I left Iraq, I had the entire chapter memorized. I chose this chapter because it was excellent instruction on how to live in mutual love, forbearance, and forgiveness. I highly recommend hiding these words in your heart. I did this because I wanted to invest my time in something eternal as well as something practical for today. In addition, I would attend weekly Bible studies in Saddam Hussein's previous throne room. The irony of this experience did not escape anyone who attended.

My deployment ended, and I was suddenly back home. This deployment bolstered my retirement, and I was able to leverage this position to work another full-time active duty job at Wright Patterson AFB. For the next nine years, I was able to string one full-time active duty assignment after another. I went wherever the Air Force needed a worker and met wonderful people along the way. I took only one three-year break to attend Capital University Law School in Columbus. By the spring of 2016, I had accomplished my goal to create a retirement. On October 1, 2016, I received my first retirement check. God is good!

Over the second half of my military career, Carrie worked selflessly at home to care for Mitchell. Although Mitchell's cycle of surgeries ended, his ongoing seizure control and difficulty breathing brought a slow decline. Somewhere along the way, Mitchell became a young man and then an adult man. By his early twenties, his facial hair hid the rest of his childlike features. Nonetheless, Mitchell was still my baby … still Carrie's baby. I still hold Mitchell when I can in the quiet of the evenings or early mornings. Mitchell stills surrenders his entire stress in my arms and quietly groans his satisfaction.

God gave us this incredible gift nearly three decades ago. Mitchell never crawled or walked. Mitchell and I never played catch, and he did not scare me while learning to drive. Mitchell never married or gave us a grandchild. Not once did Mitchell say I love you. It turned out that Mitchell gave us something better. He showed us how to love God and not to lean on our own understanding. He taught us how to pray, serve, and love others more than ourselves. God entrusted Mitchell with this important job, and I believe someday he will hear, "Well done, good and faithful servant."

Chapter 8
Life Goes On - Mom

Mitchell turned twelve on October 6, 2001. This was a big day for our family. We gave Mitchell a huge "I-am-still-here" birthday party. We invited all our friends to say thank you for praying for him. We did not know it at the time but Mitchell would never have another major surgery. Life was beginning to look up, and 2002 would turn out to be a wonderful year for our family. It would be an especially good year for my tired back and bruised legs. In May, Craig and I went to the Ford dealership and picked up our new van that people from our community and church had gotten together to purchase for us. As we drove into the Ford parking lot, I saw a full-size green Econoline van parked by the entrance. My heart was so full of gratitude, and I could not stop the happy tears from falling down my cheeks. Happy tears are so much nicer to have than sad tears. It was nice to have some happy ones for a change. Accepting that van was a very humbling experience. I desperately needed a vehicle lift for Mitchell's wheelchair. My back was getting so sore, and I was very afraid of doing permanent damage. I could not afford back trouble if I were to continue to care for Mitchell full time. Many people would come to us when they saw Mitchell in a wheelchair, mostly moms, complaining of severe back injuries from caring for their special child. We have learned that if someone comes up to us or Mitchell, that person likely has or had a special needs person in his or her life. Having this large van capable of holding a wheelchair lift now meant we could apply to the state to pay for and install a lift. This was one of the benefits of Mitchell's

Independent Options Waiver. Oh glorious day! We have since traded that van in for a different vehicle, but we still have that same lift. Both Craig and I are forever grateful to everyone who served our family in such a tangible way. This van was also a great example to our children of giving and serving others.

That same year, the Make-A-Wish Foundation provided another blessing to our family. While we were on one of our family vacation trips to Disney, the staff kept asking if we were visiting through Make-A-Wish. We had not ever heard of the Make-A-Wish Foundation. After arriving home, Craig researched what it was all about and learned the foundation grants wishes to children with life-threatening medical conditions. Mitchell was indeed eligible for a wish! Craig applied for Mitchell's wish and soon after, we received a call to schedule an appointment with wish makers. While waiting for our meeting, our family began to think about what Mitchell would like. We all agreed a huge screen television was the perfect wish for Mitchell and his family. We knew how much Mitchell loved watching his cartoons and movies on television. The day came when two wish makers arrived at our home. They brought with them gifts for each of our children and a huge box of baked goods for the entire family. The wish makers spent time asking us about Mitchell and getting to know him. They agreed that a huge television was perfect for Mitchell, and they set out to make his wish a reality. Our entire family loved that television. We used it for Mitchell and for our Friday family-night movies. A tradition combining two of Mitchell's favorite past times: watching a good movie and spending time with his family.

In the fall of 2002, Mitchell became a teenager. Wow! I never imagined a thirteen-year-old Mitchell. He had gone through so much in his lifetime – more than most adults I know. God had taught me quite a bit in thirteen years – lessons I needed to learn and lessons that would help me get through the next thirteen years. Somewhere about this time, I stopped thinking each year would be Mitchell's last. He had already lived longer than anyone had expected. By this time, it was becoming obvious to Craig and me that God had a ministry for Mitchell and that he had more to do. It was time for us to be still and learn from Mitchell.

In June 2003, Taylor graduated from high school and entered the Marines. It was very exciting to see your child pass this milestone in his life. At the same time, it was sad to see him leave the nest. As a mom, I was excited and proud for Taylor. This event was a reminder of what Mitchell would not accomplish. I did not feel sad for myself but had a sadness for Mitchell. I am sad at times for things that he will never get to do – be a husband or dad. Just the other day my five-year-old grandson Miles said to me, "If Mitchell were like my daddy he could be married and have a baby, and I would have another cousin." Yes, Miles, so true. I have come to terms over the years that Mitchell really is not missing anything. It was a journey for me to get to this place ... a journey that I think is normal when raising a non-normal child ... journey that was full of tears and heartache. I had to learn not to compare Mitchell to other children his age or even to my other children. This was easier said than done at times, but very important. I know that Satan loves to discourage people who walk with the Lord. I stopped comparing Mitchell with others years ago. I confidently can say that Mitchell has not missed anything but has been doing just what he was created to do.

June also brought a new medical adventure for Mitchell. He had been on the Ketogenic diet for a little over two years. Supposedly, after two years, a patient would remain seizure-free after coming off the diet. Mitchell's ketogenic team planned to decrease his carbohydrate ratios slowly until he was completely off the diet. This took about four weeks. It seems like it was right at that four-week point that Mitchell's body complained. One day, he started having an increase in seizure activity, and it continued to increase all day. I was not at home. However, I was keeping up on Mitchell's condition through Pat and Grace. When I was finally able to get home, I saw for myself the amount of seizures Mitchell was having. I felt helpless as I watched his body stiffen. By then Craig had made it home, and we decided to drive Mitchell to Nationwide Children's Hospital so his neurology team could see him. Craig, Grace, Mitchell, and I loaded into the van, and we sped away at top speed to Columbus. This was usually an hour drive, but we made it there in a little over a half hour. I had called the emergency department ahead of time, and they were ready for Mitchell as soon as we arrived.

When we arrived at the emergency department, nurses quickly took Mitchell to a room, and he was given a shot of an anti-seizure drug. As soon as that drug entered his blood stream, he instantly started having the worst seizure he had ever had. I could not believe what was happening. That was a strong anti-seizure medicine, and it had not worked. The medical staff leaped into super-fast mode. Before I could say "Mitchell", they had him out of his wheelchair and onto a bed while another doctor ran into the room. I heard the doctor yell for them to get Ativan. I remembered the name of this drug from past encounters. Ativan was the drug that successfully brought Mitchell's body back to its no-seizure state in the past. Mitchell reacted to the Ativan wonderfully as his seizures stopped instantly. By this time, tears were streaming down my cheeks, and I said thank you to the doctor. The doctor turned out to be the daughter of one of Grace's high school teachers. She is one of my favorite doctors to this day.

After getting his seizures under control, Mitchell was admitted to the hospital. After this incident, the ketogenic team needed to determine Mitchell's new course of treatment. During his hospital stay, I met with Doctor Tsao, the lead physician on Mitchell's ketogenic team. I remember standing in the hallway talking with him – well, pleading with him – to put Mitchell back on the diet and to keep him on it for good. He agreed that Mitchell's seizures were best controlled by the diet, and Mitchell began the process of returning to his seizure-controlled self. Mitchell spent a week in the hospital before they let us go home. He is still on that ketogenic diet today, and it has worked miracles for his type of seizures. I am glad to report that Mitchell has more seizure-free days than seizure-filled days.

I am grateful for medical professionals who work with their patients outside of the traditional methods of treatment. Mitchell has participated in ketogenic studies over the years to assess the effect of the diet on a body over long periods. I am glad that his experiences can help doctors learn how to treat future patients. Mary Kerns, one of the nurses who cared for Mitchell during his major seizure episode, is now a nurse practitioner in the Ketogenic Clinic. She still remembers Mitchell's emergency hospital visit that day and speaks of it often.

The next several years brought many changes to our family dynamics. Taylor was sent to Iraq shortly after he graduated from military police school. He was away serving our country for nine long months. It was again a time of trusting God. This time it concerned Taylor's life and not Mitchell's. Every night, Craig and I prayed together for Taylor. I tried to write to him every day, and we sent many care packages to him. We were so excited when we would get a rare phone call from him.

During Taylor's deployment my parents moved to Cedarville. I had been begging them for years to move this way. I am an only child, and I wanted them close so I could care for them as they grew older. Now that my dad has cancer, I am extremely thankful they decided to move nearby. When Taylor safely returned home from Iraq, he enrolled at Cedarville University to begin his college education. There he met his wife, Amanda. They were married in August 2005. It was nice to add another daughter to the family. The same year, Grace graduated from high school. She tried college, but God led her in another direction to serve in The Luke Commission in Swaziland with the VanderWal family. Two of our four children were now technically out of the house. It was an adjustment to say the least.

June 2005 brought another hospitalization into Mitchell's life. This time it was not for a surgery or seizures, but for pneumonia. Pneumonia is an illness we always fear. We still have a healthy distaste for any respiratory illness that comes Mitchell's way. Through the years, we have met many parents of deceased severely handicapped children. They usually tell us that pneumonia was the culprit that took their loved one away. Fortunately, after about a week in Dayton Children's Hospital, Mitchell was well enough to return home.

Four months later, Mitchell turned sweet sixteen. This was amazing we thought as our family celebrated his birthday one evening. Speaking of birthdays, Mitchell loves the "Happy Birthday" song. No matter whose birthday we are celebrating, we look at Mitchell as we sing. His face lights up with joy. Sometimes we sing "Happy Birthday" just to see that smile on his face.

Grace started working with the VanderWals full-time in 2006. It was a perfect fit for her. Not long after, our entire family fell in love with the VanderWal family while helping them prepare to travel to Swaziland to serve the medical needs of the country's remote population. Little did I know at the time I would soon have another child in a foreign country. I remember how Grace's face lit up with excitement when she came home to tell us that Echo VanderWal had invited her to join them on their trip to Swaziland. I was sad to see her go, but very proud that she was following God's leading in her life. Shortly after Grace left, Mitchell must have needed some excitement because pneumonia once again landed him in the hospital. After another week at Dayton Children's Hospital, he was home again. I know it was tough on Grace being so far away while her favorite brother was sick. It stretched her faith in a good way.

Mitchell gave us a hospital break in 2007. I am grateful he did because that became my year for surgeries. In April, I had a full hysterectomy that included a few complications. Craig was already scheduled to leave for Iraq the week after my emergency surgery. God knew in advance and took care of me. Abbey (Pyles) Goins was living with us at the time, and Pat Tompkins was still caring for Mitchell. Our church family at Faircreek Church also took great care of us in the meals department. I remember Levi wondering each day who was bringing dinner and what it would be.

Grace came home from her mission's adventure a few weeks after my surgery and, as usual, was a great help. I did not know at the time but another surgery was in my near future. In October, Mitchell and I were home alone, sitting on the couch watching a college football game, when I had a terrible gall stone attack. This is not a good situation to be in with a severely handicapped teenager propped up beside you. I called my daughter-in-law, Amanda, and she called 911 for me. Craig arrived home as the rescue squad arrived. A few weeks later, I had surgery to remove my gall bladder full of stones.

I knew these surgeries were nothing compared to Mitchell's surgeries. Even so, both were a small reminder to me of what Mitchell had gone through. I remember thinking that I always knew beforehand I was having my surgeries. Mitchell, on the other hand, really could not understand what he was about to face. All he knew was the people who cared for him took him on a trip, and he woke up in terrible pain. I often try to put myself in Mitchell's place and try to imagine what he is thinking or feeling. This has turned out to be a great technique. When Mitchell is ill, he cannot communicate how he is feeling or point to his pain. I know God has given us a special ability to figure out where Mitchell is hurting.

Mitchell's eighteenth birthday arrived this year – what a milestone. We were so sure that this would be his last milestone birthday. Of course, I laugh now for thinking this. We had a big birthday party for him at our church and invited everyone we could think of who had been a part of his life. Many people came that afternoon to see Mitchell. It is amazing how many people love and pray for our son. Although he has never talked to any of them, he has influenced their lives.

God also has brought especially helpful people into my life at just the right time. I call Lois Jacobs my kindred mom. Lois also raised a special needs child, a daughter named Christi. Christi has Downs Syndrome and is forty-seven years old. She lives at home with her parents. Lois and I have children with very different disabilities, but our lives are still affected the same. We can laugh and cry about our children's situations that come our way. We understand how each other feels with just a look. Lois and I met twenty-six years ago. Watching Lois and her family care for Christi helps me to be a better mom to Mitchell. I love Lois and thank her for being an example. Moms with a special needs child, I encourage you to find your kindred mom and learn from her.

In 2007, we finally began our lives as grandparents. Taylor and Amanda gave us Emma Minor that April. I must say that being "Grams", as I am affectionately called, is one of my all-time favorite roles in life. It has also been wonderful to see Mitchell teach the next generation the lessons we have learned about God's character through him, especially unconditional love, faithfulness, and service to others. After Emma came Madeline Minor in 2008. Anna Becknell and Paige Minor joined the family in 2009. Lucy Becknell arrived in 2011, followed a year later by Miles Becknell. Victoria Minor arrived triumphantly in 2013. Finally, Levi and Sarah's first child and son, Lincoln Mitchell Minor, graced our lives in 2017. I knew one of our children would use Mitchell's name! It was no surprise that it was Mitchell's best friend Levi. Over the years, Mitchell's wheelchair and Hoyer lift have become a jungle gym set to our grandchildren. All our grandchildren love their Uncle Mitchell very much and are always asking to help with his care. Feeding him is their favorite. If you counted, you now know Craig and I are blessed with six granddaughters and two grandsons – eight grand-blessings so far.

Mitchell would have three more hospitalizations at Dayton Children's Hospital. The first of the three was very different from his previous hospital stays. One February evening in 2008, I started to change Mitchell's diaper. To my surprise, I found a diaper full of bright red blood. I called for Craig, Grace, and Abbey to come and look. We all knew something was wrong so I called the Star Pediatrics after-hour telephone number and reached Doctor Hesz. She told me that if it was more than a tablespoon of blood Mitchell needed to go to the emergency room. It was closer to a cup of blood. We loaded Mitchell into the van and made the familiar drive to the hospital. Once there, we waited for what seemed like an eternity. All emergency room visits feel this way to a parent. Once back in the triage area, Mitchell's blood was tested for all kinds of infections to try to determine what had caused his bleeding. Finally, Mitchell was admitted to the ICU, and a colonoscopy was ordered for the next morning.

Preparing an incontinent person for a colonoscopy is not a walk in the park. Let me begin by saying it is a very unpleasant experience for both the patient and the caregiver. Mitchell was given a laxative through his G-Tube called Golytely (pronounced go lightly). It does not live up to its name at all. Craig calls it "go lotly". While this was taking place, the nurses were trying to insert an IV line into Mitchell's arm without much success. Mitchell has never been an easy stick for an IV line. Finally, one of the nurses sighed and said that she would go and get the charge nurse to get Mitchell's IV going. A few minutes later, in walked a friend of ours from church, JoAnn Davis. She was the charge nurse that evening. I was so glad to see her. She is amazing. God seems to place his people for encouragement at just the right time for our family. JoAnn was able to get Mitchell's IV going with just one try. I was very thankful. She also stayed with us, most of the night, to help with all the problems the Golytely was causing. I think you can use your imagination to figure out what that means.

The next morning Mitchell went for his colonoscopy. During this procedure, it was determined Mitchell had acute gastrointestinal bleeding due to ulcers in his colon. For several days the doctors thought Mitchell had developed Crohn's Disease, which is a chronic inflammatory disease of the bowel that affects the lining of the digestive tract and causes ulcers throughout the digestive tract. Fortunately, this was not the case. After a week of medication to heal the ulcers, Mitchell was released from the hospital, and we came home. Thankfully, Mitchell has never had any more issues with ulcers in his colon.

In May 2008, Grace, our only daughter, married a Naval officer. I knew when they started dating that a future with Scott would mean my daughter, one of my best friends, would be moving far away. Both Craig and I knew Scott was God's choice for Grace, so her moving away would be okay. They did, however, move back in 2014 and now live just a quarter mile down the road. Yes! They both are always great support caring for Mitchell. In addition, Grace's children get to grow up near their favorite uncle. In our family, Mitchell is everyone's favorite person.

All three of the other children played sports year-round in high school. Football, wrestling, and volleyball were my favorites. We took Mitchell to watch every sporting event. Mitchell loved going. He especially loved the whistle any referee blew. It would make him laugh. I think it was important for our children's friends to see Mitchell. I know our children talked about Mitchell to their friends. When Levi was in wrestling, his coach, Mr. Rose, gave Mitchell an honorary team shirt to wear. Mitchell wore that shirt to every wrestling match. It was sweet to see those tough athletic high school boys melt with kindness as they would pass by Mitchell and say hi or give him a wave. Levi did not care what others thought about him or his wonderful brother. He would walk right by Mitchell, in his wheelchair, and plant a kiss on his cheek and give him a hug. I noticed others around us watching. It was a great teaching moment.

Levi had another teaching moment in high school during his senior year of football. Coach Basinger, Levi's football coach, always had the seniors make a speech during the last home pregame dinner. Mitchell, Craig, and I were at the dinner, and I wish I had had made a video to capture this precious moment. When it was Levi's turn, he stood up and looked toward Mitchell. Most of what I remember him saying was how Mitchell could never play football or any sport, so Levi played for the both of them. He continued to explain how Mitchell was the inspiration for him to give his one hundred and ten percent effort to whatever he was doing. Levi was saying these words through tears. As I looked around the room, there was not a dry eye among all the parents, coaching staff, and players. After that tearful speech, adults, and teammates went up to Levi to say how much his speech meant to them. I remember one of the staff members coming over to meet Mitchell. He said to me that he had wondered what drove Levi to excel. He said that now he understood. Levi went on to play football for two years at Ashland University, an NCAA Division Two school. Mitchell attended every home game.

We moved into what I refer to as my dream house in August 2011. Built in the late 1800s, I asked God for this very house fifteen years earlier. In general, older homes do not have a bedroom on the first level. This one did because of the home's unique history. Our new home was once the home to our town doctor, Doctor Donald F. Kyle, who was the doctor in Cedarville for fifty years. His office was on the first level of our home along with a patient waiting area and a bathroom. The previous owners of our home turned this area into a master suite, and it is perfect for Mitchell's care.

Shortly after we moved into our antique home, Mitchell once again had a fight with pneumonia. This time it was a mild case, and he only needed to spend a few days at Dayton Children's Hospital. For Mitchell, discovering an illness early is the key to getting over it soon. Sometimes it is not apparent that he is ill. He never cries or complains. In addition, he has never had a fever with any of his illnesses.

Early in 2012, Mitchell had his last Dayton Children's hospitalization. This time it was not pneumonia. Mitchell and I were home alone that evening. Craig and the boys had gone out to a movie about forty-five minutes away. I had just fed Mitchell his last feeding for the day, which meant I was right next to his left arm. His arm looked fine while I was feeding him. Several minutes later, I went into his room to put him into bed. As I picked up Mitchell's left arm to move him, I noticed his elbow was bright red, swollen, and very hot to touch. A bug bite was my first thought so I started looking around for proof. I found nothing that looked like a bite. I looked all up and down his arm and side to see what could have caused such a thing.

Next, I did what any good mom would do; I asked Google. After reading Google, I decided to call his doctor. I called the after-hour number and spoke to Doctor Tripplett. She told me to take Mitchell to the emergency room right away. I called Craig to have him meet us at the hospital. It is about a thirty to forty-five-minute drive to the hospital, and since I was home alone, I called my friend Cheryl to travel with me. She's the friend you can call anytime of the day. Her husband, Mark, drove her right over, and we headed on our all too familiar drive. Mitchell was taken back right away in the emergency room. A flood of doctors and residents began to visit Mitchell to solve this mysterious swelling. Everyone loves a good mystery. I remember thinking I wish each staff member visiting Mitchell's exam room would not ask the exact same question as the person before. Then it happened. Something I did not want to bring to their attention. Somewhere during these questions, they determined that Mitchell was twenty-two years old. At that time, the cut off age at Dayton Children's was twenty-one. I do not know what their policy is now. We have never wanted an adult hospital to care for Mitchell. All his medical conditions are from birth, and pediatricians seem to be more up-to-date on the treatments of life-long chronic disabilities. My heart sank as I thought of the possibility of Dayton Children's Hospital's sending us away that evening. Despite my fear and after some discussion with the administrators, Mitchell was admitted to determine the cause of his swollen elbow. They were doing tests to determine if it was an infection of some kind. An ultrasound of his arm was scheduled for the following morning as the doctors decided to look for a blood clot. During the ultrasound, the technician looked up and down Mitchell's arm from his shoulder to his fingertips. Nothing seemed out of the ordinary. The staff continued to treat Mitchell for an infection as they considered other possibilities. Several days later, Mitchell was released, and he continued an antibiotic until his swelling disappeared. Later that week, tests would reveal Mitchell had a blood clot in his chest area and not his arm. Things were calm again, but I knew we had narrowly avoided another major disaster.

During this hospital stay, it was also determined that Mitchell had high blood pressure. Our other children joked that it was because Mitchell still had to live at home with his parents. As you know by now, we are a family that tries to find some humor in every situation of life. Mitchell's high blood pressure would require Mitchell to graduate from his pediatrician to a family practice doctor. I was very hesitant to make this move. I thought if Mitchell did not have a pediatrician for a doctor, he would not be allowed in the future to go to a children's hospital. I started praying for a family practice doctor who would understand my concerns and agree with me. I decided to try Doctor Pinkerton, our new family doctor in town. I had heard nice things about him, and one of my best friends, Becky, had known him when they attended Cedarville University together. I made an appointment. My favorite consideration about this change was that his office was only a mile away.

I was rehearsing my speech to Doctor Pinkerton. I knew his practice was affiliated with an adult hospital, and I was going to tell him that a children's hospital was best for Mitchell's care. Doctor Pinkerton walked in, and immediately I could tell he felt very comfortable around Mitchell. We started talking about Mitchell's complex medical history, and Doctor Pinkerton mentioned that one of his daughters, who was close to Mitchell's age, had a serious medical condition. His daughter went to Cincinnati Children's Hospital for her medical needs. My heart leaped for joy. Mitchell's new doctor would totally understand my desire for Mitchell! I thought, "God, you are so awesome and take care of all the details for me; why was I even worried?" Doctor Pinkerton was Mitchell's primary care doctor for the next three years.

Later in spring of that year, a new small surgery adventure interrupted Mitchell's life again. As I was getting Mitchell ready for an appointment with Doctor Pinkerton, I noticed as I was changing his diaper a large weird looking bump at the end of his tailbone. During Mitchell's appointment, I mentioned this to Doctor Pinkerton, and we put Mitchell up on the exam table. By this time, the bump was triple in size, and it was clearly full of puss. Right away, Doctor Pinkerton said it was an abscessed pilonidal cyst and surgery would be necessary to remove the cyst. Pilonidal what? There are not many dull moments with Mitchell. The doctor's staff contacted Nationwide Children's Hospital to set up the surgery. In May, Mitchell had his only outpatient surgery to remove the abscessed pilonidal cyst. This surgery was a breeze compared to Mitchell's previous surgeries. The healing process was another story. Mitchell's cyst was very deep, and he came home with a wound vac attached to his tailbone where the cyst had been. The area needed to heal from the inside, much like a pressure sore. There was a sponge packed into the opening where the cyst had been removed that was attached to a suction tube constantly sucking the moisture from the wound. We would need to replace the sponge at least once per week.

For twelve weeks, a home health care nurse came once a week to help replace the sponge. Because Mitchell is in diapers, the sponge needed changing more often because it was a challenge to keep the area clean. God had brought me a long way since Mitchell's first surgery needing a bandage change around his feeding tube. That was nothing compared to this. However, I was able to change Mitchell's wound vac sponge by myself. This was a great reminder that my calling was not nursing. Mitchell's tailbone area healed nicely, and he has not had any other problems with cysts since.

During this time, it was hard for Craig and me to attend church together. Mitchell no longer enjoyed going to church, and he would often interrupt the service with his sounds. Many people told us that they were not bothered by his sounds, but it was a huge distraction for us. When Mitchell made disturbing noises in church, one of us would take Mitchell to a quiet corner of the building. Since we were missing church anyway, we decided instead that one of us needed to keep Mitchell at home. At the time, Brie Ahlgrim was attending the nursing program at Cedarville University, a Christian school located in our town. We knew her family, and she had been Mitchell's classmate in elementary school. Brie had known Mitchell all her life. I decided to contact Brie and ask if she would be able to come sit with Mitchell every other Sunday so we could attend church together. She was delighted to do so and started sitting with Mitchell on a regular basis. This is what Brie had to say about her time with Mitchell and our family:

> If there is one life lesson I have learned over the years from being around Mitchell and the Minor family, it is that is everyone deserves to be loved. The amount of love the Minors have and demonstrate for Mitchell is astounding. He is never looked at as a burden despite the number of collective family hours they are spending caring for his every need. If everyone loved people as the Minors love Mitchell and each other, I believe this world would be a changed place.

My memory of Mitchell goes as far back at elementary school. We were in separate classes, though, so I mainly just saw him in passing. My mom has kept my elementary school yearbook, and I love seeing Mitchell's pictures when I look back on those childhood years.

I got to know the Minors more when their son, Taylor, opened a coffee shop in town, as it quickly became a town favorite. My senior year of nursing school Carrie asked me to hang out with Mitchell on a few Sundays throughout the semester so they could go to church. I leaped at the chance…knowing that I'd get to use my new-found nursing skills to help my childhood friend and his family. My Sundays spent with Mitchell were some of my favorite college memories. We would sit on the front porch and watch the cars drive by on Main Street, watch a movie as I gave him his g-tube feeding, or just spend an hour making him laugh and smile. Even though Mitchell has Cerebral Palsy, that does not inhibit him from interacting, communicating, and being joyful. God created each person to be loved, no matter their physical appearance, medical diagnosis, or level of communication.

There is so much fear of people in this world who are different. Let us be like the Minors and replace fear with love.

Over the years, we have had a few special people offer to do this for Craig and me. What a blessing! Several years ago, I was speaking with Doctor Lynn Roper, who taught special education classes at the University. I mentioned to her that I thought it would benefit her students to have exposure to a severely handicapped individual like Mitchell. She agreed and asked in class if anyone might be interested in sitting with Mitchell a couple of times a month so his parents could attend church together. Right away, four students volunteered, which began our season of having Cedarville University education majors sit with Mitchell every other Sunday during the school year. The beginning of each new school year, one of the previous year's students would contact me and send me a list of the students and their schedule's for the upcoming semester. Without fail, four young women would sign up to serve Mitchell. It has been a complete blessing. Several students have graduated and gone on to become teachers. I know that Mitchell has blessed them as well. Mitchell always smiles when he sees his college girls arrive. I do think he has developed a crush on a few of them over the years. Cheyenne Brooker had this to say about her time with Mitchell:

> As I was asked to write about my time with Mitchell and the impact that he had on my life, I had a hard time forming the correct words that would bring justice to my experience. During my time as a student at Cedarville University, I worked for Mitchell on Sundays for four years. By work, I mean hung out, because I do not consider being with Mitchell and helping take care of him work. Sooner than I ever thought imaginable, Mitchell began to be such a blessing in my life. The love that God has for each one of us shines through Mitchell's smiles and giggles so brightly. The strength that Mitchell exudes every day gave me confidence to fight my battles. The humor that Mitchell has brightened my day! I mean come on; he thought it was quite funny always to laugh when we would be feeding him! He has the best sense of humor! Most importantly, the love and familial feel that he gives each person that steps into his life is irreplaceable and demonstrates God's unending love for each one of us. I cannot be more thankful for the time that I had with Mitchell. I do

not think of it as a time of me serving him, but of Mitchell serving and teaching me. He changed me, molded me, and created me into more of the person that God wants me to be every day! Now that I am living in Michigan, I sure miss the Sundays spent with Mitchell tremendously. Mitchell and the Minor family have played an enormous role in my life that will never be forgotten.

The year 2014 began a new chapter in Mitchell's life. I call it the battle of the lungs. One morning in June, Mitchell began to have difficulty breathing. He already had a neurology appointment at Nationwide Children's Hospital that day so I did not make an appointment for his breathing issue. Instead, I thought I would have the neurologist listen to his lungs and go to the Urgent Care later if needed. Because I try not to drive him by myself to any appointments, my mom went with Mitchell and me to his neurology appointment. The nurse practitioner came into the exam room and immediately noticed that Mitchell was working hard to breath. Instead of our usual Keto Clinic appointment routine, she listened to his lungs and said she was going to send him down to the Emergency Department. She called to let them know she was sending Mitchell with us.

The Emergency Department took Mitchell right away and hooked him up to a pulse oximeter. His oxygen level was in the low eighties. We spent several hours in the emergency department. They put Mitchell on a BiPAP machine, drew blood, and took x-rays. Unlike a CPAP machine, which only offers pressure for inhaling, the nurses used a BiPAP machine, which applies pressure for both inhaling and exhaling. The mask for this machine made Mitchell look like he was in a fish bowl. He did not like it at all and looked scared and panicky. His next stop was the pulmonary ICU. In the pulmonary ICU, he was given a sedative so he would not fight the BiPAP machine. For the first time, Mitchell's body was not fighting off the dreaded pneumonia with only antibiotics. This time, Mitchell would need additional help from the BiPAP machine. The staff was surprised someone as severely medically handicapped as Mitchell had not had pneumonia in the past several years.

Among the staff was our friend JoAnn Davis. She was now a nurse practitioner at Nationwide Children's Hospital working in the pulmonary ICU. Since we were friends, I had to let her manager know that I did not mind JoAnn being on Mitchell's medical team. Respiratory therapists came in every four hours to try to get Mitchell to cough using a cough assist machine. Mitchell hated this machine and the way it made him feel. They also started giving him treatments using a vest that completely wraps around and shakes his chest. Mitchell loved this treatment. He was also getting medicines through a nebulizer machine and IV. Despite all efforts, Mitchell's oxygen levels kept going down. In response, the doctors kept increasing the amount of his oxygen and raising the settings on the BiPAP machine.

My mom stayed with me until Craig could get to the hospital from his military duty at the Pentagon. Grace managed to come to the hospital even though she had just moved into her new Cedarville home and was trying to unpack with three little children running around. Levi and Sarah came up. Levi wanted to make sure his best man prospect for his upcoming December wedding was not trying to back out on him. Our family always rallies around Mitchell when there is a medical crisis. We just do. Each one of us loves Mitchell dearly. Mitchell's nieces and nephews are too young to visit him in the hospital and, of course, this always makes him sad. It was during this hospital stay that I noticed a difference in the approach of the medical staff. In the past, I always felt as if medical professionals had an air of superiority. It is hard to explain. The mentality was more like me against them. This time, and since then, we have been more like a team. I am guessing the approach to patient-doctor relationships is taught a little differently today in medical school. I really like it. I first noticed this change when staff would enter Mitchell's room and introduce themselves. It was no longer "I am doctor so and so or nurse so and so." Now it was, "I am Mitchell's doctor, and my name is Jeff."

After about two days in the ICU with no improvement, Mitchell's doctor came in and started talking about how the BiPAP machine was maxed out. He said the next step would be a breathing tube inserted into Mitchell. I think my face must have drained of all color because next he said that he could tell by my reaction that we had never discussed this issue before. The doctor decided to end the discussion and said he would be back in a bit. I thought, "No, we had never talked about a breathing tube before." I am always hesitant to mention to anyone that Mitchell might not live far into adulthood. My denial and reality fought for control. I started getting that pit in my stomach again the one that makes you want to be sick. I knew these hard things needed to be talked about but talking about them was too real for me.

When the doctor returned, he came back with information about the hospital's palliative care department and told me this department would be an excellent resource for my family as we start to think about the type of care we want for Mitchell at this stage of his life. I had not ever heard of palliative care before. I learned it is for patients and their families who are facing life-threatening conditions. It offers extra support in symptom management, emotional support for the entire family, and end of life care. The last support claim really got to me. Was I even going to be able to talk about end of life care? First, I needed to talk to God about all these emotions going through my head.

After a few days, Mitchell improved and was able to wean off the BiPAP machine except during the night. Fifteen long days after admission to the hospital, Mitchell came home. This time Mitchell came home with a BiPAP machine, oxygen generator, a vest treatment machine, and a few new medicines to make his breathing easier. Mitchell officially entered his lung battle years. Because of his severe scoliosis, he has the oxygen capacity of only one lung. In addition, he has gained weight in his chest area making it even more difficult to take normal breaths. Honestly, I consider it a gift from God Mitchell did not start his lung battle years ago. Once home, Mitchell continued life on the BiPAP machine while requiring one liter of oxygen. After about four weeks, he did not need oxygen during the day. This was good. However, he did need suctioning a few times a day. Grace, Sarah, and I learned how to do this through his nose or down his throat. He also needed vest treatments at least four times per day. Fortunately, Mitchell loved his vest treatments. We call it his carnival ride. Our grandchildren love to put their cheeks on his vest in order to hear their voice vibrate.

During his hospitalization, I learned of a relatively new department called Complex Care. Complex Care scheduled Mitchell's first appointment immediately following his release from the hospital. The Nationwide Children's Hospital website describes the purpose of complex care perfectly:

> Patients with complex problems need services that are holistic, coordinated, continuous, and family-centered. The Complex Health Care Program at Nationwide Children's Hospital helps patients achieve the best possible state of health and quality of life. Patients and their families are the most important drivers of the care team, which includes their primary care provider and often an extensive network of specialists. Our program helps patients and their families be informed of medical services, avoid duplication and make care choices in keeping with the child's and family's goals. (https://www.nationwidechildrens.org/specialties/complex-care)

Mitchell's first appointment was with Doctor Grace Walton. I decided after this appointment that I liked this medical group. Now he sees either Doctor Gary Noritz or Doctor Elizabeth Lucas. Mitchell's complex care professionals are only a call away. I have loved having them as part of Mitchell's care during these past four years.

I woke up on September 7, 2014, thinking it would be just a normal day. I went downstairs to start Mitchell's morning routine. I noticed he was working hard to breathe. It had now been three months since Mitchell's last breathing problem landed him in ICU. I started doing all the preventive measures that I had learned over the summer. He still did not seem to respond well. I called Grace over to get a second opinion. I never want to rush to the hospital unnecessarily. My family tells me that I tend to wait too long. Grace came over, and we decided to call the doctors at the complex care office.

I spoke first with a nurse, and she had Doctor Lucas call me back. After Doctor Lucas heard what Mitchell's oxygen levels were and knowing how quickly Mitchell declines, she asked me to take him to the closest hospital to stabilize him for transport to Nationwide Children's Hospital. The closest hospital? Oh no, one of my worst fears: taking Mitchell to an adult hospital. My heart started racing, and I was mad at myself for not acting sooner that morning. Doctor Lucas told me what to tell the doctors when we arrived at the closest hospital. I was sure I would tell them we needed to go to Nationwide Children's Hospital, and they would laugh and say something like, "Right, no way, lady."

Grace and I loaded Mitchell and his oxygen tank into his van and off we went to Greene Memorial Hospital in Xenia, Ohio, only a short eleven miles away. We arrived in about fifteen minutes and I was already nervous about how they were going to react to my request. I do not like confrontation, but I was getting myself ready. Grace and I rolled Mitchell into the emergency area, signed him in, and were taken to triage right away. I began to explain to the nurse that I was only at Greene Memorial to get Mitchell stable enough to make the trip to Nationwide Children's Hospital. She immediately said she understood and that would be fine. She took his vitals, went to speak with someone, came back, and took us to the treatment area where the doctor met us. I told him about my conversation with Doctor Lucas and her recommendation to come there. I was met with absolutely no confrontation or negativity at all. The doctor said he agreed with her assessment. He said he had done his pediatric residency at Nationwide, and he thought that was a great hospital and a great plan. He would call Doctor Lucas to start working on the details. Meanwhile a nurse arrived and was giving Mitchell an IV and seeing to his breathing needs. I was so relieved – once again, a needless worry. It took several hours to get Mitchell's transportation worked out. The staff at Greene Memorial took great care of Mitchell while he was there, and I am so grateful. Nationwide Children's Hospital sent a MICU (mobile intensive care unit) to transport Mitchell. I was able to ride with him, and Grace followed behind.

Once at Nationwide, Mitchell made a short stop at the Emergency Department then headed straight to the ICU. Here we were again. Mitchell had already maxed out the BiPAP machine, and the attending doctor asked if I would consider a breathing tube. Oh no, there was that question again, and we had not yet come up with a plan. I told her I really did not understand what a breathing tube would entail and asked if she could please explain it to me. She gave me a thorough explanation with great kindness in her voice. She then asked if she could send someone from the palliative care team to speak with us. I shook my head yes, not really wanting to, but knowing it was the right time. We were about to talk about a subject I had been avoiding for years.

The next day, while Craig was at the hospital, we met with the palliative care chaplain for the first time. She was so sweet and put us right at ease. She explained their program and educated us on what end-of-life care meant. I sat and listened with tears running down my face. My tears always flow and never drop nicely like on television. We agreed to meet the next day with a palliative care doctor to start making some hard, but necessary, choices for Mitchell. We wanted to make them now, not in the heat of the moment. By now, Mitchell was improving, and the term *breathing tube* did not need to come up again during this hospital stay.

Craig and I nervously waited for the palliative care doctor and chaplain. I was nervous because I did not want to talk about Mitchell's dying. Talking about it made it real, and I was not ready for the flood of sad emotions. The two women who came to speak with us were so understanding and very caring. They knew this was a hard topic for families to discuss, and they tried their best to make it as emotionally pain free as possible. I first had the doctor explain to me what exactly happens when a person as medically involved as Mitchell gets a breathing tube. I was sure I knew the answer, but I needed to hear it from a doctor. Her explanation was very simple. Once Mitchell needed a breathing tube and had one put in, he would not get better but would require that tube for the rest of his life. Healthy, normal people use them while recovering from an illness or injury – not so when your body is permanently compromised. She went on to explain how families would then have a harder decision of removing the tube. We had watched Mitchell fight a BiPAP machine. We had watched him go through many surgeries to improve his quality of life. We can tell Mitchell does not like being in a hospital because he visibly becomes anxious. Craig and I had already decided never to intubate Mitchell before we spoke with palliative care, but talking with them made the choice easier. They explain how each family chooses based on their child, and each family may make a different choice. The palliative care team did not leave us feeling guilty for choosing never to intubate.

On September 11, 2014, Craig and I signed a Do Not Resuscitate Comfort Care (DNRCC) order for Mitchell. We have it hanging on the wall by his bed. It reminds us of how fragile Mitchell really is today. Making this decision has given us a peace of mind. I know that one day God will call Mitchell home. I pray that Mitchell has a painless transition to heaven. God knows my heart, and I can only trust him. Since learning to talk of Mitchell's death, Craig and I have also arranged for Mitchell's memorial service. Then when that time comes, we can grieve for ourselves and rejoice for Mitchell's newfound joy in his new body. It took me years to get to this point. Even though I have always known Mitchell would probably not outlive us, it was extremely difficult for me to discuss the possibility of my child's death.

When Mitchell came home from the hospital, he was on two liters of oxygen. He improved each day, and by December 13, 2014, he was off his oxygen tank and tube-free as he made his best man debut for his baby brother's wedding. Craig pushed Mitchell everywhere he needed to be in the ceremony. Mitchell was very handsome on stage with his dad and brothers. It was a statement of love that Levi and Sarah included him in all the festivities of that day. All in attendance could see his family's love for their brother.

Mitchell was now twenty-five years old, living twenty years longer than predicted so many years ago. We celebrate each birthday of Mitchell's with gusto – Mitchell-style gusto. We always have a cake, even though Mitchell cannot enjoy it with us. Of course, we sing his favorite "Happy Birthday" song. At every birthday, our children fought over who would open his gifts. Now our grandchildren have this battle. We started three years ago taking Mitchell to the National Air Force Museum located near Wright Patterson Air Force Base for his birthday. As Mitchell gets older, he seems to get nervous around large crowds. As such, the wide-open spaces of the museum become a great outing for him and his family.

Mitchell's health was stable as he began 2015 until July. Mitchell once again caught a respiratory virus and was in Nationwide Children's Hospital Pulmonary ICU. By now we were all familiar with hospital nurses and other staff. Everyone knew the routine very well. Mitchell began to wear a BiPAP twenty-four seven, and his oxygen was cranked up while being loaded up with antibiotics to help fight his war inside, not to mention the normal routine of suctioning his airways, vest treatments, and the cough assist machine. It was about his third day in the hospital when one of the staff members came to talk with me. Her voice was very serious. I saw her swallow several times, and then she put her hand on my shoulder and said that she thought I should call the rest of family to come because Mitchell was at a point that if he did not improve, he would not likely make it through the night. I immediately went pale after hearing the words a mother never wants to hear. I felt sick and cried a deep cry. She hugged me and let me cry on her shoulder. My mind raced with names of who to call and what to say. I dreaded each phone call, but I called them all one by one: Craig, my parents, Levi, and Taylor. I waited to call Grace because Craig told me she was already driving to the hospital. I was glad someone was already on the way. I then called our church to get people praying. The church secretary, Lynn, prayed with me over the phone and reminded me that God was still in control. She got the word out to our prayer warriors. I remember standing beside Mitchell's bed holding his hand and praying for him. I asked God not to take Mitchell home yet, but if he did, to please help me and the rest of the family get through the pain.

I decided Grace must be close enough to call. It turned out she was in the parking garage elevator when she answered.

Through my tears, I was able to tell Grace what the doctor told me, and I waited for her to arrive. I did not want to be by myself if Mitchell passed away. She arrived with tears already flowing. We hugged, cried, and then saw the palliative care doctor in the hall coming toward Mitchell's room. The staff had called and informed her of Mitchell's condition. I am so glad that they take care of those details. She very gently took us around the corner to speak with us in private. Grace and I sat side by side on a padded bench in front of a window, and our palliative care doctor sat across from us. I do not remember who spoke first. I do remember her saying what would happen next if Mitchell did not take a turn for the better. I could not concentrate on anything she was saying. Fortunately, Grace started talking and asking the right questions – the same questions I would have asked if my mind were not back in Mitchell's room wondering what was going to happen that night and how fast our lives would change. I remember Grace saying, "You mean we just watch him die?" We were both flooded with tears. We listened as the doctor tried to make it sound like a normal part of life. She was doing the best job she could, and I appreciated her being with us and her kindness. She stayed nearby in case we needed her as the rest of the family began to arrive.

In Mitchell's usual style, he began breathing better about five hours later. We all began breathing better. During those hours, one of our pastors arrived to pray with us and encourage us. My friend, Becky, came to see Mitchell and visit with us. We received text messages and phone calls from people who were earnestly praying for Mitchell. I know modern medicine is powerful, but there is nothing more powerful than the prayers of God's people. I am forever grateful to our prayer warriors.

I have learned something about prayer through situations like this. When you know people are praying, it gives you an inward hope and strength. For this reason I always pray for someone when asked. If I say I am going to pray for you, then I do. I have also learned to let people know that I have prayed for them. It is encouraging to have someone say, "I prayed for you." It is truly empowering.

Mitchell did recover from his near-death respiratory illness, but he entered a new normal as we call it. Mitchell was not able to wean off the oxygen as he had done previously. Requiring two liters of oxygen around the clock. Mitchell was noticeably more fragile than before. October arrived, and Mitchell turned twenty-six. With each passing birthday, God reminds me of his faithfulness and that Mitchell's ministry is not over. God is still teaching through Mitchell.

It took a bit of time to adjust to Mitchell's need for oxygen. The oxygen concentrator makes a loud constant hum and puts out heat. Oxygen tanks for the wheelchair are now in Mitchell's closet with tubing to store and change. We must be more observant of Mitchell since his nasal cannula (the part of the tube that blows the oxygen into his nose) can easily fall from his nose. Of course, Mitchell cannot tell us when this happens. It is now second nature for everyone in the family to walk by him and give a once over to make sure it is all in place. Even his nieces and nephews will check and let me know if something needs adjusting or if they already fixed it.

After our eye-opening year, 2016 arrived without much fanfare. Mitchell and I had adjusted to his new normal, and we were living our normal day-to-day activities – or as normal as our family gets. I was so happy that Mitchell was having a healthy spell. The daily tasks of keeping Mitchell healthy had increased, especially during the past three years, but as with anything, we made it all work. It was especially nice having Sarah to help with all the added things to remember to do. Then out of nowhere, Mitchell caught a cold, a plain old cold virus that brought him to ICU for a week. Oh no, here we go again, I thought. I do not like to admit that I am getting older, but I am. I do not function as well with less sleep. No one ever gets rest sitting by his or her child of any age in a hospital. This stay, I was especially tired. Craig saw how tired I was and stayed one night. I came back to Cedarville to get more clothes. I could not stay in my house alone; it felt weird without Mitchell around, so I had a sleep over at my parents' house. After Craig, Grace offered to stay the night with Mitchell. I knew she was knowledgeable on Mitchell's medical information and would be fine. It was just different, but I welcomed the opportunity for another full night's sleep. When I went to the nurses' station to say that Mitchell's sister would be staying the night, the comment was that siblings are not allowed to stay overnight. I know, but this sibling is 29 years old and a mother of three children. I let the nurse know while half laughing that Grace has known her brother his entire life. The nurses laughed in turn and responded with, "Oh, sorry, we are not use to siblings of that age." Grace did stay all night. She was glad to help, and I was thankful for the help. Once he found out Grace stayed with Mitchell, Levi offered his and Sarah's overnight services. This was sibling rivalry to my benefit. I am grateful that they take seriously their sibling bond and are thoughtful about their mom's health too. Once again, Mitchell improved with the extra medical help, and it was not long before they sent us home again. This time Mitchell came home on three liters of oxygen, taking another small but permanent step backward.

Shortly after returning home on three liters of oxygen, Craig and I left on a near local getaway. We had planned a getaway for the following weekend well before Mitchell was hospitalized again. With Grace's encouragement, we decided to go ahead and go. Craig and I know how important it is to get away, but it is always difficult for both of us – maybe a little more difficult for me. We decided it would be okay since we would only be an hour away, and Mitchell was doing well with his new normal. Scott was deployed, so Grace and her three children came over to stay with Mitchell. After some hugs and kisses, we left Grace in charge. It was so relaxing to get away. I love Mitchell dearly, but it is so nice to get a break from taking care of someone's daily needs when you have done it regularly for over twenty-five years.

We went to a beautiful bed and breakfast. It was quiet and peaceful. The next morning Grace called. Grace never calls anyone; she would rather text. I answered right away. Grace did not sound panicky but began telling me about Mitchell's previous night. As she started telling me Mitchell's near-death story, I interrupted with, "Why didn't you call us to come home?" She assured me that we needed a break, and it was ok. This is what Grace told me as I listened in shock. Evidently, Mitchell had respiratory failure that night, and she had to shake him to get him breathing. After he started breathing, again his seizure activity greatly increased. She asked me to call his doctor and let her know what happened and to get advice. Grace assured me that we did not need to rush home, just finish out our day as planned and then return. I told her I agreed if the doctor thought everything was good. I called a number that I had saved in my phone when Doctor Lucas called me last over some medical issue. It happened to be her private desk phone, which she promptly answered. I have not called this number since, but I am thankful it was in my phone that day. She and I spoke about what happened the night before, and she agreed to call and speak with Grace. We then set up an appointment for her to see Mitchell the following day. She also asked if she could invite a Palliative care team member to be there as well. I agreed. Craig and I finished our sightseeing and headed home that evening. Once home, Mitchell seemed himself, just extremely tired. The following day, Craig, Grace, Mitchell, and I headed to Nationwide Children's Hospital for Mitchell's new appointment.

Grace's experience exposed a problem we knew needed solving. Grace told us how she felt having no one close by to call during Mitchell's sudden respiratory failure while we were out of town. Mitchell has a DNRCC, but just like Grace, we all thought it was not a good idea to call 911. That night she finally decided to call Levi and Sarah despite the fact they lived forty minutes away. Of course, they came right away, but this did not solve the problem of not having someone to call in an emergency. This would be the case for Craig and me as well. We all expressed our concern over how fragile Mitchell was becoming and that his current respiratory problems put him on the edge. Grace knew this first-hand all too well. We all knew Mitchell was not bouncing back as he had from previous illnesses. We all agreed that someone coming to our home to assess Mitchell for the upcoming months was a good idea. The Palliative care nurse brought up the word hospice, but I was not ready for anything that included the word *hospice* in it. I know it is just a word, but my heart could not take that. Accepting terms like *Palliative care, end of life care, DNRCC,* and *hospice* is a process for anyone, especially for a parent concerning their child. Doctor Lucas and the nurse were very understanding and patient with me and suggested they look for a palliative care nurse who could come check on Mitchell every week. With a heavy heart and tears flooding down my checks, I agreed. The next week a person from the hospice agency came to do Mitchell's intake into their agency, which also included palliative care. That meeting was very emotional. I got through it with lots of tissues. By agreeing to palliative care, we were finally resigning ourselves to the fact that Mitchell's time was short. The following week, Mitchell began having weekly palliative care visits for three months. Why only three months? Mitchell had not finished his work for God. Mitchell improved enough during this time and no longer qualified or needed palliative care services.

Mitchell's respiratory failure on Grace's watch became a blessing in disguise. I smile with joy as I tell you. This story reminds me of God's sovereignty over our lives. A week later, I was feeding Mitchell when Levi came into the room. Levi lifted Mitchell's arm as he was saying hi to his brother. Levi let go of Mitchell's arm and then lifted it again. He then asked, "Mom, what drug have you given Mitchell?" My response was that I had not changed any of his drugs. Levi showed me repeatedly how easy it was to lift and stretch Mitchell's arm. Puzzled, I started moving Mitchell's arm and then moved his right leg. I was able to easily move his leg and bend his knee. Levi called for the rest of the family to come and see. We were all amazed, wondering why Mitchell was so loose on his most spastic side. After a couple of appointments, the doctors gave us an explanation. During Mitchell's respiratory failure ending in seizures, Mitchell sustained brain damage, brain damage to the exact area that controls muscle tone on his right side. While it may sound terrible, it was a blessing for Mitchell. As a result, the doctors cut Mitchell's muscle relaxer in half, and Mitchell did not need his Botox injections in his hip. This was also a blessing to the rest of us. It was no longer a wrestling match to get his clothes on. God gave Mitchell this new normal!

As I write this, Mitchell is still is on three liters of oxygen, no longer needs a BiPAP machine at night, still gets vest treatments, and is still on the ketogenic diet. As we care for Mitchell, he rarely has a seizure-free day and retains all his diagnoses with an infectious smile on his face every day. Mitchell has never spoken a word, never taken a step, never sat up, and never rolled over, but he has taught my family and me more about God's unconditional love than I ever thought possible. Years ago, I claimed this verse for Mitchell: "For I know the plans I have for you," declares the Lord, "plans to prosper you and not to harm you, plans to give you hope and a future" (Jeremiah 29:11). Also, beside Mitchell's bed hangs a verse I read daily as a reminder of how special Mitchell is and how perfectly he is made. "Before I formed you in the womb I knew you, before you were born I set you apart" (Jeremiah 1:5).

I am forever thankful that my God did not answer my prayer years ago and give me the future that I had planned. God's steps for my life are much better than I ever could have imagined. I am reminded, "In his heart a man plans his course, but the Lord determines his steps" (Proverbs 16:9). Our family has cared for Mitchell through financial and medical adversity for nearly thirty years. In this time we have learned to trust and lean on God. Craig and I can tell you, we are no longer *Overwhelmed.*

MITCHELL'S
FAMILY ALBUM

Mitchell October 1989 Wurtsmith AFB, MI

Minor children 1993

Minor Family 1994

Amberlynn (Baum) Fritts holding Mitchell, Sarah (Baum) Small, Heather (Harkleroad) Schenkenfelder, Levi, and Grace at home in Cedarville, OH

Minor children on a picnic with their grandparents
(Ernest and Hilda Taylor)

Levi and Mitchell taking a nap

Grace sharing her dolls with Mitchell

Mitchell working hard at Four Oaks

Snuggling with Dad

Mitchell enjoying his swing

Mitchell and Eli Pyles in their matching body casts

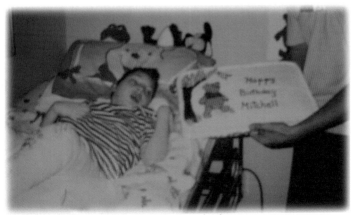

12th Birthday in a body cast

Family Christmas Disney Trip 1999

Linda & Norma from Make-A-Wish Foundation

Grace & Levi with their tattoos of Mitchell's name

Overwhelmed

Mitchell holding his first niece, Emma Minor

Minor Family 2010

Levi & Sarah visiting Mitchell at Nationwide Children's in Columbus, OH

Minor Family 2013

Mitchell & 5 of his nieces

Levi & his Best Man 2014

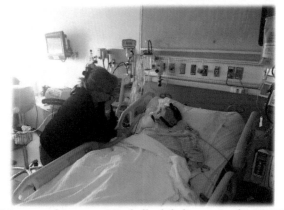

Mom watching over Mitchell while he was in the PICU

Mitchell enjoying Lincoln & Anna

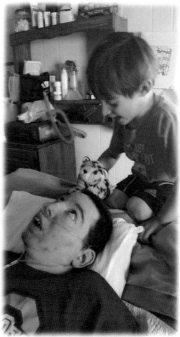

Mitchell watching Miles play

Mitchell & Grace at Levi's Ashland University football game 2011

Minor Family 2014

Overwhelmed

Mitchell's Memoir

LOVE BINDS A FAMILY

Chapter 9
Fear and Faithfulness – Sister

Dates and time do not neatly divide my childhood memories. Like most children, the concept and burdens of time will come soon enough. Someday I would see all of this as an adult. I remember my childhood as a collage of many experiences until I left home. In addition, how I saw things then and how I interpret them today reveals my richer understanding of how God brought our family through very difficult times. This is Mitchell's memoir, and I lend my voice, together with my parents, Levi, and Abbey, to speak for my brother.

After reading my parents portion of *Mitchell's Memoir*, you might think we had a horrible childhood. It was the complete opposite. We had a wonderful childhood where horrible things happened. My brothers and I had responsibilities most adults could not imagine. We had to grow up fast, thereby, forfeiting some of our childhood. My mom leaned on me for extra support caring for Mitchell and duties around the house. My brothers often helped my dad with carpentry side jobs and helped maintain our five-acre lot. My parents also owned a few small businesses where we all frequently worked. During all the financial hardship, surgeries, near death moments, and hard work, my parents always pointed us to God. I never once doubted my parent's faith or my own faith.

Having a sibling with special needs is all I know. It is my normal. My normal was and continues today as I care for my brother's physical needs by changing his diapers, bathing him, making his special ketogenic food for seizure control, feeding him through his G-Tube, giving him his long list of expensive medications, and going to what seems like endless doctor appointments. We would often joke and ponder, "What do other families without a handicapped child do with their time?" Then we would laugh and say that their life cannot be as exciting as ours! I would not change my normal for someone else's normal. Now and when I was young, Mitchell's needs were mainly my mom's responsibility with help from my dad. My little brother Levi would help some when he was old enough. He would eventually be the only one able to lift Mitchell. Looking back, and hearing the stories, I now know it was overwhelming for my parents. Now that I am a parent, I cannot imagine going through such hardship with the grace my parents did. However, as a child it was not overwhelming for me because I never knew Mitchell was the source of any hardships.

My parents loved Mitchell and taught all of us how to do the same by tirelessly caring for him without complaining. Therefore, it was through my parents that I personally learned unconditional love and selfless service. To this day, we all continue to care for Mitchell in the same way. We have, however, added a few helping hands along the way. My husband, Scott Becknell, is a loving and caring brother-in-law. Sarah Minor, Levi's wife, serves Mitchell most every weekday. We all are proud of Scott and Sarah because they seamlessly came alongside to care for Mitchell as though he was their own sibling. Of course, they knew beforehand that marrying into the family meant Mitchell was part of the equation. I remember telling Scott that if we get married, Mitchell becomes our responsibility if my parents die. Now that Sarah and Levi are married, our families agree each will care for Mitchell six months out of the year. Levi likes to tell people jokingly that he gets the top half of Mitchell and I get the bottom half. Anybody who knows our family knows we cope with humor. As a family, we have survived the last twenty-eight years with lots and lots of humor.

Mitchell now has six nieces and two nephews with the unique opportunity to see their Grams (my mom) and Poppy (my dad) show them the same unconditional love and selfless service I had the privilege to witness. As a bonus, they get to see this same service from Levi, Sarah, Scott, and me. It warms my heart to see Mitchell teaching another generation how to see God in all situations, good or bad.

In comparison to my parents, my experience during Mitchell's first few years of life is as different as night is from day. They held the guilt, financial burden, and heavy weight of what it means to have and care for a profoundly handicapped child. From my perspective, I was given a best friend whom I could take anywhere with me. He could not say no! From the moment my parents brought Mitchell home, we were inseparable. I only remember having fun with my new baby brother, not the tears my parents shed those first few weeks after Mitchell's diagnosis. All I knew was that I had another life-long friend.

From the very beginning, you could always find Mitchell by my side; I was either holding him, putting bows in his thick black hair, or sleeping in his crib with my forehead pressed lightly against his pacifier. I used to hold his pacifier in place with my forehead while we both slept so it would not fall out. Of course, I did not know or understand that my brother had trouble sucking because of his cerebral palsy. All I knew was that holding the pacifier in place helped Mitchell sleep through the night. This, in turn, allowed my parents to sleep all night as well.

Mitchell was always a part of my childhood adventures. I remember pushing Mitchell in his wheelchair while rollerblading up and down our long gravel driveway. Several times, I remember tying a rope to his wheelchair and then to my bike. This never ended up working quite as I planned. I have a wonderful memory of a red and yellow Little Tyke's baby swing hanging from our big maple tree in the front yard. This was one of Mitchell's favorite spots, and I can still picture his little hands clenching the blue and white ropes, his thick black hair blowing in the wind, and his sweet laugh as everyone took turns pushing him repeatedly. From this swing, he could watch all of us play in the yard and see our black lab, Midnight, running around as well. My brothers and I always made sure Mitchell was involved in everything we did. To us Mitchell was and is simply our brother.

Our play did not always turn out the way we envisioned it to go. One day, when Levi was about two years old, he was trying to play catch with Mitchell. He was not using a soft ball but instead a can of Ensure, which was Mitchell's food at the time. Levi didn't realize Mitchell would not be able to catch something hurling his way because everyone else he threw things to caught them. Yep, Mitchell caught that Ensure can all right. Right in the forehead! Our neighbor, Andrea Harkleroad, patched Mitchell up with a butterfly stitch. Today, Mitchell still carries that memory (scar) on his forehead, just above his left eye.

I was six years old when Mitchell's first surgery put a Gastrostomy Tube (G-Tube) in place. I learned to feed Mitchell right away through his *button*. As a child, I always loved helping take care of Mitchell. Now, as an adult, God has opened my heart and eyes to understand what it means to care for Mitchell: it is a direct service to our Lord and Savior, "caring for the least of these."

My childhood memories are wonderful, but they also include great anxiety. I lived my whole childhood thinking Mitchell was at death's door. My identity was tied to Mitchell, and I could not imagine life without him. My parents would talk to us about the day Mitchell would go to heaven, simply to prepare us for what that day might look like. I knew that day would eventually come, and it would be a joyous time for him with no more pain and no more limits. Heaven was hard for me to grasp as a child. I guess some adults cannot even wrap their heads around this idea. I remember wanting my brother to be able to run and walk, but I was not ready back then. I am not sure I am ready yet today, although my reasons are slightly more complex. My children love Mitchell with all their being, and it will be a soul-crushing conversation to have with them. We speak of Mitchell's entering heaven often, but just as I could not grasp the complexities of death, they will also have a difficult time.

I must admit, looking back and digging into my Mitchell memories has been very emotional. Most people who knew me as a child would classify me early on as a painfully, shy child. I was the child that you would look at and think that she must have been through a trauma. Well, I was, but no one could see it, and I would not open up about my fears. I hid my anxiety well behind my people-pleasing personality while my parents focused on keeping Mitchell healthy and alive. Dad was working millions of hours so we could have food on the table, and mom was preoccupied with my very complex brother. Being shy was my way of hiding from it all.

I understand today that my shyness was purely from fear. I was so fearful that Mitchell would enter heaven when I was not home. I never liked going to school, church camp, or any activity that had me far away from Mitchell. I was only nine years old when Mitchell had his first hip surgery. During the surgery, Mitchell stopped breathing from the weight of his body cast suffocating him in his hospital bed. I cannot recall my exact emotions during this surgery, but this near miss reaffirmed and increased my fear. Every surgery after this code blue experience left me anxious inside.

Mitchell's next major surgery was at Nationwide Children's Hospital to correct his scoliosis. Leading up to this surgery, Mitchell lived in what we referred to as the *taco shell.* The taco shell was a hard-plastic back brace that Mitchell wore to try to slow down the progression of his curving back. Of course, it did not work. By this time, I was twelve years old. I was pleading with God to keep my brother alive. My anxiety was continuing to build, and I was now even better at hiding my fear.

Somewhere in between all the stresses in our childhood, my parents found time for morning family devotions. Every Saturday morning we would pile up in my parents' bed and listen to *Adventures in Odyssey* on the radio while my dad made breakfast. We were always very involved in church and went as a family when Mitchell's health allowed. When Mitchell's health interfered, mom or dad stayed home while the other took the rest of the family to church. It would have been easy for my parents to use Mitchell as an excuse and not put God first in our lives, but that was never the case.

In addition, my parents always made time for our family vacations. Despite all our financial trouble, medical crises, and hard work, dad always found a way to set aside money for a vacation. I remember him saying that if we worked hard, then we played hard. Most of my childhood memories revolve around our family vacations – these vacations created memories that will last my lifetime. I remember dad reading Frank Peretti children's books at night or listening to them on tape as we drove to our vacation spot. From one of the stories, I can still picture the large, fire-breathing dragon flying in and out of the cave. I think I had nightmares for weeks following that particular book!

One year, my parents asked us if we wanted to leave Mitchell with my grandparents so we could go on a family vacation, a vacation that was not wheelchair friendly. The three of us thought it was ludicrous to go on a *family* vacation without Mitchell. We decided to leave Mitchell for one day and night while we hiked Luray Caverns in Virginia near my grandparents' house in Charlottesville, Virginia. This vacation did not feel right, and we all decided afterwards never to leave Mitchell behind again.

It would have been easier to leave Mitchell home while we went on vacations, especially, for my mom. The night before each vacation, mom and I would pack all of Mitchell's medical equipment, medicines, food, and clothing. We double-and-triple checked everything, but inevitably we would forget something! Dad wrote about our neighbors, Joe and Andrea Harkleroad, and his description is right on. Mom would call Andrea, and she would overnight whatever we forgot. One time it was even Mitchell's food and, to this day, there is still a debate as to who *actually* forgot it!

In addition to our vacations, we also went to Uncle Steve and Aunt Sharon's house for nearly all our Thanksgivings. Military friends become family quickly; I have always known

Steve and Sharon as my uncle and aunt. I am so thankful God put the Baums in our family's life at just the right time. I would always look forward to Thanksgiving at the Baum's house. We could relax and just have fun. Uncle Steve and their girls (Lisa, Amberlynn, and Sarah) always met us at the door; each would fight to get to Mitchell first! He was everyone's favorite; his bright brown eyes and joyous smile made it no competition. Aunt Sharon was in the kitchen with snacks ready, no matter what time we arrived. She usually had a fresh baked batch of Buffalo Chip cookies waiting for our arrival. To this day, if we visit them or they visit us, she has those freshly baked cookies.

While visiting, mom and Aunt Sharon would spend their days designing and making crafts or going to antique stores. Dad and Uncle Steve would go deer hunting and then antiquing with the moms after they came out of their tree stands. One year, the four of them put on matching outfits and went out on a double date! The Baums are those kinds of friends – once in a lifetime! We never missed a Thanksgiving with them until the year 1999, when Mitchell had back surgery that fall. Instead of spending Thanksgiving with them that year, we went to their house for Christmas. I do not remember the gifts we opened that year, but I do recall the love that was always on display.

When I was fourteen years old, Mitchell started his new ketogenic diet and I/O Waiver. After the I/O Waiver, life was a little more peaceful. Pat Tompkins became a home health care provider that year, faithfully caring for Mitchell day in and day out. This was the first time a non-family member cared for Mitchell long term. She took such good care of Mitchell and was a part of our family for thirteen years. I am not sure she knows the blessing she was to Mitchell and our family during her time. The quality of care she gave Mitchell is commendable. We all love Pat, and her Christian faith was a source of wisdom for me. I always enjoyed our long conversations about life and faith.

Mitchell's next home health care provider was Abbey (Pyles) Goins. Abbey was eighteen years old when she started working for Mitchell through the I/O waiver. Her family had already played a big role in our lives as her little sister, Elisabeth (Pyles) McNeely, was my best friend since kindergarten. I still consider them both very close friends. In fact, both were bridesmaids in my wedding. When Elisabeth is in Ohio visiting, we all get together and enjoy fellowship over coffee while our children play.

For the first time, Abbey went on vacation with us that year to care for Mitchell. This was my mom's first *real* vacation. We all piled into our white Aerostar minivan – all seven of us – with an emphasis on mini! Abbey and I sat with Mitchell propped up between us. My other brothers sat in the backbench seat. Luggage was in piles all around us because Mitchell's wheelchair took up the entire back of the van. Mitchell hated riding in the car at night, so dad rigged together the first portable CRT TV/VHS player. It rested snuggly on the armrests of the front captain's chairs. Once we arrived at our Florida destination, Beverly Hillbillies style, we fell out of the van and onto the parking lot. What a sight we were to all the onlookers – a family of brunettes with a handicapped child and a token blonde! We were already used to the stares, so we laughed and unpacked.

Abbey later moved in with my parents, Levi, Mitchell, and me so she could help care for Mitchell while saving money to finish nursing school. The timing was perfect because dad would deploy to Iraq. Not only did she alleviate some of the burden of Mitchell's care, but also she became like a sister to me. Growing up with three brothers, I longed for a sister! I finally had someone from whom I could borrow clothes and make-up as well as share anything in confidence. We know each other's secrets, just as sisters would. I am so thankful she followed God's prompting and came alongside our family to help in the capacity she did.

Fall of 2001 was an emotionally draining time for me. I started my first year of high school, and a month later Mitchell would have his fifth and final surgery. I was just starting my journey through high school when my secret train of emotions hit me head-on after Mitchell did not wake up from his hip surgery. I distinctly remember visiting him after his surgery and hearing the nurses tell us while he lies there unconscious, "Handicapped people are just lethargic like that." I knew this was not the case with Mitchell. My brother was bright-eyed and full of life and not the pitiful little boy I saw lying in the hospital bed. He would not even respond to Dad's voice, and he always responded to him. A few days passed, and he still didn't wake up from anesthesia. I was visiting Mitchell at the hospital when his primary care doctor, Dr. Nancy Hesz, called my mom back and promptly called the nurses station to order a neurology consult. Once she made the call, nurses and doctors came flooding in and immediately put Mitchell in ICU. Mitchell had blood work ordered, and once it returned, the nurses began to listen to our concerns. His blood work showed that his liver and pancreas were failing. He was suffering from chemical pancreatitis because of the seizure medicine he had been on for years. We were already familiar with Children's ICU. No children could visit, but the nurses kindly made an exception for us. All I could think was that here we are again; Mitchell is not going to make it. I was not ready for him to leave. My pleading with God began again.

My mom never left Mitchell's side when he was in the hospital. This meant my brothers and I went home at night with my dad. My dad is not someone with whom you cry; it is just not him. We are both very stoic, so dad would be my last choice to have a good cry with over Mitchell. I would then cry myself to sleep, still pleading with God, and wake up the next morning like all was right with the world and go to school. All day I would stare at the clock waiting for the school day to end so I could get to the hospital. Looking back currently, I do not recall any teachers or coaches asking me how I was doing. Surely, they knew my brother was in the hospital fighting for his life, but then again, maybe they did not know the severity of what was happening in my world. I distinctly recall thinking, "Does anyone believe that Mitchell is at death's door again?" It seemed to me that others around us thought we were crying wolf, so they did not respond with concern. In our case, there was a wolf. There was always a wolf. Mitchell improved quickly, and I tucked my fear away as I had done so many times before. I will deal with this another time, I thought. By the way, this is not a good approach.

By my sophomore year, I was heavy into sports: volleyball, basketball, and track. My parents never missed a game, and Mitchell loved coming to as many games as he could. My teams also loved having Mitchell at our games. Everyone would always pass by Mitchell and tell him hi. He was our *undesignated* mascot. In the fall of 2003, Mitchell's dietician and neurologist concluded that Mitchell had been on his ketogenic diet long enough. Evidently, it is harmful to other organs, especially the heart, to stay on a high fat no carb diet for so long. The weaning off the diet began.

I remember what happened next as if it were yesterday. I arrived home to Pat and Mitchell. Pat had already called Mom to tell her that Mitchell was having too many seizures throughout the day, and they were not stopping. Pat then asked if I would monitor him with her. However, within a few minutes, he began to have a non-stop seizure. Mom came home moments after Mitchell started his non-stop seizing. Within minutes, Dad arrived home responding to his urgent call from mom. We needed him to be at Nationwide Children's Hospital, so we opted to load him in the big green van and speed to the hospital. We arrived at the Emergency Department via the ambulance entrance. By this time Mitchell had been seizing for almost an hour. Yes! We arrived that fast! The staff quickly administered an anti-seizure medicine. Instantly, his body completely locked up with a life-threatening seizure. Mitchell could not breathe, and he was turning blue. We were back at that dreaded moment where my fear was happening right in front of my eyes. Panicked, the doctor administered Ativan – the medicine for which my mom originally asked – to counteract the other anti-seizure medicine. Just as quickly as before, he was back, breathing shallow but alive.

After everything calmed down, the doctor noticed my Cedarville Indians volleyball t-shirt. We chatted a bit and discovered her dad, Mr. Harris, was my history teacher. She had saved my brother's life, and I will be forever grateful. Mr. Harris was already one of my favorite teachers, but from that day on, he was my all-time favorite.

My mom told the neurologist he was staying on the ketogenic diet, and we were not going to wean him off ever again! After all, she is a redhead! Mitchell is still on the ketogenic diet to this day. For years, we have had to double check every medicine or IV solution administered to my brother while he is in the hospital. Anything with sugar in it will send him into a seizure. Mitchell's medical chart lists sugar as one of his allergies. Today, the ketogenic diet is a mainstream therapy for seizures, and nurses are alert to the issue of how sugar will undo the diet. Despite this fact, we still double check everything before it touches Mitchell.

In 2005, a few months after I graduated high school, I got a phone call from a woman, Echo VanderWal, looking for someone to watch her four boys – not just any four boys, but four-year-old triplets (Luke, Jacob, and Zebadiah) and a one-year-old (Zion)! We talked a few minutes, and she told me she got my name from a mutual friend. Echo was a Physician's Assistant at Star Pediatrics. Mitchell's primary care doctor was part of Star Pediatrics. As the story goes, Echo casually mentioned to a patient's mother that she was looking for a nanny for her boys because her husband, Harry VanderWal, was in his second to last year of medical residency, and she was working part-time at Star Pediatrics. The patient's mother knew our family from Cedarville. She told Echo I had cared for my handicapped brother for years, and I might be a good fit. I agreed to meet Harry and Echo. On a trial basis, I watched their boys for a few weeks that summer.

Late that fall, Echo's cousin moved to Ohio to care for the boys. That same fall, I started at Clark State University in Springfield, Ohio, for nursing. By spring, I did not want to return to school. My dad said I had to have a job or sign up for spring classes. A week before spring registration cut-off, I got a call from Echo. Her cousin could no longer watch the boys, and they needed a full-time nanny right away. I was more than happy to accept her offer and started watching the boys the next week. I quickly became a part of the VanderWal family. Harry was finishing medical school, and they were already planning to head to Swaziland, Africa, as missionaries to operate mobile medical clinics under the name, The Luke Commission (TLC).

During the beginning of summer 2006, I not only watched the boys during the day, but also on weeknights and weekends, I helped Harry and Echo prepare for their first TLC mission. I remember helping sort and prepare clothes from The Children's Place. These clothes and medical supplies were in storage units just down the road from their Xenia, OH, home. As July approached, the storage units were overflowing with clothes and medical supplies ready to load onto an empty forty-foot trailer container due to arrive later that month. It would be a big task to load the container, and I assured Echo that my family would be there to help load. After making this promise to Echo, I let my family know. Leading up to loading day, my family began to help in the evenings and weekends. Over the next week, we helped box medical-related supplies and equipment including preparing two pull-behind trailers. I remember dad working with Harry to build fixed shelving in one of the trailers and to apply the vinyl TLC logos to the exterior of both. My entire family was there to load the trailer. Even Mitchell was keeping a watchful eye from his wheelchair. He enjoyed watching the VanderWal boys run circles around us. On a squelching hot summer Saturday, we all arrived early to organize the contents of two large storage units. Echo told us we had one shot to load the trailer because the semi-trailer driver would pull up, wait for us to load, and then drive away no later than a specified time. Echo also said that we could not pack any air. Therefore, in roughly four hours we hurriedly packed this enormous trailer, filling every space imaginable. I recall they had to pull the wheels off the axel of the big trailer for it to fit. Without a minute to spare, we swung the big doors closed while pushing on the contents. The semi drove away and headed to a shipping port to start its long journey over the Atlantic Ocean.

It was now August 2006, and the VanderWals would be heading to Swaziland soon. I was surprised when Echo asked if I wanted to go with them. I said yes! Echo sat me down thinking that we needed to assess my debts and get them paid off. To her surprise I assured her that I carried no debt, including credit card debt, and that I had paid cash for my car. My parents had always taught us to make wise financial decisions to avoid the burdens of debt. With that conversation out of the way, Echo and I began to plan my joining TLC.

I was leaving home, and my life serving Mitchell would need to adapt. God was calling me elsewhere, but He always left a part of Mitchell in the corner of my heart. My service in Mitchell's ministry would now be from afar, encouraging my parents, and hands-on whenever I visited home. The faith my parents were living during my childhood journey was now my own. Making lots of mistakes along the way, I navigated my faith, and I grew through those mistakes. I was getting ready to leave the country on my first mission trip to Africa. It did not escape me that my brother's ministry now intersected with the TLC ministry and that God had prepared me to serve something bigger through Mitchell!

In late August, the VanderWals and I flew to Swaziland, Africa, spending two months operating rural mobile medical clinics. On our arrival back to the States, I travelled with the VanderWals raising financial support as they drove up and down the east coast to Canada and out to Idaho. That December I stayed home for Christmas and met Scott Becknell for the first time at Faircreek Church (FCC). I spent the month of January 2007 in Idaho helping care for the VanderWal boys. Scott and I emailed back and forth a few times. In February, I flew home to Ohio for a month before we left for Swaziland. Scott happened to be visiting Ohio for President's Day weekend, so we planned to meet for dinner. We continued to email, but communication in Swaziland was spotty at best. Dad also deployed to Iraq for five months while I was gone that spring.

When I returned home the last week of May, my mom had run into Scott at church and told him I would be there the following Sunday. That Sunday, he asked me out on our first date for the next evening. Scott planned our date to be at the Spaghetti Warehouse in Dayton, Ohio. Unbeknownst to him, this was special to me because as a child I have fond family memories of the Spaghetti Warehouse. When I was young, dad traded picture framework for gift cards, so we spent many birthday celebrations there. Scott would be moving to South Carolina in a month to start submarine training. My plan was to meet the VanderWals in Idaho for the summer until we left for Swaziland that fall. Instead of going to Idaho, I had to make the hard decision to stay in Ohio and help my mom with Mitchell because my dad had deployed. The VanderWals had become my family, and it was not an easy thing to do. I felt like I was letting them down. Scott asked me to marry him in December 2007. My last trip with The Luke Commission (TLC) was for two months during our five-month engagement. A few nights before I left Swaziland for home, Echo and Harry told me they would not make it back for my wedding. Opportunities arose, and they were extending their time in Swaziland. On the day I flew home to the States, I can still clearly see the boys as they stood at the wrought iron fence with their hands on the bars, faces pushed tightly against the fence, and tears streaming down their little faces. Harry, Echo, and I were sobbing as well. I returned home the last week of April, and Scott and I were married on May 31, 2008. The VanderWals are still following God's vision for TLC to this day. They are still my family, and I love them dearly. If not for Mitchell I would have never met this dear family or my husband.

My prayer, "Lord, PLEASE let me be home when Mitchell leaves this world!" began while on my first trip to Swaziland in the fall of 2006. During my stay abroad, a respiratory infection put Mitchell in the hospital. This would be the beginning of Mitchell's pulmonary issues. After my wedding to a naval submarine officer, I spent the next six years not living near Mitchell. You guessed it. There are no submarines in Ohio. We called the East Coast home the entire time and welcomed our three children (Anna, Lucy, and Miles) to the Becknell and Minor family. We managed to move five times in six years and bring each child into the world in a different state.

My prayer about Mitchell was always in the background when Scott began to think about leaving active duty. While Scott was making plans to leave active duty and transfer to the Reserves, my vote was to move to Cedarville. After much prayer, we decided that Cedarville would become our new home. In February 2014, the children and I moved in with my parents and Mitchell. The following month, Scott joined us and continued his job search in the Dayton area. By God's grace, he found a job in the Dayton area, and in May we finalized our house search and bought our forever home.

July rolled around, and it was time to move into our new home. A few days prior to our move-in date, a serious respiratory infection put Mitchell in the hospital. During one of my drives up to Nationwide Children's Hospital, I could not help but think about what I had prayed eight years ago. I asked God then not to let Mitchell die while I was living out of the state. God and I had a serious talk on my hour-long drive to the hospital. Laughing and sobbing through tears, I said aloud, "Lord, I didn't mean it was ok for Mitchell to die when I was literally moving into my house. I guess I should have been more specific!" God wants us to be specific in our prayers. I have always known this, but I fail to practice this in my prayers. Every so often, God gently reminds me of this. I wanted my children to know and remember Mitchell. I wanted to spend more time with my brother. "I am not ready for this!" I continued. I know my prayer was selfish, but I was honestly not ready to let go of Mitchell.

After spending a week in the hospital fighting pneumonia, Mitchell came home with a few more daily medicines to add to his already long list. During Mitchell's hospital stay, the family learned of *palliative care* and had to decide whether to prepare a *Do Not Resuscitate (DNR)* order. This was new to all of us. My parents, Levi, and I decided to make decisions concerning Mitchell, together. We have chosen what we think is a loving and non-invasive end-of-life path. The doctors at Nationwide Children's Hospital continue to be supportive of all our decisions.

The morning of September 7, 2014, I received a call from mom asking if I could give her a second opinion on Mitchell and help her decide if he needed to go to the hospital. Mitchell and mom hate hospital stays. She tends to wait if possible, hoping he will turn around to avoid a hospital stay. When I arrived, his breathing was visibly labored, and he was declining quickly. We called his Complex Care doctor, Dr. Lucas, and she advised us to go straight to the nearest hospital, so he could be stabilized. Mom quickly panicked because the nearest hospital was Greene Memorial, an adult hospital. One of her biggest fears is Mitchell's being admitted to an adult hospital. Dr. Lucas assured her that they would just stabilize him for transport, and Nationwide would pick him up. Upon arriving at Greene Memorial, the nurses rushed us back right away. My mom explained we were only there to stabilize him enough for transport to Nationwide Children's. The nurses and doctors at Greene were wonderful and were very supportive of our plan. They called Dr. Lucas and planned to have a helicopter or MICU (mobile intensive care unit) pick Mitchell up. Hearing *helicopter* made me realize the severity of Mitchell's condition. Ultimately, a MICU from Nationwide arrived, and he and my mom were off to Columbus. I followed behind in Mitchell's red transit and made all the calls to family. Dad was stationed at the Pentagon at the time, and I remember calling him and telling him he needed to head to Columbus right away. Here we were again, just three months later, on the Pulmonary ICU floor. Mitchell continued to improve from his respiratory virus and had a relatively short stay that time.

In the summer of 2015, just when we thought we had made all the hard decisions, Mitchell once again found his way back to the emergency department. Mom and Grandma took him to a routine neurology appointment, and within minutes of seeing the doctor, she advised them to take Mitchell straight to the Emergency Department. From there he went right to the PICU. The x-rays and tests started to determine if he had pneumonia or a virus. In the meantime, he was started on an antibiotic, and as his condition worsened, more antibiotics. Eventually, a test came back showing he had the rhinovirus, a common cold, and all we could do was let it run its course.

A week into this hospital stay, I decided at the last minute to ask my mother-in-law to watch my children so I could visit my brother and mom during the day. My mother-in-law is especially quick to say yes when she knows Mitchell is sick. It is comforting for me to know that my children are having fun with their grandparents when I am away. I could feel God orchestrating my visit to the hospital this day. His timing, I have learned, is always perfect. I have no idea why I ever doubt Him!

I was just entering the elevator from the parking garage when my mom called and said, "Are you close? Hurry!" Evidently, dad called mom to say I was on my way. My parents had coordinated the timing of my call so I was not driving at the time. I could not get my visitor tag quickly enough, and I could not have prepared for what I was about to see next. I walked into his room, and there was Mitchell's near lifeless body with nurses working all around him. The nurses were working frantically to recover his oxygen level. His oxygen saturation was in the low sixties. Mom said to me that the doctor suggested she call the family, Mitchell was likely not going to make it. The next thing I knew the palliative care doctor was at the door and wanted to talk with us. She took us down the hallway to a bench that sat in front of a large window to tell us that their next step was to keep him comfortable. I said, "You mean sit and watch him die?" By that time, streams of tears were rolling down our cheeks. She sweetly assured us that it is not like that and that he would not be in pain. Soon after our conversation with her, the rest of the family arrived, and we waited. Of course, Mitchell did what he is accustomed to doing at every hospital stay – he went right up to death's door and then turned around and came back. All I can do is thank God for giving us a little more time to serve Mitchell. Mitchell's oxygen levels crept up slowly and then stabilized in the eighties. The doctor discharged Mitchell a few days later. However, this time, he was on oxygen permanently.

The holidays were more special that year. We had almost lost Mitchell the summer before and lived those fall months caring for Mitchell's new respiratory needs. He stayed healthy until April 2016. I was watching him that day because mom had taken Papa to a chemotherapy session. When I arrived that morning, Mitchell's breathing was labored, and my mom told me to decide whether he needed to go to the hospital. After a few hours of suctioning and breathing treatments, he wasn't improving, so I drove Mitchell to Nationwide Children's Hospital Emergency Department while my mother-in-law cared for my children. After an initial assessment, Mitchell went straight back to a swarm of nurses and doctors. I knew his breathing was labored, but I did not know the severity of the situation. Once again, there was the question how far do we go, meaning do we just use the bi-pap machine, ventilate him, or nothing?

After stabilizing Mitchell, the Pulmonary ICU (PICU) took him to the same place he was the year before. Mom joined us as soon as we made it to the PICU floor, and that was the beginning of our two-week tag team sleepovers. Mitchell is non-verbal, so mom will never leave him alone overnight.

Despite my top priority, my three children at home, I knew she needed extra support both physically and emotionally. We found a way to make it work and get all the children covered.

During this hospital stay, my husband was a month in to his six-month deployment. My children stayed with my parents, and I stayed with Mitchell. This would be the first time my mom would let someone, other than her or dad, stay with Mitchell at the hospital overnight. It took some convincing, but she and I both knew she needed the rest. She also could just enjoy being a grandma to my children and not have to worry about Mitchell. Next, we had to assure the night guard that I, a sibling, could stay the night. He called up to the PICU, and they assured him it was ok.

Mitchell was discharged on a Thursday, and my parents were due to go on a weekend trip for which they had been planning for weeks. I assured my mom it was best if they still go and that I would watch Mitchell for the weekend. On Saturday evening, I put my children to bed and then got Mitchell changed, fed, and ready for bed. By 10:00 PM, I was finished with everything and went to the living room to relax and watch a movie. Around 10:20 PM, when I heard Mitchell's pulse oximeter beeping, I went to check his oxygen level and see if he was sleeping. When he falls asleep, his oxygen levels tend to hover around the high eighties. Much to my surprise his levels were in the sixties but within seconds climbed back to the low nineties. I sighed a breath of relief, but that breath came too soon. His levels plummeted again to the sixties and climbed back to the nineties just as quickly. This pattern continued for ten cycles. The tenth time he did not climb back so quickly; his fingers and lips were turning blue, and his face was as pale as a sheet. I shook him slightly while repeating his name over and over to get him to take a breath. I quickly removed his bi-pap mask so I could put his oxygen directly to his nose. Then I cranked his oxygen machine to four liters, knowing full well that this was not a recommended amount to be on at home.

My mind was going a mile a minute as panic set in. Most who know me would say I am not a person who panics easily, but in this moment, I could not think straight. I could not think of a single local person to call. He had a *DNR*, so I was not going to call 911. Scott was deployed. My grandfather had just finished a round of chemo the Thursday prior. Since it was almost 11:00 PM, he would have been in bed. I had been texting Levi and Sarah while the ordeal was happening, but they lived forty minutes away. By the time I got Mitchell breathing again, I told them I wanted them to come stay the night with me, but, thankfully, they were already on their way. My thoughts were that if Mitchell was going to die tonight, I did not want to be alone. I also prayed, "Lord, I know I said I want to be here, but I didn't mean I want to be the ONLY one here!" They arrived, and Mitchell was completely back to his normal happy self, laughing and bright-eyed, but I was noticing many small seizures happening consecutively, and they were lasting too long. Normally at this point, Mitchell is given a seizure medicine called Diastat; it acts as a sedative to stop his seizures.

When it is given to him, he becomes very lethargic, and his breathing becomes shallow. There was no way I was going to give him that after he nearly stopped breathing only minutes before. Sarah and I decided it was best just to watch him and hold off on the medication until we could ask his doctor. We got him settled for bed and gave him to the Lord and his guardian angels for the night.

The following morning I called mom. No, I did not tell her while it was all happening. There was not a thing she could do from afar, and she would have insisted on cutting their trip short. I asked mom to contact his primary care doctor about administering his Diastat, because we were still noticing increased seizure activity. She assured us it was better to lessen his seizure activity with this medication, so we administered it and waited. He peacefully slept most of the day while his body recovered. God still was not ready to take Mitchell home, but faithfully taught me a lesson through this experience. I need only to find my strength in God and not others around me – not even my husband or my parents. I was not alone while Mitchell was having respiratory failure. I felt God there helping me navigate this unthinkable situation.

Through Mitchell's journey, we never imagined he would make it this far. God has been so faithful in allowing us time to grieve and prepare (as much as we can) for the day Mitchell will enter his glory. My personal faith has been stretched and strengthened though Mitchell's life and journey. We are better people for all the hills and valleys we have faced together as a family because of Mitchell. The adversity we faced as a family taught me to look at others going through adversity with grace, not to assume I know all the details of their lives. I learned to get close to those families and figure out where I could step in and help. If I didn't know, I would pray and ask God to show me where the need was.

For any parent expecting a child with special needs, know that your other children, present or future, will be blessed. The number one question friends will ask me is if I ever felt like I missed anything in life because of Mitchell. My answer is simply *absolutely not!* If anything, those without a special needs sibling have missed something spectacular. Your special needs child will help build your other children's character and shape who they will become. Do not rob them of this blessing.

I had the opportunity to grow up in a unique family. We were not the norm, and people often did not know what to do with us. People still do not understand our family dynamic, but I have learned that we do not need to explain ourselves. If others really want to understand, they must get close enough because that is the only way to come to a full understanding. I am thankful that my parents taught us to do this and how to serve, not only Mitchell, but others as well. Amid serving and caring for Mitchell, my parents were always serving friends and family. I am thankful for this example, because it taught me to care for all the people in my life, not just Mitchell. To Mitchell, I say, "Thank you for all of the life lessons about trusting God, selfless service, guardian angels, and the hope of eternal life."

Mitchell's Memoir

Chapter 10
Love Crosses All Barriers – Caregiver

Just coming out of high school, I was approached about the possibility of being a caregiver for Mitchell. Growing up knowing the Minor family kept Mitchell's complex care and health issues from being intimidating to me. His siblings, Taylor, Grace, and Levi, were always doting and loving on Mitchell. They are so proud of their brother. I remember seeing Mitchell at sporting and school events, just like any other sibling. This was helpful to me, and I am sure to others. Seeing their love and care for their brother naturally put others at ease. This made it more comfortable to interact with Mitchell. After being approved through the county, I began caring for Mitchell the summer of 2001. Carrie was a wonderful teacher. She and the rest of the family taught me the specifics of Mitchell's care and how to prepare his food and medication.

The Minors quickly became like a second family to me. Over several years, I was frequently in their home caring for Mitchell, assisting with doctor appointments, and traveling with them on several family vacations. Preparing for vacation, we did what was needed. Looking back, I honestly do not know how we made it work. We had to have been quite the sight. Seven people, a wheelchair included, packed into a minivan. Along with all the normal luggage was Mitchell's canned food for a week, breathing machines and supplies, and a TV hoisted up between two seats to keep Mitchell occupied. Off to Florida we went. We not only survived, we all still liked each other! Those are memories I will never forget.

Several years later, I moved in with the Minors as extra help caring for Mitchell while I worked and later went back to school. At the time, I did not fully appreciate all the blessings and the lessons my time with them would teach me. Looking back, I could not be more thankful. Having cared for Mitchell is what first interested me in healthcare. This was an unexpected blessing. I have Mitchell to thank, as I have now been working as a nurse for over ten years.

Another blessing was the close friendships that continue to this day. Carrie became like a second mom and Grace another sister. When I had my son this year, Carrie and Grace came to visit. They said they would bring a meal. I told them no need to go to any trouble; I was just looking forward to seeing them. They insisted, saying, "We are bringing three meals, standing in for each of your sisters who are out of town." I should not have been surprised; that is just how they are. They are truly servants, not only to Mitchell, but also to those around them. I continue to learn from them to this day!

What I have learned from Mitchell is invaluable. One of the greatest lessons is that love really does cross all barriers. Mitchell's physical barriers are extreme as he is unable to communicate verbally or show typical affection. This does not keep him from showing love. I will never forget when I would be near the back of the house in Mitchell's bedroom, and Craig would get home from work. Mitchell would hear his voice coming down the hall. His body would tense, his eyes brighten with excitement, and a huge smile would come across his face. Sometimes he would make an excited squeal. There was no denying his love for his dad. No words were needed. I also learned, and am still learning, that despite all our differences, we are all God's children. He loves us all the same. In a world that is so quick to judge based on physical differences, limitations, social status (and the list could go on), we have no place to judge. It is not our job. We are called only to love.

Craig, Carrie, Taylor, Grace, and Levi are wonderful examples of not letting struggles define you. Despite the stresses and hardships having a complex handicapped child brings, I have no doubt that they are thankful God blessed them with Mitchell. Some of the struggles I saw were obvious as they learned how best to treat Mitchell's seizures, the emotional stress of hospital stays and surgeries, the physical stress of 24/7 care, and the lifting of Mitchell as he got older. I remember they could never make a trip without first planning either who would watch Mitchell, or all the planning and time it would take to get Mitchell ready to go. I never saw them treat these things like a burden. For them it was what you do for a child you love. Other stresses with which they dealt I am still learning of today because they never talked about them. They did not focus on their struggles or let it define them. They focused on love and service – loving and serving Mitchell and each other unconditionally despite all the distractions. I am so thankful for their example.

I am confident of a couple things. First, Mitchell could not have been born to a better family. God says he will not give us more than we can handle. I am sure there were doubtful times, especially in those early days of Mitchell's unknown diagnosis. However, the Minors have kept their faith and are proof God's Word is true. Second, we are all here for a purpose. One might look at Mitchell, see only his limitations, and wonder about his purpose. I am reminded how the Minors were told he would only live to be five, but Mitchell is still serving his purpose today and teaching those around him how to love unconditionally and serve without boundaries.

Chapter 11
Unlikely Motivation – Brother

Though it may not look like it, I am Mitchell's younger brother. Mitchell, as you know by now, is not your typical big brother. He cannot throw a ball, talk about girls, or give life advice. What he can do, and continues to do, is inspire me to become the best version of myself. Even though he cannot throw a ball, he inspired me to pursue sports and do so to the best of my abilities. Even though he cannot talk about girls, he helped me find my amazing wife, Sarah Minor. Even though he is unable to give life advice, he has taught me more about what it means to live than anyone ever could. You may be asking yourself how Mitchell could have done all those things when he cannot even move or talk. In the following pages, I hope to answer this question by telling you how I became Mitchell's big brother and how he became my best friend.

Some of my earliest memories of Mitchell are from before I started kindergarten. I used to go with my mom to all his doctor's appointments and take him to the special needs school he attended, Four Oaks. One of my most vivid memories from these trips was taking Mitchell to school. Four Oaks is a circular building with one main hallway and classrooms on either side. I remember walking down this hallway on our way to pick Mitchell up from class. I also remember, on more than one occasion, playing with some of the children from the school in a gymnasium while my mom would be talking with Mitchell's teachers. I also have many vague and blurry memories of being in doctors' offices, typically playing with some toy while my mom spoke with the doctor. When on these trips, my mom would usually take me to grab a quick and cheap bite to eat (we could only afford McDonald's dollar menu).

When I started school, I no longer went with my mom to Mitchell's appointments with such frequency. Kindergarten through seventh grade I went to the Cedar Cliff Local School. There were about fifty students in my graduating class, and my other siblings had already had all the same teachers as I did. I have a lot of great memories of this time, including family vacations and getting Mitchell to laugh as semi trucks drove by my family's coffee shop.

Family vacations were a coveted luxury. Before we could afford any type of real trip, we would always go to the Baum's house in Missouri for Thanksgiving and Christmas. We would leave early in the morning so that we could sleep most of the way there. Before we had a fancy van with a wheelchair lift, Mitchell sat in the car as anyone else would, except surrounded by pillows and blankets to conform to his crooked body. His wheelchair took up all the available space in the back, which means we had to pack light. My favorite vacation memory was our first trip to Disney in December 1999. It was Christmas time, and the hotel pool was shaped like Mickey Mouse. What was even more amazing was the way the Disney staff treated my family. We were escorted to the front of every line, and they gave us free stuff. Disney goers on the other hand, children and adults alike, would spread like the red sea when they saw Mitchell's wheelchair coming in their direction. People would always stare – that was a given – but many people treated us as if we carried a deadly virus. I remember my sister and I would catch people staring at Mitchell, and we would just stare back at them until they were uncomfortable and looked away. That is just one of the things you must get used to when you have a sibling like Mitchell. While I never saw him as being anything other than my brother, strangers were all too quick to run in the opposite direction.

That Disney trip was one of many we would take over the years – each trip better than the last. I remember one time my parents sat through timeshare presentations just to score free Disney tickets. I know this was not fun for my mom and dad. Though I did not know or understand at the time, I did notice that we were starting to stay at nicer places, and my parents did not have to sit through any sales presentations to get tickets. By no means were we rich, but life was noticeably easier after the state began picking up the slack on Mitchell's medical bills. I do not envy what my parents had to go through emotionally and financially during the early years. I would not wish that on my worst enemy. Regardless of how hard it got for them, I never felt that I was anything less than loved. I cannot think of a single instance where I felt pushed aside or left behind because of the amount of time and energy Mitchell consumes. It is a cliché to say "The world doesn't revolve around you." However, it did revolve around Mitchell. I do not fault my parents in any way – that is just what had to be done to keep him alive. I just fell right into orbit, loving my brother unconditionally, doing anything I could to help take care of him.

Growing up, my parents owned a small coffee shop in Cedarville. I was too young to do any meaningful work, so I was tasked with keeping Mitchell entertained. This usually consisted of keeping a movie going on the television in the back room or sitting outside on the sidewalk and watching the cars go by. Mitchell has always loved loud noises, such as truck horns, and would laugh uncontrollably when he heard them. To our benefit, Cedarville is located on a road that connects two major semi truck routes. Every truck that would come by, I would motion the universal honk the horn sign. Mitchell would crack up laughing, and we would play this on repeat for hours.

My childhood was by no means a fairytale of happy memories, but rather was fraught with heartache, difficulties, and emotional lows. While I do not remember every hospitalization, surgery, or near-death experience, I remember enough. Two memories stick out to me the most. The first was Mitchell's leg surgery, which turned into a full body cast, and the second was seeing my brother's lifeless pale body lying on a hospital bed.

Because of Mitchell's diet prior to the ketogenic diet, his bones were extremely vulnerable to breaking. I remember going with mom to the original surgery; I believe my grandma was there as well. I vaguely remember mom trying to explain to me how the doctor accidently broke Mitchell's leg. I also remember seeing Mitchell in the full body cast for the first time. The cast came up to his G-Tube and had a bar running from one knee to the other, which was a convenient handle for moving him around. Oddly enough, my best friend at the time, Eli, broke his femur during football practice and was in a body cast too. We have a picture of both of them in their casts. I cannot even begin to imagine how this surgery affected my parents. They had already been put into an impossible situation with Mitchell's congenital defects, and now they had yet another hurdle thrown in their way.

I have always been able to make Mitchell laugh; I could look at him a certain way or make a noise, and he would smile from ear to ear. In fact, at some of Mitchell's appointments, I would have to make him laugh to give the doctors an idea of his cognitive abilities. I pride myself in being able to make him laugh to this day. So, when I was unable to make him laugh, or even smile, while he lay in front of me lifeless, his skin so pale it practically blended in with the white hospital bed, I thought the worst. I remember the moment well.

Anytime Mitchell was in the hospital for a long period of time, my grandparents would drive in from Virginia to help. I would stay with them in the hotel on Wright-Patterson AFB so that my parents did not have to worry about where I was or what I was doing. My grandparents took me to the hospital and walked me into the room where Mitchell was lying. I now know that it was because Mitchell might not wake up. I remember walking into the room; mom was sitting in a chair on the right side of the room, and Mitchell was lying on the bed in the middle of the room hooked up to as many cords as you could imagine. This was nothing out of the norm, and I had seen him like this before. However, when I moved in closer and put my hand on his, he was cold, and I could see he was breathing slowly. I remember feeling sad and helpless. I could not help but think this was Mitchell's last visit to the hospital and quite possibly the last time I would see him alive. As the tears began to form, my mom asked me to talk to Mitchell to see if I could get him to respond to my voice. For the first time, I could not.

Whenever Mitchell has been in a life-or-death situation, I always find myself pleading and bargaining with God. By now, I have gotten out of the way all my whys and how God could do this to Mitchell and my family. What you must realize and come to terms with is that God has a plan – whether we like it or not.

I remember thinking about heaven when I was younger and how it had to be a real place or what was the point? What I mean by this is the only way I will ever be able to play or have a conversation with my brother is if heaven is real. If it is not, it is almost impossible to cope with the emotional strain of it all. God knew that, so he also gave my family and me a sense of humor to make the best of the worst situation. Without being able to laugh at yourself or the situation you are in, how can you truly enjoy life? Growing up with Mitchell, this is even truer. The rule in our house is if you are not laughing, you are crying. I would urge anybody who has a handicapped child or sibling to find laughter within themselves, because if you do not, reality will crush you.

I will give you an example of just how funny we really are, and I give you permission to laugh. When Mitchell has a big seizure, he makes a very distinctive sound, one that can be heard throughout the house. When my mom would wash the dishes in one end of the house, my siblings and I would be in Mitchell's room on the other end. At a young age, I had mastered the seizure sound, and I had no shame. I would make the sound as loud as I could. We would hear the dishes drop and my mom running through the house yelling, "I'm coming, I'm coming." Of course, when she arrived, Mitchell would be fine, and we would be cracking up rolling on the floor. I could write a book on this topic alone, but I will spare you. I just ask that you keep everything in perspective; do not take life too seriously, and most importantly, do not forget to laugh!

Jokes aside, above are just some of my earliest and most memorable moments I have with my wonderful brother – his infectious smile, his knock on heaven's door, and the beginning days of our friendship. However memorable those moments were, Mitchell's influence on my life truly started to take shape when I began high school. By that time, my entire personality and work ethic had been forged from my experiences with Mitchell, and I was just beginning to understand how. I met my high school sweetheart, because Mitchell taught me what to look for in a girl.

By the time I entered high school, all my peers knew I had a brother in a wheelchair. I never tried to hide the fact or felt embarrassed about it. Mitchell was always around, from sporting events to cookouts. Even if I wanted to hide the fact that my brother was different, there was no way on earth I could with the big red van my mom drove. My mom would drop me off at school or football practice in our goofy-looking red van, and heads would turn. This never bothered me, because I was used to people staring by now and had developed a very thick skin. Other than my best friend Mitchell, football was my passion in high school, and I made the decision to pursue it to the best of my God-given talents.

Football was hard, both physically and mentally. The August heat during two-a-days was unbearable, and the early morning workouts were grueling. Nevertheless, I had to fight through the sweat and pain in order to achieve my goal of playing college football. One thing I never lacked was internal motivation to get me through the toughest of times. What I came to realize is the motivation came from Mitchell. Either being bound to his bed or his wheelchair, one thing Mitchell never lacked was a smile. I remember thinking about this all the time. Out of all the people in the world who could be angry or just plain sad all the time, Mitchell had the best excuse of them all. I would especially remember this when I was too tired to keep going and just wanted to quit. But, how could I quit? I would never know true pain or exhaustion the way Mitchell does. This was my mantra. I would not give in to my own physical and mental weaknesses, so I pushed through the pain and always came out alive. You may call it giving one hundred and ten percent. I call it Mitchell's day-to-day struggle to breathe. I call it Mitchell's tireless seizure episodes that leave him exhausted, but unable to sleep. I call it motivation by Mitchell.

That motivation and uncompromising attitude are what led me to find my wife, Sarah. I have seen time and time again the way people react when they see Mitchell. They are typically nervous, and they do not know what to say and ignore him all together. While Mitchell does not understand or care about the way people treat him, it matters to me and my entire family. Even just a nod or a simple hello will do. Most people do neither, so it is refreshing when you come across a person who treats Mitchell like a human being. Sarah did more. She treated him like a brother.

Sarah and I met at church youth group. It was not long after we started dating that Sarah met Mitchell for the first time. She did not shy away, but quite the opposite. When she said hi to Mitchell, she leaned in and touched his hand. This is not the norm. People are typically afraid they are going to somehow catch what Mitchell has, so they get as far away as possible. However, in that moment, I saw a tender heart in the woman I knew then I would one day marry. Over the years, Sarah's bond with Mitchell has grown exponentially. Mitchell is no less my brother than he is hers. So, when Mitchell's caregiver of fifteen years retired, Sarah was the natural replacement. She now takes care of Mitchell on a regular basis, taking on the day-to-day tasks that can only be done out of love. Sarah knows how much I care for my brother, and she strives to do the same. I cannot thank Mitchell enough for showing me the qualities to look for in a girl.

When I graduated from high school, I was fortunate enough to go on to play NCAA Division II football at Ashland University in northeast Ohio. I attribute this achievement not to myself, but to the life lessons Mitchell engrained in me at a young age. Without taking what I learned from Mitchell and implementing it into my daily life, I never would have been able to do the things I wanted to do like play college football.

Being in Ashland was the first time I was away from Mitchell for any meaningful time. Because of my rigorous football and academic schedule, I was not able to make it home as often as I would have liked. I was not able to come home while Mitchell was in the hospital in the fall of 2011. I had to rely on Sarah to keep me updated on his progress or lack thereof. I am used to the daily thought of Mitchell dying, but when he is in the hospital, the emotions become all too real. The feelings of helplessness only grow with distance. If Mitchell did not pull through this time, I might not make it home to wish him farewell.

After being plagued by injuries, in December 2012, I decided to continue my education closer to home at Wright State University and leave football behind for good. Playing college football with some of the best athletes in the game was an amazing opportunity, but it was time to set my sights on a new goal. I always knew that I wanted to go to law school. Now it was just a matter of putting the work in to set myself up for success. I put my competitive drive and grinding personality to the task. I was now using the lessons I learned from Mitchell to pursue a new passion: my education and future career. Now that I was closer to home, my future with Sarah began to take shape as well.

Naturally, when Sarah and I got married in December 2014, I did not have to think for more than a second before deciding on my best man. It had to be the person who told me that Sarah was the one I was going to be with for the rest of my life. It had to be Mitchell. Now, technically, Mitchell never said yes when I asked him to be my best man. But, he did not say no either, so I took that as a yes. He also did not make a very good best man speech during the reception. At least, nobody could understand what he was saying. Nevertheless, it was a very special day for so many reasons.

From the time I moved back and got married, Mitchell was in and out of the hospital. He was never in the hospital for just one night. It was usually for two to three weeks. It seemed like his twisted frail body was finally getting the best of him. Each time he was in the hospital, my emotions would rush back. Constantly thinking Mitchell was going to die and thinking I would never see my brother's smile again were my prevailing thoughts. Those feelings never really go away. Those feelings just tend to rear their heads when times are tough. The only thing you can do is think of the happy memories and pray to God that he dies peacefully and without pain. The last thing Mitchell deserves is to be in any more pain. Death's grip has yet to be strong enough to take him away from us.

The reality of possibly losing Mitchell was the most real to me in September 2015. I remember these moments as if they were yesterday. I was working during the day in Vandalia, Ohio, and going to class at night. My mom would text me often, but when Mitchell is in the hospital and she calls, I usually hesitate to answer. I do not want to hear the news I have been dreading my entire life. I was sitting at my desk when I got the call. I answered, and I could tell my mom was crying. I immediately thought the worst. Through the tears she finally said, "You need to come to the hospital; the doctor said Mitchell probably won't make it through the night." My heart sank into my stomach, and I began to feel queasy. I grabbed my stuff, told my boss I had to go, and I ran out the door. The drive from Vandalia to the Children's Hospital in Columbus is a modest hour drive. Not that day. I called Sarah to break the news. The tears in my voice said it all as I struggled to tell her what my mom had told me moments before.

I walked into the hospital room, not too different from when I was a child. Mitchell was lying in the bed attached to a countless number of tubes and machines. His oxygen was so low he had no pigment in his skin, and his lips were a bluish purple. He was pale and cold. I thought to myself, "I have been here before." I have watched my brother struggle for decades, and he was finally going to run and dance in heaven I thought. There is a kind of peace that accompanies the sadness in thoughts like that. The room slowly filled with family as we talked about many of the family memories you have read in this book. However, once again, Mitchell pulled through and came out the other end alive. He has tried to die so many times. I am beginning to think he likes the attention a bit too much.

Regardless of his hidden motives, that hospital visit changed Mitchell and our family. Mitchell now must be on oxygen 24/7, and we must monitor him very closely to make sure his oxygen saturation number does not get too low. After that visit, my parents were confronted with new realities such as a *Do Not Resuscitate (DNR)* and the meaning of *palliative care*. Mitchell has since been in the hospital for things as small as a common cold, which for him can be deadly. Due to the way Mitchell's body is twisted, he has diminished lung capacity. Every breath is harder than the last, but he keeps on chugging along with a smile on his face.

I am especially thankful that Mitchell made it through this hospital stay, because if he had not, he would have never met my son, Lincoln. When Sarah and I were dating, we talked about getting married, buying our first home, law school, and having children. We never knew if our children would get the opportunity to meet Mitchell and build memories. In the fall of 2016, Sarah and I found out we were expecting our first baby in May 2017. We were staying at my parents' home that week. We were on Mitchell-duty when Sarah found out. Mitchell knew our exciting secret before anyone else, as he is the best secret keeper. It thrilled both of us to know that Mitchell might get to meet our son.

When Lincoln was born and we made our way home for the first time, it was a priority for Mitchell to meet his newest nephew. My parents brought Mitchell over that evening, and we all took as many pictures as we could. We would prop Lincoln up in Mitchell's arms to get the best pictures. Lincoln now helps Sarah take care of Mitchell by patting on Mitchell's chest, wiping off his spit with a washcloth, giving him the gentlest hugs, and making him smile the same way I do. Lincoln and Mitchell have already become best buds, and Lincoln has even inherited Mitchell's infectious smile.

Mitchell's smile will not be the only thing that endures long after he enters the gates of heaven with his new body. Mitchell's legacy is greater than any amount of words can describe. Everybody who meets him changes for the better. His laugh inspires those who struggle with sadness, and his joy for life makes life worth living. I have learned so much from my baby brother over the years. I hope that I can teach my children the same way Mitchell has taught me. I cannot thank Mitchell enough for being the best friend anyone could ask for. He has blessed me with the skills to conquer any task that comes my way. He helped me find the woman of my dreams. And most importantly, he has taught me what it means to be alive.

Thank you Mitchell! I love you with all my heart, and I cannot wait to walk beside you in the warm glow of heaven's glory.

Mitchell's Memoir

BEFORE MITCHELL WAS BORN

Chapter 12
Preparing Mitchell's Dad

I was fourteen years old and at church camp that summer. My aunt invited me to go with my cousin, and I was thrilled. My family never attended church, so I did not understand the camp's religious connection at all. All I knew was children my age went to the wilderness and had fun. The camp leaders told us stories about this man named Jesus. The last night we sat around the campfire, and the camp leader asked if anyone wanted to accept Jesus into our lives. I raised my hand, we prayed, and something amazing happened.

Everyone who knew me before this moment would have told you I was good kid but undisciplined. My grades at school were Cs and Ds at best. I had failed third grade, and my teacher told my parents I was dumb. I finally learned to read the summer before sixth grade because I really wanted to read the Hardy Boys mysteries. I struggled with each page, but I was able to piece together the story using a dictionary. By seventh grade, I finally memorized the multiplication table. I had just stopped wetting the bed every night the year before. I remember being a happy young man, but for some reason learning and memorizing was difficult for me. I was blissfully ignorant.

The next morning after accepting Jesus, I woke up and the world was noticeably different. It was as if a fog lifted off my brain. I saw everything around me with incredible clarity. I instantly understood things that had escaped me before. With a new heightened sense, the world was brighter and more colorful. I looked up at the trees, and I saw their leaves in incredible detail. Of course, I saw leaves before, but not like this. There were millions of them, and they moved noisily with the breeze. The trees and each individual leaf glowed a golden color. I did not know what was happening.

A month later, I advanced to eighth grade at Chantilly High School in Northern Virginia. By this time, the golden glow had disappeared but not my new awareness. On the first day of my math class, as the teacher passed out our general math books, I told the teacher that I understood general math now and that I wanted to start algebra. She looked up my last year's grades and shook her head, making it clear that my D average would not let this happen. I lost that argument. However, I came up with a plan. I took the math book home and in less than two weeks, I completed every single question in the book. I reasoned that they could not keep me in general math if I did the entire year's work. I handed my teacher a one-inch thick binder of ruled paper filled with math problems. Soon, three teachers huddled together in the corner of the room. Every few moments they would take turns glancing my way. Next, the teacher from the algebra class next door walked over and led me to my new desk in algebra that morning.

That was the beginning of my wonderful high school years – innocent years filled with joy and discovery. Unbeknownst to me, my art teacher submitted a piece of art I made in class, and it won first place in some art show. The Monday after the show, she handed me a blue ribbon. I never had one of those before. In my physical education class, we did the presidential physical fitness measurements. I remember running the 600-yard dash with reckless abandon. The next day the track coach approached me to run track. It turned out I ran the fastest time in the school that year. In my choir class, I found my true passion, which I perfected in my backyard. We lived in an old secluded farmhouse on ninety acres of land. Our driveway was one hundred yards long. Behind our house was a large field, and every night I would walk out into the field, and I would sing for hours until a song's tone and syncopation was perfect. My eight brothers and sisters used to make fun of this spectacle. By my junior and senior year, my practice paid off; I was an all-state vocalist in Virginia. In my junior year, I remember all my teachers in Chantilly High School putting together a thousand dollars to buy me clothes. This was an incredible act of kindness. In that same year, my music teacher, Betty Davis, died of cancer, and she bequeathed me a thousand dollars a year for college. I loved my teachers at Chantilly High School, and I am extremely grateful for the love they showed me.

I left home during my sophomore year, and wonderful families invested in me while I finished out my high school days. Several families treated me like a son. I remember Steve Marcy, who was my age, driving out to our remote farmhouse to pick me up and take me to school events. I worked as a carpenter for Steve's dad during the summers and on breaks. The entire family – Alvin, Laura, Laura Lee, Steve and Grace – taught me how I was to model my approach to family. Steve, Laura, and Grace are my eternal siblings. They taught me service before self, and Carrie and I named our daughter, Grace, in honor of this family.

My junior year Lee, Carol, Clay, and Marla Cromley took me into their home – another great family to model. Their son Clay was my best friend in high school. Clay was brilliant and a great vocalist. He was like what I wanted to be. Carol, whom I affectionately call Mom-C, taught me a lot more than this book can hold. Mitchell's middle name is Lee in honor of this family. The last family I stayed with for a few months was the Gilberts. Again, I saw another family working together seamlessly in love. I remember they put together an amazing breakfast every morning. I copied this tradition to serve my family a great breakfast on Saturday mornings.

Reading between the lines, it is clear that my life before leaving home was less than the gold standard. I was the oldest of nine children, giving me advantages my other brothers and sisters did not have. I am thankful for my childhood and decided long before I can remember to leave behind the bad and carry forward only the good. This is akin to never keeping a record of wrongs. Life was tough for my parents, and *poor* is too rich a word to describe their lives. I would like to say this about my dad and mom whom I love unconditionally – out of all the people ever born, or yet to be born, God in his wisdom chose my dad and mom to be my earthly parents. For this reason my parents are perfect for me and worth every honor I give God himself. Amen!

I did not understand in those days why my salvation experience and change were this dramatic or why so many people invested their lives in me during my high school days. I was completely unaware of my unusual life at the time. Only now do I see the obvious. Simply. God had a work for me to do and these were the skills and experiences necessary for that work. I know today that my job on this planet was to lead my family and keep it all together during difficult times to protect God's purpose for Mitchell and the rest of my family. God showed me his love my entire life. I testify to his love because it was tangible and real. Therefore, I can proclaim to you that God loves you as much as he loves me. I have no hesitation in my spirit, and if I could look you in the eye, my message to you is this: Jesus wants a relationship with you! Not a casual relationship but a tangible heart-to-heart relationship. You need only to ask Jesus to fellowship with you just as I did around that campfire many years ago. I recommend that once you call on Jesus, talk to him about where you fall short of God's standards. Of course, he already knows this about you. You see, articulating your shortcomings helps you own what you have done wrong. This step not only begins to heal you, but it heals the one you have wronged. Final healing comes when you ask for forgiveness to restore the relationship. After you restore your relationship with God through Jesus, you can begin the lifelong process of replacing your old nature with God's nature. Using this model, you can begin to restore your earthly relationships as well.

After graduating from high school, I left for Averett College (now Averett University) in Danville, Virginia. It was a wonderful and carefree time! I learned much about myself and met my bride of now thirty-six years. I remember seeing Carrie one day, and I thought, "She is the one!" By this time in my life, I had stitched together my vision of the woman I was hoping to marry from examples I had seen in several families. I know my approach is not that romantic; nonetheless, I had a list of emotional, intellectual, and physical attributes for which I was looking. Stop laughing. It gets better. I had never dated anyone steady, because I did not want to waste the time or money on anyone that did not fit my model of a wife. After a few hall conversations and impromptu talks at some parties and events, I was convinced and asked Carrie out for dessert and coffee. She said yes! I remember that afterward a poor impression of Santa was handing out red Santa-rings. I gave

Carrie this ring pretending to propose in my mind. The next day I asked her to marry me. She said yes! Of course, I never recommended this approach with my children. Definitely not! However, Carrie and I had a date with destiny, and God was in the middle from the start. By next summer, we were married, and I finished my last year at Averett receiving my Bachelor of Science degree in Chemistry.

Shortly after graduating from college, I remember driving by an Air Force recruiter office in Danville, Virginia. Carrie had said to me on several occasions that she did not mind what I did for a living so long as it was not the military or being a pilot. I thought, "What are the chances of that happening?" Carrie's dad was a retired Air Force Chief Master Sergeant, and she did not want the transient lifestyle of the military. It was now six months after graduation, and I was having a difficult time getting a job. A career in chemistry really begins after more advanced degrees. I did not want to go back to school. I decided to poke my head in the recruiter's door. The next thing I knew I was set up for an entrance test. I took the test and when the scores came back, he said that I had scored in the ninety-eighth percentile for being a pilot. He suggested putting together a package to get a pilot spot. I said nonchalantly, we could try it. Sure enough I received orders for pilot training. I was shocked. I had never considered being a pilot, but the job sounded interesting. Now, I needed only to tell Carrie. Let us just say that you should never tell your wife certain things while she is holding a knife cutting chicken. Carrie used the knife as a pointing stick to remind me of her only request. After a lot of discussion, we both decided I should go for it. I remember getting on a plane for the first time to head to a program called the Flight Screening Program

Officer Trainee (FSPOT pronounced *fish-pot*). As I looked out the window of the airplane, I thought, "This is cool. I can do this for a living."

This was the beginning of my Air Force career. I began to fly B-52 missions in the spring of 1986 at Wurtsmith AFB. Taylor was one year old when I started flying bombers as a copilot. Grace joined the family a year before I upgraded to aircraft commander in 1988. When we first arrived, we bought a tiny home in Greenbush right on Lake Huron. Life was simple, and our family was just beginning to take shape when we found out Mitchell was on the way. We decided beforehand to sell our home and move on base in anticipation of getting routine orders to move to another location. I distinctly remember Carrie's first trimester. One night I had an extremely vivid and very troubling dream about our new son being profoundly handicapped. I told Carrie about my dream, which she quickly dismissed as any mother would do. However, I was convinced something was wrong with Mitchell and waited for his birth with mixed anticipation. The second Mitchell was born I felt relieved. I was glad I was wrong. Well, you already know the rest of the story.

Mitchell's Memoir

Chapter 13
Chosen To Be Mitchell's Mom

I grew up in a military family. My dad was in the Air Force. Although I was born in California, I never considered that my home. I was six months old when I moved from California, and I grew up at various Air Force bases, mostly in the southern states. Our last base before my dad retired was Andrews Air Force Base in Maryland. It was there that I met my Savior.

I was thirteen years old when we lived on Andrews Air Force Base. One Saturday morning a group of young teens about my age came to the front door to invite me to District Heights Baptist Church. Their ministry was a church bus ministry, so the invitation included a ride to church the next day. At that time, my family did not attend church, but they agreed that I could go. Sunday morning the bus came to pick me up, and I started my faith journey. I quickly became friends with the teens on the bus ministry and began to attend the youth group on Sunday evenings. It was not long before I joined the bus ministry team, traveling on Saturday mornings to invite others to attend church. I am still in touch with our youth leaders from that time, Barbara and Don Sturm. They both helped me develop a love for our Savior. I am grateful for the time they spent teaching and loving the youth group. Beverly was also part of the youth group, and we became good friends. Beverly and I stay in touch to this day. Approximately twelve years ago, I reconnected with two other friends from my youth group, Mary and Julie, who are sisters. It was Mary, Julie, and Beverly who came to my door that Saturday long ago. I am eternally thankful for their faithful bus ministry work.

It was at District Heights Baptist Church that I realized my need for a personal Savior. The exact date I do not remember, but I do remember the event. It was during a revival service when one week out of the year, we had services nightly from Sunday through Friday. The purpose was to encourage the church and to present the gospel to friends you invited. This evening the speaker was describing a tour through hell. He was a very dynamic speaker, using words that created vivid pictures in my mind. I remember his imagining walking through hell and describing those he met. He started with the most vile people, those you would expect to find in hell, carefully describing all kinds of criminals. Then, he moved to another section of hell. This section was full of nice people – the ones who did much for others, good people based on the world's standards. I was thinking to myself, why are these people there? It was as if the speaker heard my thoughts. He stated plainly that good works do not get you into heaven. It is only through the blood of Jesus Christ and His forgiveness of our sins that you can get to heaven. He went on to explain that no matter how much good each one of us does, it is not enough to make us good. Only through Christ can we ever be good enough. I realized he was talking about me. I had tried hard to be good. I was busy working in church doing good works for God, but I had missed the big picture. I knew I was a sinner in need of a Savior, a Savior who loved me so much He died on a cross for my sins, rose from the grave to defeat death, and reigns in heaven today with our God and Father. All I needed to do was call on Jesus' name, ask him to forgive me, and He became my Savior. Simple enough! During the altar call that evening, I chose Jesus – a decision that changed my life forever. The Scripture I claimed that moment was "For it is by grace you have been saved through faith, and this is and not from yourselves, it is the gift of God—not by works so that no one can boast" (Ephesians 2:8-9).

I went home excited that evening to tell my parents about my decision. My dad and mom had made similar decisions years ago as children. However, when they moved away from home, they did not attend church regularly. After that evening, this all changed! My parents felt terrible for not being part of my life-altering night. They began attending church with me the next evening. My dad and mom have been faithful and have grown in their faith since that day. We enjoyed attending church together as a family.

When I was almost sixteen years old, my dad retired, and we moved to Charlottesville, Virginia. Both of my parents had grown up in Dillwyn, a small town in Virginia. They wanted to retire close to their families, and I was very excited to do the same. Because I grew up an only child, I longed for that bigger family feel. We were now only a short thirty-minute drive from my many aunts, uncles, cousins, and grandparents. I loved it! My mom's sister lived in Charlottesville as well. Therefore, I became close to my Aunt Sallie and Uncle Jimmy Dean and their only child, Sarah Dean Litten. Although Sarah is my cousin, we are more like sisters and remain a part of each other's daily life despite the fact she lives six hours away. During high school, I made many trips to hang out with my cousins, some days skipping school for the experience. I have too many cousins to name them all. I love each one of them on both sides of my family. I am blessed to have a large extended family, and I know each one is only a phone call away.

When we moved to Charlottesville, we started attending the same church as Jimmy, Sallie, and Sarah. Laurel Hill Baptist

Church would become my church family. My Uncle Jimmy was my Sunday school teacher, and I went to church camp each summer with my friends. Laurel Hill Baptist Church was a very traditional Baptist church, opening its doors every Sunday morning, Sunday night, and Wednesday night. We wore choir robes, held hymnbooks, and had a church piano and organ. I met my high school best friends Mary, Terry, and Becky; and Craig and I were married at Laurel Hill Baptist church. I loved my church!

After graduating from Albemarle High School in 1981, I attended Averett College in Danville, Virginia, now Averett University. Averett seemed so far from home then, but it was only two hours away. My friend, Mary, also went with me to college, and we were roommates our first year. I thought of studying nursing but quickly changed to special education after looking at the class selection list. I have always had a love for people whom God designs differently. I wanted to help teach the special needs individuals and their parents to help them reach their potential. One of my favorite college memories is helping coordinate and work in vacation Bible school for the adult mentally challenged. I just loved the women with whom I worked. Their smiles and joy were contagious.

During my first semester at Averett, I met Craig Minor. He was a junior, and I was a freshman. I say it was "love at first sight". We did not date very long before we were engaged that winter. We married that next summer. We lived in Danville for Craig to finish his senior year. The following year, we moved to Charlottesville to wait for Craig to leave for Air Force basic training. We attended Laurel Hill Baptist Church while we lived in Charlottesville.

In October 1984, we moved to Columbus Air Force Base in Columbus, Mississippi, where Craig began pilot training. While there, we welcomed our oldest son, Taylor Minor. We did not attend church regularly that year. I went occasionally to the base chapel. Our first real assignment came after pilot training in 1986. Craig's assignment was to Wurtsmith Air Force Base in Oscoda, Michigan, to fly B-52Gs. We went from the extreme hot south to the extreme cold north. We loved our time in Michigan. Our first Sunday we visited Oscoda Baptist Church and knew right away it was a great fit for us, because it was a good mix of military and non-military families. Both Craig and I grew spiritually in our new church, making lifelong friends along the way while creating great memories. Grace joined our family in February 1987. By the summer of 1989, Craig and I settled into a routine with our friends and our church. Life was simple. Life was good. Little did I know what God had in store for us on that wonderful day, October 6, 1989.

I leave you with two of my favorite verses. "Praise be to the God and Father of our Lord Jesus Christ, the Father of compassion and the God of all comfort, who comforts us in all our troubles, so that we can comfort those in any trouble with the comfort we ourselves receive from God" (2 Corinthians 1:3-7), and "He will cover you with his feathers, and under his wings you will find refuge: his faithfulness will be your shield and rampart"(Psalms 91:4).

Chapter 14
Poison in the Wells...In the Womb

During a child's development in the womb, the potential for birth defects from even small amounts of chemicals is a well-known danger. The first trimester is especially critical. Like most moms, Carrie was careful not to take any over the counter drugs and consumed no caffeine or alcohol. Of course, doctors would not prescribe any medications to Carrie back then. During our time at Wurtsmith AFB, Carrie and I do not recall anyone telling us the groundwater was contaminated. Had we known, Carrie would not have drunk the well water. Knowing what we know today and because Mitchell's handicaps began in the womb, the story of the cause begs consideration. Without it, *Mitchell's Memoir* would seem incomplete. This chapter begins twelve years before our son Mitchell was born and ends with a drink of water.

While living on Wurtsmith AFB, Michigan, something happened in the first trimester of Carrie's pregnancy. As God was knitting Mitchell's brain together in Carrie's womb, a foreign substance crossed the placenta. Time would reveal the profound damage to Mitchell's brain. In the early years, Air Force doctors would suggest the cause of Mitchell's microcephaly (small head) and profound handicaps was a virus. For years, we accepted this possibility, providing us with some amount of closure as our heads were down fighting for stability. However, recent revelations point to chemical poisoning as the more sinister cause.

Carrie and I did not learn of this groundwater contamination until part-way through writing *Mitchell's*

Memoir. We sat stunned in front of the television as the national news began to report on a Department of Defense letter about significant groundwater contamination on 126 military bases across the United States. Wurtsmith AFB was on the list where the only source of drinking water was from the many wells scattered across its seven-square-mile landscape. After reading the U.S. Geological Survey's (USGS) 1983 and 1986 reports on the groundwater contamination at Wurtsmith AFB, the cause of Mitchell's profound handicaps began to crush our hearts.

Next, we read the Agency for Toxic Substances and Disease Registry (ATSDR) "Public Health Assessment for Wurtsmith AFB" report published in 2001. This report was published eight years after local citizens complained about the groundwater contamination left behind after Wurtsmith AFB closed its doors June 30, 1993; three years before, we were quickly moved by the Air Force to reach critical medical support for Mitchell in Ohio. It took 23 years after the groundwater contamination was first discovered in the faucets of base housing residents before its impact to veterans and their families was first assessed. The next health assessment came 17 years later on July 27, 2018. This assessment, called a reevaluation, arrived part-way through writing this chapter, recognizing for the first time the possibility of birth defects at Wurtsmith AFB from short-term chemical exposures in the first trimester of pregnancy. What follows is an introduction to the groundwater contamination at Wurtsmith AFB when it first came into view and then unfolded around our lives. Because the contamination issue continues to express itself in the lives of our nation's warriors and their families, this is not the end of the story, but rather only the beginning of Mitchell's story and the life of his veteran family left to pick up the pieces and fight for their lives.

The base began military operations in 1923 as Camp Skeel, a training area for overseas combat fighting with a gunnery range and landing field and officially became Wurtsmith AFB in 1953. Over the years, the base was an airfield accommodating many different types of aircraft to include a weapons storage area. B-52s arrived at Wurtsmith in May 1961, which I began to fly in the spring of 1986. During our time in Oscoda, the base was the dominant industry situated near the west shore of Lake Huron, less than 170 miles north of Detroit. Roughly, 8000 civilians and military lived and worked on Wurtsmith AFB during our tenure. The dominant base landscape is sandy soil, roughly eighty feet above the level of Lake Huron, with beautiful waterways and lakes forming its borders. It was clear from above that fresh water was the area's richest asset. As a B-52 pilot, I routinely flew over the Wurtsmith AFB area marveling at its beauty as the sun's reflection sparkled off the region's freshwater surfaces. We did not know that lurking beneath the surface were chemical contaminates insidiously altering this pristine freshwater landscape and the people who occupied this small patch of federal land.

Our daughter, Grace, was born at the Wurtsmith AFB hospital. When Carrie was pregnant with Grace, we lived far north of the base in Greenbush Township. We owned a small home on the shore of Lake Huron. Before Mitchell was born, and during Carrie's first trimester, we sold our house and moved into Wurtsmith AFB housing. We made the move because our two-bedroom home was too small for three children and because a mandatory career move to another military Air Force base was likely a year away. Even before moving on base, Carrie spent most of her days visiting a friend at her home and me near the alert facility on base. The base was the center of all our daily activities. Carrie's exposure to contaminated water crisscrossed the base from the hospital, recreational buildings near the alert facility, shopping areas, and base housing.

Today, Wurtsmith AFB has fifty-eight known chemical contamination sites. Some contamination sites are more significant, resulting in large groundwater plumes in the space between the top soil and roughly 65 feet below the surface where clay creates a nearly impermeable barrier. Think of a groundwater plume as an underground contamination ballooning or expanding outward and downward as groundwater naturally carries the contamination along. It was not until 1977 that any chemical contamination of the groundwater became an unavoidable issue at Wurtsmith AFB. After complaints that the tap water smelled and tasted bad, the base civil engineering group tested the water. Test results confirmed chemicals were pouring out of the base housing faucets. The offending wells were taken off-line. By October 1977, investigators discovered the source was a leaking 500-gallon underground storage tank full of a chemical used to degrease engine parts next to Building 43. The tank was in the ground from 1962 to 1977. When investigators dug up the tank, they discovered a leak near the filler pipe. When the tank began to leak is unknown. Once the tank was full, reports state that the contents of the tank were disposed of in an approved manner. However, there are no surviving records of when the tank was emptied after it was thought to be full. Investigators would estimate that 5000 gallons of used engine degreaser went into the tank while in service. Because the leak was somewhere before the filler pipe (meaning the leak was somewhere near the top of the tank before the filler pipe), it is not hard to imagine airman pouring used degreaser chemicals that would leak directly into the soil after filling the tank up to the level of the leak. Unless the filler pipe was overflowing, there would be no indication that the tank was full. According to the USGS report, there were too many unknowns for investigators to estimate the amount of used degreaser entering the groundwater. In the beginning, the Building 43 underground storage tank leak was known as the "Building 43 Plume". Building 43 was the Jet Engine Repair Shop at Wurtsmith AFB. After the base closed in 1993, this contamination plume was renamed the "Arrow Street Plume". Eventually, the site simply became SS-21. The chemical content of the Building 43 tank was trichloroethylene (TCE) loaded with the remnants of other contaminants from degreasing aircraft and equipment parts. Once the contents of the tank hit the subsoil's groundwater, the chemicals stratified where the more dense chemicals (denser than water) descended deeper into the aquifer than the less dense chemicals. Over time, decomposition of the chemicals produced new chemicals.

The base immediately stopped using the water from the wells spoiled by the Building 43 Plume. Five months later, Civil Engineering would use a couple of the decommissioned wells to try to purge the TCE from the aquifer. These wells were not located near the tank. For this reason, the purging process did not significantly begin until roughly seven months after digging three new purging wells near the location of the leak. By August 1979, the base would add three more purging wells around the same location, bringing the total to six. The contaminated purge water went to the base's wastewater treatment plant and after treatment to a seepage lagoon.

Sometime after the first purging began in March 1977, the construction of two aeration reservoirs would begin to remove some of the TCE present before sending the water to the waste treatment plant. In the fall of 1979, Civil Engineering added carbon filtration after the aeration reservoirs to remove the remaining TCE before sending the water to the waste treatment plant. Unfortunately, the first two-and-a-half years of pulling TCE and other contaminants out of the groundwater resulted in transferring an untold amount of TCE back into the groundwater at the seepage lagoon. By November 1981, the USGS estimates the removal of 580 gallons of TCE from the groundwater near Building 43. By June 1985, a year before we moved to the area, the USGS claims to have removed another 320 gallons. This and other TCE plumes remain above safe drinking levels, and purging continues to this day.

Because of the Building 43 underground storage tank leak, broader testing of all the base water sources led to the discovery of more groundwater contamination plumes. USGS's reporting ended in 1985. While the USGS was finishing its second and final water resource investigation, Wurtsmith AFB officials took the lead on the contamination issue by initiating an official Installation Restoration Program (IRP) in October 1984. IRP is an Air Force wide program to identify, characterize, and remediate past environmental contamination on installations. By April 1985, Wurtsmith IRP officials published their first administrative report after conducting a base-wide records search. The records search focused on collecting past waste handling records to determine disposal practices and included interviews with past and present base employees. Problem Identification and Records Search was the first phase of the four-phase program. The other phases were Problem Confirmation and Quantification, Technology Development, and Corrective Action. That same year, USGS published its final water contamination report. Building on the 1985 results of the USGS water reports and the IRP records search report, the IRP officials identified 53 potential contamination sites: 7 leaking underground storage tanks, 9 landfills, 2 fire-training areas, 29 spill sites, 4 surface impoundment areas, and 2 sludge drying areas. This is roughly all base officials knew about the contamination problem in 1986. After reading the official contamination and health reports from 1983 to present, it is clear that officials were only beginning to understand the depth and scope of the base-wide contamination problem when we arrived in the spring of 1986. The ultimate goal of remediation or correctives was a long way off. The story of the Benzene Plume is a good example of how little base officials knew when we arrived.

The USGS discovered the Benzene Plume in 1979, which led investigators to suspect the base Petroleum, Oil and Lubricant (POL) Bulk Storage Area. The POL storage area stored jet fuel, heating oil, gasoline, diesel, and deicer. The storage area had aboveground storage tanks (AST) and underground storage tanks (UST). Over time, other nearby tanks were considered part of the POL storage area because of their proximity to each other, the shared portion of the aquifer, and the leading contamination from the overall area was JP-4. As defined, the storage area was comprised of the following:

- 1.26-million-gallon jet fuel AST
- 568,000-gallon jet fuel AST
- 210,000-gallon heating fuel AST
- 315,000-gallon heating fuel AST

- 2,000-gallon military operational gasoline (MOGAS)
- 2,000-gallon waste heating oil recovery UST
- 10,000-gallon diesel fuel tank UST
- 12,000-gallon gasoline tank UST
- 550-gallon diesel tank UST

After laboratory testing in 1979, it was determined that the Benzene Plume was from jet fuel. The military jet fuel at Wurtsmith AFB was JP-4, which is half kerosene and half gasoline. JP-4 was the primary military jet fuel for the Air Force from 1951 to 1995. According to early USGS, Wurtsmith AFB water contamination reports, Benzene is only 1-2 percent of the chemical composition of JP-4. This estimate is likely high as material data sheets list Benzene as only 0.50 percent of JP-4. To put this in perspective, finding a gallon of Benzene underground means that roughly 200 gallons of jet fuel is the actual amount of the underground contaminate. Investigators decided in 1983 that the cause of the JP-4 in the groundwater was from a spill and not from a leaking tank. At the time, Wurtsmith AFB did not implement the purging schema suggested by the USGS.

By 1985, the Benzene Plume was somewhat larger and had shifted northward. This time, JP-4 was floating on the surface of the water table near the bulk-fuel storage area. This was a new development that investigators had not seen up until this time. The presence of jet fuel was not in question because it looked and smelled like JP-4. Tests confirmed the obvious. Again, investigators decided the fuel was not from a leak of a storage tank or the Harrisville pipeline leading to the tanks. Investigators eliminated the pipeline as the source of the leak after digging up and inspecting the section of pipe near where the JP-4 floated on the aquifer. Again, USGS investigators decided the jet fuel was from a surface spill and not a leaking tank in the bulk-fuel storage area. In 1986, USGS investigators again recommended a modified purge plan, and Wurtsmith AFB did NOT implement the plan.

It was not until six years later, in 1992, that base officials would discover a leak in the 1.26-million-gallon JP-4 AST. This led to the removal of the tank by the summer of the same year and the addition of a Benzene pump and treatment system shortly thereafter. It would take thirteen years for investigators to discover this leaking tank after finding Benzene in the aquifer in 1979. How long the JP-4 tank was leaking before this time is unknown. How much went into the groundwater is also unknown. Two years earlier in May 1990, base officials had already discovered and removed two other leaking tanks in the POL area: The 2,000-gallon waste oil recovery UST and diesel fuel UST. When and how long these tanks leaked is also unknown.

Shortly before Carrie and I arrived at Wurtsmith AFB base, officials did not know of any active leaking storage tanks. By 1990 when the Air Force moved our family from Wurtsmith AFB to access better medical facilities for our newborn handicapped son, base officials identified seven leaking USTs and would discover a leaking AST a short two years later. The removal of the leaking tanks took place shortly before and after the base closure activities, which officially started in July 1991. Wurtsmith AFB closed its doors two years later in June 1993. Shortly after the base closed, a Final Environmental Impact Statement depicted an IRP site map of Wurtsmith AFB. The map shows the Arrow Street Plume and POL Storage Area Plumes discussed above. In addition, the map depicts the

Mission Street Plume, Operational Apron Plume, Inactive Weapon Storage Area Plume, Pierce's Point Plume, Northern Landfill Plume, and Fire Area Training Plume. Contamination plumes cover roughly one-third of the base public working and living area.

The above survey of the contamination at Wurtsmith AFB is brief, but it shows how pervasive the contamination problem was then and is today. Based on the record, Carrie and I arrived on the scene precisely when the severity of the problem first came into view in 1986, and we moved from Michigan precisely when base officials began to take actions to remove leaking tanks in 1990. The record shows very little activity between these dates. In fact, all Wurtsmith specific contamination assessment and health reports through today (there are many) reference many past authoritative reports and records before 1986 and after 1990. The absence of reports during our time at Wurtsmith is conspicuous at the least and is likely the time when base officials were assessing the scope of the contamination before beginning any real action. According to the *Oscoda Press*, a few months after we moved to Ohio, Wurtsmith began providing drinking water to base residents affected by water contamination. A September 1993 Final Environmental Impact Statement writes how the Air Force distributed drinking water to affected residences until they were connected to the Oscoda municipal water supply by the end of 1992. The base officially closed in 1993, and its remaining occupants were no longer drinking the water from its wells.

The real issue, however, is whether groundwater contamination made its way to the kitchen faucets and drinking fountains on base. Did Carrie and the residents and workers at Wurtsmith drink poisoned water? After reading contamination and health reports from 1983 to today, the answer is undoubtedly yes. Veterans and their family and visiting friends were drinking contaminated water from sometime before the contamination was discovered in 1977 until the well water was replaced by Oscoda's municipal water supply.

The next issue is whether enough contaminate was present long enough to harm the civilians, warriors, and families living and serving on base. Before 1977 the evidence is clear: TCE and other contaminates in the tap water exceeded safe levels and caused harm. After removing the Building 43 leaking 500-gallon used degreaser tank, shutting off the more severely impacted wells, and installing new purging wells, the contamination reaching the kitchen faucet was considered below a calculated minimum risk level. It is important to consider that the minimum risk level did not consider children in the womb. Veterans and their family and guests were continuing to drink water with TCE until the base closed. The TCE contamination, however, is only part of the larger contamination story. Other volatile contaminates were leaking from eight other tanks storing hazardous chemicals unknown to base officials at the time. No doubt, the groundwater was transporting the hazardous contents of these leaking tanks in the aquifer long before their removal in the early 1990s.

Past reports do not state whether water testing was continuous or frequent enough from October 1977 through June 1993 to account for known and unknown chemicals transiting a dynamic and ever-changing aquifer. The water below the surface was transient, moving roughly 5 to 10 inches a day to the closest body of surface water. In some areas, the movement of the aquifer was more than 12 inches a day. To the northeast was Van Etten Lake and to the south was the Au

Sable River. Eventually, all water and its contents made its way to Lake Huron. The introduction of purging wells at various depths in the aquifer partially changed this normal flow of groundwater, which transported contaminates underground in less predictable directions. In addition, the water table below would rise and fall roughly three feet a year depending on the rainy and dry seasons. Chemicals entering the aquifer would stratify, as the less dense constituents of a chemical mixture would move up higher in the aquifer. For example, Benzene is less dense than water and would migrate and pool underground near the top of the aquifer. Of course, this means denser chemicals would descend deeper. To complicate matters further, chemicals would react with the soil and other chemicals to form different chemicals. Some of these new chemicals were hazardous and others benign. Chemicals would also cling to the sand and rocks below while some of the chemical would move with the water. Purging wells could not pull much of the chemicals clinging to the subterranean surfaces of gravel, sand, and dirt. Add to this that the depth of the wells was different, and you begin to understand that the aquifer, extending to roughly 65 feet below the surface, was a dynamic and ever changing environment, where the concentration of chemicals from tank leaks or random spills could rise and fall in concentration as they passed by the screens of the drinking wells. For these reasons and more, making absolute determinations as to the amount and length of human exposures to chemical contaminates is likely not statistically valid.

In addition, past reports do not state that testing was so comprehensive as to test for every hazardous chemical present in the water. Early USGS reports would write about testing along a base/neutral priority pollutant analytical scheme. Think of this as testing for some subset of chemicals. Therefore, Benzene led to the discovery of JP-4 in the soil when Benzene is only a fractional component of JP-4. One look at the complex chemical mixture of JP-4, and you realize that there are many more chemicals trapped and moving about the aquifer than any testing sought to reveal. In general, the focus of past testing was to detect volatile chemicals in the groundwater in order to determine the type and source of the contamination and not necessarily to isolate each chemical that could cause health problems. For example, firefighting foams (PFOS – Perfluorooctanesulfonic acid and PFOA – Perfluorooctanoic acid) used to put out fires are not volatile chemicals. The military began use of this chemical in the early 1970s. Wurtsmith AFB water contamination reports in the 1980s did not seriously consider firefighting foams when these chemicals were clearly present in the groundwater. The health impact of this class of nonvolatile chemicals is only now making headlines as the complete story of the scope of contamination and its human toll are still being written.

The July 27, 2018, ATSDR report is the most recent Wurtsmith AFB reevaluation of the human impact of volatile chemical exposure, which now recognizes that pregnant women were susceptible to harmful TCE exposure to "include decreased body weight, liver and kidney defects, and neurological, immunological, reproductive, and developmental defects." The report adds that previous "studies of women living in areas where the drinking water was contaminated with TCE, as well as other VOCs [Volatile Organic Compounds], have suggested an increased risk of several types of birth defects."

On September 28, 2018, Congressman Dan Kildee, representing the fifth district of Michigan, introduced to the House of Representatives bill H.R. 6994. The bill was sent to the Committee on Veterans' Affairs for review. The bill seeks "to amend title 38, United States Code, to furnish hospital care and medical services to veterans, members of the reserve components of the Armed Forces, and dependents who were stationed at Wurtsmith Air Force Base in Oscoda, Michigan, and were exposed to volatile organic compounds, to provide for a presumption of service connection for those veterans and members of the reserve components, and for other purposes." The bill recognizes those "in utero while the mother of such family member resided at such location during such period and was exposed to such a substance...."

As Carrie and I step back and look at the past groundwater chemical contamination at Wurtsmith, we are saddened. We understand now that more likely than not Mitchell's handicaps are a result of the Wurtsmith AFB groundwater contaminations. Our family's story begins when Mitchell was born, October 6, 1989, and the doctor first noticed he had a slightly smaller head than normal. It was another six months before doctors knew for sure something was wrong. In the end Mitchell's diagnosis became microcephaly (small head) because his head and brain were growing slower than his body, causing his now obvious developmental delays. Mitchell's initial diagnosis was only the beginning of our family's journey that would span nearly three decades.

At the beginning, a doctor said Mitchell would not live past five. When Mitchell was six years old, doctors suggested Mitchell would not live to be a teenager. After Mitchell's thirteenth birthday, the doctors stopped guessing. Mitchell is fast approaching thirty and lives at home. Today, Mitchell's complete diagnosis is microcephaly, infantile cerebral palsy, spastic quadriplegic cerebral palsy, scoliosis associated with his condition, generalized convulsive epilepsy with intractable epilepsy (Lennox-Gastaut syndrome), and respiratory insufficiency.

Clearly the contamination story at Wurtsmith AFB is part of a larger story affecting military families across decades. Our family now realizes that the frontline of the Cold War was military installations like Wurtsmith AFB. Like all wars, there is a loss of blood and treasure. During the Cold War, it was the civilian, the soldier, and their families working and living on military installations that were in harm's way on the battlefield. History will likely record that the groundwater chemical contamination on military installations harmed our veterans like Agent Orange in Vietnam and the Burn Pits in Iraq. Unlike the chemical contamination of veterans on foreign soil, the groundwater contaminations at home unfortunately impacted the warfighter's families and the surrounding communities. American civilians were unknowingly on a battlefield, becoming conscripts in a Cold War. Our nation has a duty to address this issue with the same veracity expected by our young men and women on the battlefield. Too often our country owns an issue of this magnitude only after the affected generations are nearly gone. Here we are, approaching thirty years since the end of the Cold War with only studies and reports to show for it. If chemical contamination of this magnitude happened on the land of an American company, our people's pursuit for justice and restitution would be veracious. At a minimum, the Cold War chemical contamination of veterans and their families should challenge and expand our nation's calculus when tallying the costs of freedom. From our perspective, Mitchell paid the ultimate price for the freedoms our great country enjoys today.

Sources

United States Geological Survey (USGS), 1983. Ground-Water Contamination at Wurtsmith Air Force Base, Report 83-4002.

United States Geological Survey (USGS), 1986. Assessment of Groundwater Contamination at Wurtsmith Air Force Base, Report 86-4188.

Montgomery Watson, 1993. Final Environmental Impact Statement, Disposal and Reuse of Wurtsmith Air Force Base, Michigan. September.

US Department of Health and Human Services, 2001. Public Health Assessment Wurtsmith Air Force Base, Michigan. April.

Air Force Real Property Agency (AFRPA), 2004. First Five-Year Review Report for Installation Restoration Program Sites at Wurtsmith Air Force Base, Michigan. September.

US Department of Health and Human Services, 2015. Evaluation of Drinking Water near Wurtsmith Air Force Base, Michigan. September.

US Department of Health and Human Services, 2018. Re-evaluation of Past Exposures to VOC Contaminants in Drinking Water Former Wurtsmith Air force Base, Michigan. July.

House of Representatives Bill H.R 6994, 2018, Care for Veterans Act of 2018, 115th CONGRESS 2d Session. September

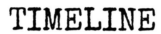

TIMELINE

A Ministry is Born

(January 1989 – June 1990)

1989

Oct 6   Mitchell Born @ Wurtsmith AFB

1990

May 14   Microcephaly Diagnosis

Jun   Orders to Wright Patterson AFB

A Time of Transition

(July 1990 – October 1995)

1990

Aug   Arrive Wright Patterson AFB; Start 4Oaks;

Aug   Start Attending Grand Heights Baptist Church

Oct 6   Mitchell's 1st Birthday

1991

Apr   Mitchell's Seizures begin

–   Mitchell's First Wheelchair

Oct 6   Mitchell's 2nd Birthday

Nov   Moved on Wright Patterson AFB on Longstreet Lane

1992

Jun   Move to Cedarville; 3653 Route 42 East

Sep   Grace Starts Kindergarten

Oct   Mitchell's 3rd Birthday

Nov 29   Levi is born

1993

—   Surgery #1 of 4: Mitchell's G-Tube &
           Fundoplication; Pneumonia 2x before

Oct 6   Mitchell's 4th Birthday

1994

Oct 6   Mitchell's 5th Birthday

1995

Oct   Craig Leaves Air Force

Oct   Mitchell's 6th Birthday

Years of Adversity
(November 1995 – December 2000)

1995

Sep   Mitchell starts Kindergarten

1996

Winter   Surgery #2 of 4: Mitchell's First Hip Surgery;
           Code Blue!

Oct 6   Mitchell's 7th Birthday

1997

Oct 6   Mitchell's 8th Birthday

1998

Oct 6   Mitchell's 9th Birthday

1999

Fall   Surgery #3 of 4: Mitchell's Back Surgery:
           Nationwide Columbus Hospital

–	Financial crisis, auction off most household Items
Oct	Mitchell's 10th Birthday
Dec	Christmas with the Baum's – Big Snow Storm Heading Home

2000

Jun	Craig Starts Full-time Work @ Cedarville University
Oct	Mitchell's 11th Birthday
Dec	First Official Family Vacation: Disney in Florida

Finding Peace in the Storm
(January 2001 – Present)

2001

Mar	Mitchell put on I/O Waiver
–	Hospitalized: Start Ketogenic Diet
Aug	Pat starts working for Mitchell
Sep	Surgery #4 of 4: Mitchell's Hip Surgery; Leg Fractures; Chemical Pancreatitis
Oct	Mitchell's 12th Birthday: I'm Still Here Party!!

2002

May	Mitchell's Make-A-Wish: Big screen TV
–	Green Van gift: Church Benevolence Gift
Aug	Craig Starts Wright State University MBA
Oct	Mitchell's 13th Birthday
Fall	Carrie starts working @ Cedarville University

2003

May	Taylor Graduates from Cedarville HS
Summer	Taylor Begins Marines
–	Mitchell's Massive Seizure-Tried to take off Ketogenic diet
Oct 6	Mitchell's 14th Birthday

2004

Jan	Taylor Leaves for Iraq
Oct 6	Mitchell's 15th Birthday
Sep	Taylor Returns from Iraq
Nov 20	Craig Graduates From Wright State University

2005

May	Grace Graduates from Cedarville HS
Jun	Hospitalized: Respiratory Pneumonia – Dayton Children's Hospital
Jul	Grace meets Harry & Echo VanderWal
Aug 6	Taylor and Amanda Wedding
Sep	Craig Leaves Cedarville University
Oct	Craig Starts Work @ Ryan Homes
Oct	Family Attends Faircreek Church
Oct	Mitchell's 16th Birthday

2006

Jan 26	Craig Begins Reserve Air Force
Mar	Grace Begins Full Time as Nanny for Harry and Echo VanderWal
Apr	Family Moves Away from Cedarville and Sold House
Apr	Family Moves to Beavercreek and Bought New Ryan Home

Aug	Grace Travels to Swaziland with H&E – 1st TLC Mission Trip
–	Mitchell Hospitalized for Respiratory: Dayton Children's Hospital
Oct 6	Mitchell's 17th Birthday
–	Grace returns from Swaziland – 1st TLC Mission Trip

2007

Mar	Grace Leaves for Swaziland – 2nd TLC Mission Trip
May	Craig Leaves Ryan Homes
May	Craig Deploys to Iraq for 5 months
May	Grace Returns from Swaziland – 2nd TLC Mission Trip
Oct 6	Mitchell's 18th Birthday – Big party at Faircreek

2008

Feb	Hospitalized: Mitchell's Acute Colitis: Dayton Children's Hospital
May	Scott & Grace Wedding
Oct 6	Mitchell's 19th Birthday

2009

Summer	Taylor's Voluntary Honorable Discharge from the Marines
Aug	Craig Starts Capital University Law School
Oct 6	Mitchell's 20th Birthday

2010
Aug	Moved to Bellbrook
Oct 6	Mitchell's 21st Birthday

2011
May	Levi Graduates from Bellbrook HS
Aug	Moved to Cedarville – 2nd
Oct	Hospitalized: Mitchell's Pneumonia: Dayton Children's Hospital
Oct	Mitchell's 22nd Birthday

2012
May	Out Patient: Mitchell's Pilonidal Cyst
Oct 6	Mitchell's 23rd Birthday

2013
May	Craig Graduates from Capital University Law School
Oct 6	Mitchell's 24th Birthday
Oct 16	Carrie's Knee Surgery – Result of Picking up Mitchell

2014
Jan	Craig Leaves for Pentagon Tour
Apr	Idea to write Mitchell's Memoirs
Feb	Grace and Scott move to Cedarville
Jun	Hospitalized: Mitchell's Pneumonia: ICU
Sep 7-11	Hospitalized: Mitchell's Respiratory Virus: ICU
Sep	Craig Returns From Pentagon Tour
Oct 6	Mitchell's 25th Birthday
Dec 13	Levi and Sarah Wedding

2015

Jul	Hospitalized: Mitchell's cold: ICU for a week
Oct 6	Mitchell's 26th Birthday

2016

Apr	Hospitalized: Mitchell's cold: ICU for a week
Aug	Levi starts Dayton University Law School
Sep 1	Craig Retires from United States Air Force
Sep 6	Craig starts Begins work at MTSI
Oct 6	Mitchell's 27th Birthday

2017

Jul	Craig and Grace Leave for Swaziland: Two-Week TLC Mission Trip
Oct 6	Mitchell's 28th Birthday

2018

Jul	Craig and Carrie Leave for Swaziland: Two-Week TLC Mission Trip
Aug	Mitchell's Memoirs off to Publishing
Oct 6	Mitchell's 29th Birthday

Mitchell's Memoir

ABOUT THE AUTHORS

Dad – Craig Lynn Minor

Senior Analyst and Program Manager with Modern Technology Solutions Inc (MTSI), Dayton Ohio. Lieutenant Colonel, retired, 2016. Previous B-52G Aircraft Commander Pilot, NT-39A Instructor Research Pilot, and Air Force Lifecycle Management Center Acquisition Program Manager. Bachelor of Science degree in Chemistry from Averett University, Danville, Virginia, 1984. Master of Business Administration in Finance from Wright State University, Dayton, Ohio, 2004. Juris Doctor in Law from Capital University Law School, Columbus, Ohio, 2013. Husband, Father, and Poppy.

Mom – Carrie Ann Minor

Founder, Mitchell's Ministry. 24/7 Caregiver for Mitchell Minor. Averett University, Danville Virginia, 1981-1983. Wife, mother and loving 'Grams' to eight grandchildren.

Sister – Grace Minor Becknell

Founder and CEO Mitchell's Ministry. Previous missionary work, The Luke Commission, Eswatini (previously Swaziland). Wife and stay-at-home mother raising three children.

Brother – Levi Steven Minor

Law Clerk, Ameritas Life Insurance Corp., Cincinnati, Ohio. Juris Doctor in Law with Business and Compliance Law concentration from University of Dayton School of Law, Dayton, Ohio, 2019 (expected completion). Bachelor of Arts degree in Political Science and Minors in History and Religion from Wright State University, Dayton, Ohio, 2016. Property and Casualty Insurance, Life and Health Insurance, and LexisNexis Research Certifications. Husband and Dad.

Acknowledgment

Our family extends a special thanks to Chuck (Charles) Clevenger for his artwork portraying Mitchell as we expect he would look in heaven without his handicaps. Chuck is a talented pianist and retired music professor from Cedarville University, Ohio. Chuck and his wife, Rhonda, have been friends of the family for over twenty years. Chuck's vision of Mitchell leaving the confines of his wheelchair for heavenly perfection was further inspired by his own experiences with his special needs brother who passed in his childhood. Portraying Mitchell provoked some unexpected healing, through tears, as Mitchell's life silently touched yet another life.

www.clevengerfineart.com

Connect with Mitchell's Ministry

Website: www.mitchellsmemoir.com

Facebook: https://www.facebook.com/mitchellsmemoir

Instagram: @mitchellsmemoir

Email: craig@mitchellsmemoir.com
                carrie@mitchellsmemoir.com
                grace@mitchellsmemoir.com
                levi@mitchellsmemoir.com
                sarah@mitchellsmemoir.com

Mitchell's Memoir